Swift to Battle

Swift to Battle

No. 72 Squadron RAF in Action
Volume 2: 1942–1947

Tom Docherty

Pen & Sword
AVIATION

First published in Great Britain in 2009 by
Pen & Sword Aviation
An imprint of
Pen & Sword Books Ltd
47 Church Street
Barnsley
South Yorkshire
S70 2AS

ISBN 978 1 84884 087 4

A CIP catalogue record for this book is
available from the British Library

Typeset in 10pt Palatino by Mac Style, Beverley, East Yorkshire
Printed and bound in the UK by CPI Antony Rowe, Chippenham, Wiltshire

Pen & Sword Books Ltd incorporates the Imprints of Pen & Sword
Aviation, Pen & Sword Maritime, Pen & Sword Military, Wharncliffe
Local History, Pen & Sword Select, Pen & Sword Military Classics, Leo
Cooper, Remember When, Seaforth Publishing and Frontline Publishing

For a complete list of Pen & Sword titles please contact
PEN & SWORD BOOKS LIMITED
47 Church Street, Barnsley, South Yorkshire, S70 2AS, England
E-mail: enquiries@pen-and-sword.co.uk
Website: www.pen-and-sword.co.uk

Contents

Acknowledgements

I cannot stress enough how grateful I am to the following people for their contributions to this book. A large number of them served with 72 Sqn, and many are staunch supporters of the No 72 Squadron Association. Those of you already familiar with the squadron will note several names in these acknowledgements of persons who are now deceased. I have included them in the list in grateful thanks for their contributions, which otherwise would be lost to history.

Matt Adams
A.E. Allen
A. Allsopp
Roy Anderson
John Augoustis
Mick Bajcar
Jim Barton
Jeff Bird
Ted Boakes
Eric Boddice
Brian Bond
Ken Boyd
Paul Bradley
Steve Brew
Darryl Briggs
Jack Browne Jr
Ernie Burton
Mrs Casey
Chris Charland
A. Chater
Matt Clague
Malcolm Clarke
John Clegg
Jim Corbett

Jimmy Corbin
Joe Dade
C. Davis
Keith Deary
Patrick Downer
R.D. Elliot
T.A.F. Elsdon
Greggs Farish
Richard Ferriere
Vic Flintham
Diana Foster-Williams
Laurie Frampton
Michael J. Freer
Graeme Gillard
Richard Gledhill
Fergal Goodman
Des Gorham
Ernie Graveney
Eric Gray
RH Gregory
Betty Gridley
Hugh Halliday
Ian Haskell
Robert Hawkins

Acknowledgements

Ben Hitt
Tom Hughes
Angela Jobson
Jack Lancaster
David Lane
Bruno Lecaplain
Mr Lindsay
R. Lindsay
P.D. Lodge
Alan Lowe
Donald MacLean
Erik Mannings
Angus Mansfield
P. McMillan
Ross McNeill
John Meddows
Ron Mitchell
G.M. Monahan
D.C. Nichols
Roy Norfolk
Cyril Nugent
Tony Peacey
M.A. Pocock
D.E. Pool
Peter Pool

Harold Powell
Glyn Ramsden
Mark Ray
R. Rayner
Bill Rolls
Robbie Robertson
Rodney Scrase
Wallace Shackleton
M.J. Shaw
Desmond Sheen
Cedric Stone
Bert Sweetman
Ken Summers
John Sydes
Tom Thackray
Simon Thomas
Piet Van Schalkywyk
Sean Waller
K.C. Weller
Henk Welting
Jerry Wilkinson
Steve Williams
Ray Woods
Keith Worrall
Irvine Wright

Preface

I first considered writing the history of No. 72 Squadron in its entirety when I joined the squadron in 1993 and became the deputy squadron historian. At the time the squadron was in the early stages of forming a squadron association for both ex-air and ex-ground crew, from every period of its existence, as well as serving members who wished to join. Since then I have been actively involved with the association as membership secretary, a post I still fill today.

Having collated a vast amount of information over this period and spoken to members of the association ranging in service from 1937 to the present, I realized that to cover the history in one book would not do it justice. The cost of such a book would put it out of reach of most buyers! Another reason I decided to limit the scope of the book was that from the late 1960s to 2002 No. 72 Squadron was actively involved in operations in Northern Ireland and much of its activities are still classified. It seemed logical, therefore, to look for natural breaks in the squadron's existence and cover that period in detail. Following a brief existence in World War I, and preceding its period as a support helicopter squadron, No. 72 Squadron existed as a fighter unit, both day and night, for a period of twenty-five years from 1937 to 1961.

This second volume is a humble effort to record the history of the squadron during the period 1942–47 using official records and the reminiscences and recollections of those who lived and breathed No. 72 Squadron through this period of its life. I hope that fellow historians will find it a useful reference and that the reader will enjoy the story of a famous squadron and its men.

T.G. Docherty
Forres
2009

CHAPTER ONE

North Africa

No. 324 Wing formed at Maison Blanche, Algiers, on 13 November 1942, under the command of Gp Capt R.B. Lees, who had previously served with 72 Sqn. No. 324 Wing was one of six which made up 242 Group. 324 Wing and two others, 322 and 325, had been designed to be fully mobile and self supporting, and were tasked with close support of land forces in the advance towards Tunis. Maison Blanche was cleared to receive Allied aircraft on the 9th, and 72 Sqn joined the invasion on the 16th, when sixteen No. 72 Sqn Spitfires left Gibraltar for Maison Blanche airfield near Algiers, accompanied by six from 152 Sqn and two replacement aircraft. One of the pilots to go was Jimmy Corbin:

Monday 16th 8.15 a.m. left for 'drome – sorted out Spits, dirty 90-gallon tank – kit packed in after dismantling Spit. What a take-off, shaky do, nearly in drink, wallowed all over the sky – never seen as much sea-wrecks along line. Arrived Algiers/Maison Blanche 13.45, sorted Spits out. Eat – back to 'drome – nature in the raw, learnt how to cook – petrol found many uses. Most of us shagged out, queued up for food – cook our own tomorrow, to bed, scrounged blankets, slept on cement floor, what a night. A good 'drome but everyone going in circles. All types in 'drome, Spits, Lightnings, DC3s, Blenheims, Beaus, French and Italian jobs – a rough do but too tired and hungry to moan.

The following day saw their first operations, with standing patrols throughout the day over Maison Blanche and Algiers harbour. Laurie Frampton flew one of the Spitfires into Maison Blanche:

The aircraft had been shipped to Gibraltar in crates and assembled there. On 16 November, all the Squadron pilots having arrived safely, we flew to Algiers, our aeroplanes being tropicalized Mk V Spitfires fitted with 90-gallon long-range tanks.

We stayed two days at Maison Blanche, where we had the option of sleeping in the cockpit or on the ground under a wing. Someone found a newly built low building with semi-open sides and freshly whitewashed. At least we had a roof, room to stretch out, and using a Mae West as a pillow, managed a degree of sleep. We later found out that the building had been constructed as a pigsty – but not previously occupied.

Jimmy Corbin recorded the first sorties from Maison Blanche:

Off at dawn after a terrible night on the hard floor. Rain and no shelter. An hour patrol, no joy, rained like hell. I lose my kite to Wg Cdr Hugo at Bone, blitzed today by 88s and 109Gs – ten Spits for two squadrons up there – wish to hell we could go up there. Some of the boys gone to Algiers. I may tomorrow. Have commandeered three French cars – some owner is peeved. No bed yet, bombed by Jerry in moonlight. After panic, down to concrete. Awakened at 11 p.m. to pack for morning as moving to forward base – maps issued, three cheers and so to bed.

To the west by the 17th British paratroops and US troops were engaged in fighting the German forces in Tunisia. Two days later British troops were fighting German tanks thirty miles from Tunis. On the 18th the squadron moved from Maison Blanche to Bone and flew its first offensive patrol with eighteen Spitfires that afternoon. Among those taking part was the wing leader, Wg Cdr Hugo. Eight minutes after take-off, in the Tabarka area, a Ju 88 was sighted flying at 5,000 ft. Several pilots fired at the Junkers but it was Wg Cdr Hugo who made sure of the kill, closing to close range and blowing it up. The Junkers crashed in flames. This was the first victory for 324 Wing. Jimmy Corbin (EP911) noted the victory in his logbook:

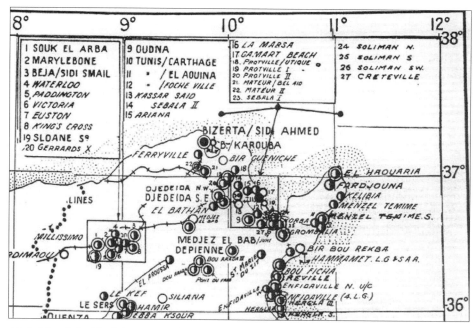

Airfields of the Tunisian campaign.

Patrol Bone. Wg Cdr Hugo got Ju 88. Several squirted. Tail off – fell in flames – no survivors.

Laurie Frampton recalled the arrival at Bone:

We flew to Bone and slept that night on the floor of a villa, at least marble tiles were more luxurious than concrete.

No. 72 Squadron's first victory of the campaign came the next day during a patrol of Bone harbour and the airfield. Blue Section, led by Plt Off Robertson (RN-H), spotted two Bf 109s at 3,000 ft coming out of cloud over Bone harbour. The Messerschmitts bounced a Spitfire and then headed east along the coast. Blue Section gave chase and was able to intercept them from slightly above and behind. Blue 2 was flown by New Zealander Plt Off O.L. Hardy, who opened fire at 150 yards, giving one of the Messerschmitts a three-second burst. He observed hits all over the wings, fuselage and tail. The Bf 109 began streaming glycol from the port radiator and then the propeller flew off. The doomed fighter made a gentle turn to the right and hit the side of a hill, bursting into flames. Plt Off Robertson was able to confirm the kill.

The Eighth Army captured Benghazi as the squadron continued patrols on the 20th and moved once again, this time to Souk el Arba, being fired at several times by understandably nervous Allied anti-aircraft gunners. Laurie Frampton wrote of the arrival at Souk el Arba:

We landed on an airstrip at Souk el Arba about twenty-five miles west of Beja, which we understood to be occupied by the Paras. The strip was a level area of hard baked earth with no signs of life, only cans of 100-octane petrol stacked in a ditch on the opposite side of the road. After an hour the first lorry of the RAF Servicing Commandos arrived; they were wireless mechanics with no gear for refuelling. Using their jack knives they prised the seals out of the cans, and together we managed to get fuel into the aircraft. In the meantime contact had been made with the local French Army unit, who loaned us two elderly bell tents and a few thin blankets. After a hectic drive through the Atlas Mountains the rest of the commandos arrived and a degree of servicing was established.

On our arrival at Souk el Arba we had selected an area on the opposite side of the road for a campsite for when the squadron caught up with us. We erected bell tents here and dug a slit trench nearby. One night in the small dark hours there was much noise. I woke up and saw a hole in the top of the tent. There was one other person in the tent; we leapt out of bed and headed for the slit trench, to be greeted by the other bods, climbing out. Jerry had dropped a stick of bombs and had now departed – no serious damage done.

Jimmy Corbin flew into Souk el Arba after a sweep of the Beja area on the 20th:

Landed at Souk el Arba, now the most forward 'drome. Arrived before RAF Commando and started to refuel ourselves out of tins. 109s overhead. Commandos arrived – those boys sure can work, trenches and refuel and cookhouse all done. Meal, then watch French erect tents for us, more talk than work – done at last and settle down for night – expecting bags of joy tomorrow. Froze like hell last night with one blanket.

There was no rest for the squadron following the move, and on the afternoon of the 21st eight Spitfires set about a convoy of four troop-carrying lorries south-west of Mateur, destroying them. The following morning eight Spitfires swept the Mateur–Bizerta road and attacked and destroyed four trucks in convoy, two of the valuable petrol tankers for Rommel's troops. Sqn Ldr Oxspring's aircraft was hit during the strafing run, and he force-landed eight miles east of Beja. Laurie Frampton (ER555) was also in trouble, and recorded in his logbook:

Sweep – Beja. Engine cut (Mags) 3 miles beyond Beja. Belly-landed in ploughed field, narrowly missing two Arabs and Mokes [donkeys]. CO pranged 2 miles beyond myself. Oil tank hit while beating up Jerry transport. PM 'drome blitzed. Eight kites damaged beyond repair.

Later he recalled more detail of this sortie and its aftermath:

21 November – Where is the Hun? – We knew the Paras were advancing to the east of Beja. To try to find the enemy's location a flight of four aircraft set off that morning on a recce, led by David Cox with Pete Fowler as his No. 2 and Chas Charnock leading me as the second pair. Nothing was visible from 2,000 ft, so Chas and I went to have a closer look from 50–100 ft. While looking for square heads under bushes my engine decided to call it a day. To port was a newly ploughed field, which looked as if it would give a reasonably soft belly-landing. I levelled off on the approach and saw off the port wing an Arab crouched against the backsides of his ox and ass, which were pulling the plough. At that moment I realized I was about to land in a dried-up wadi – not a good idea – so I rammed into the soft earth, spun through 90 degrees and came to rest. I climbed out and walked towards a road 200 yards away; as I arrived there a black Citroen drew up with two French officers, who drove me back to the squadron.

In the afternoon the airfield was attacked by twelve German aircraft, and Flt Lt Krohn and Sgt Pearson, patrolling overhead, were able to get among them. Krohn claimed a Bf 109 as probably destroyed. The two Spitfires were unable to prevent the attack, though, and 72 Squadron's dispersal was bombed and strafed, disabling eight Spitfires. Later the airfield was attacked again, and while the Germans were strafing, Plt Off Daniel jumped into his Spitfire and attempted to take off and engage them. Taking off straight ahead and hurtling

72 Sqn pilots in tented accommodation in the desert at Souk el Arba. (L. Frampton)

A group of pilots at Souk el Arba. (72 Sqn)

across the airfield, he hit a bump, tearing off a wheel just as he became airborne. Daniel chased the Germans and opened fire but had no success. After the attack only two tents survived unburnt. These were dispersed even further apart, which was as well, as the airfield was attacked again by Ju 88s during the night. Jimmy Corbin (EP911) recorded the earlier combat and the airfield attack in his log:

Aerodrome patrol. CO shot down by flak – safe. Sweep to Lake Bizerte. Pranged six lorries NE of Mateur. 109s, Mac 200s, 87s pranged our 'drome – eight kites for burton, including mine.

He also recorded in his diary:

Twelve 109s bombed and machine-gunned us at 1.30 p.m., wiped out eight of our Spits. Krohn got one. Was I scared, no cover. Cox hurt, several types killed, three burnt up as petrol dump went up. Three-quarters of an hour later 190s bombed and machine-gunned us again. 93 Sqn got it an hour later, 87s with top cover of MC200, 109s and 190s. 93 got two and several probables. We had not enough kites to get up. Dan had a go and crash-landed. Moved tents at night and attention from Ju 88.

During the 22nd the convoy carrying the remainder of 72 Squadron's pilots and all of the ground crew arrived in Algiers. Immediately Plt Off Farish set off with a group of drivers to collect the squadron transport from Bone. In the meantime the pilots at Bone would continue to rely on the servicing skills of the RAF Servicing Commandos at Souk el Arba. Meanwhile the squadron ground crew were working their way toward Souk el Arba by various means and methods, some quicker than others, as Ben Hitt remembers:

We docked at 2.00 p.m. and disembarked at 4.00 p.m. with full kit and one kitbag. The dockside was crammed with packing cases. We marched about four miles from the dock area and ended up in a large garage or shed. We slept on a stone floor with intermittent air raids throughout the night. Food was in the form of Compo rations: a box containing tins of bacon, sausages, steak and kidney, suet puddings, dry biscuits, bars of chocolate and cigarettes. Enough for twelve (often the chocolate and cigarettes were missing). Our group lit a fire and cooked breakfast and later on that morning we were issued with two-man tents, so we moved to the beach area. That night there was a lot of activity all night long with continuous air raids. The following night we had torrential rain and half of the camp was waterlogged, so we moved back to the shed, where we slept in rows of six, feeling rather damp.
    The following day a section of the ground crew boarded a destroyer and headed for the port of Bone as an advance party. Many of us spent a couple of days at the docks helping to unload and stack supplies.

Jack Lancaster also recalls arriving in Algiers and the days that followed:

After disembarking we marched about three miles east and stayed the night on the beach. The Luftwaffe visited us and the pyrotechnics were something to behold. Next morning we learned that one of the ships lying outside Algiers had been torpedoed. Some of the occupants, 13 Sqn, swimming ashore.

The following day Bill Mann, myself and some of the ground crew were taken to Maison Blanche where we boarded a C-47, which took us, flying at zero feet, to Souk el Arba, escorted by Hurricanes of 43 Sqn. On arrival we were unceremoniously dumped off the aircraft, which immediately took to the air again heading west. Only then did I realize that the hurried departure of the C-47 meant that a certain danger lurked here. We were told that the first thing we should do was dig a slit trench as the Hun would be around quite shortly. During the day the raids were carried out by 109s and 190s, strafing and bombing, but at night by Ju 88s dropping nasty little anti-personnel bombs. We had all experienced bombing in England, but not

Adding another kill to the tent pole. (72 Sqn)

strafing, however we were not to wait long as half a dozen 109s screamed across our dispersal, cannons blazing. Not a nice experience, but one we got quite used to over the coming months. No wonder we dug out our tents so that we lay about two feet below ground level. We had no radar, but if enemy aircraft were approaching from the east the Army would fire a smoke shell into the air to give us warning – fifteen seconds! However, most of the bombing and strafing raids came in from the south-west, and the 109s and 190s were difficult to see, being low down and with a hill behind them.

'Rio' Wright also recalled the difficulties at Souk el Arba:

Conditions for operating Spitfires could not have been worse than they were at Souk el Arba, what with the lack of PSP tracking, the muddy conditions and not forgetting the hill to the south of the strip, which allowed the Germans to arrive with the minimum of warning.

Laurie Frampton also remembered the numerous German sneak attacks on the airfield:

On one such occasion I was duty pilot at the northern end of the field with a bell tent, and in it an ammunition box with a field telephone. Very pistol loaded with a red cartridge and my tin hat; alongside were the crash tender and blood wagon.

When the visitor arrived I dived into the tent on my belly trying to fire the Very, ring the telephone and put on my helmet all at the same time, thinking 'I can't see him so he can't see me ergo I'm all right.' On emerging we found lines of bullet holes between the tent and crash tender, the two vehicles, and the far side of the ambulance. The crews had dived under their vehicles and none of us had been touched.

By the 23rd the Axis forces were being put under even more pressure and retreating before the Eighth Army. The *Afrika Korps* fell back to El Agheila. On the 23rd the squadron put up patrols over the airfield using the five remaining Spitfires, and on patrols the following day the pilots were able to observe the massive build-up of Allied troops advancing in the Medjez el Bab and Beja areas. By now many French troops had laid down their arms and ceased fighting; however, there was a hard core determined to fight on, and these were united under Laval as the *Phalange Africaine* to fight the Allies. It made little difference to the outcome, and Allied troops were only twenty-two miles from Tunis by the 27th.

The 25th was a highly successful day for the squadron, and was a portent of things to come. The pilots flew twelve sorties, during which they destroyed five enemy aircraft, probably destroyed two and damaged one. The score sheet was as follows:

Plt Off J. Lowe	1 Ju 88 destroyed
Plt Off 'Robbie' Robertson (RN-P)	1 Bf 109 destroyed
Plt Off S.W. Daniel	1 Bf 109 destroyed
WO 'Chas' Charnock	1 Bf 109E destroyed
Flt Lt I.R. Krohn	1 Ju 88 shared destroyed and 1 Ju 88 damaged
Sgt Laurie Frampton (ER603)	1 Ju 88 shared destroyed
Sqn Ldr R.W. Oxspring	1 Bf 109 probably destroyed
Flg Off D.G.S.R. Cox	1 Bf 109 probably destroyed.

Laurie Frampton noted in his logbook:

Sweep covering army advance. Bounced 8 Ju 88s over Djedeida. Shared one with 'Killer' Krohn. Johnny Lowe got one. Flg Off Cox, Roy Hussey 109 each.

On the 26th the squadron had yet another highly successful day, with Sqn Ldr Oxspring damaging a Ju 88 during an early-morning sweep of the Djedeida and Tunis area. An hour and a half later Flg Off D.G.S.R. Cox set about a Bf 109F he encountered at 6,000 ft. Giving the Messerschmitt a twelve-second burst, he observed sparks coming off the engine, followed by the port wing collapsing at the wing root. At the same time Sgt R.J.H. 'Roy' Hussey attacked a Bf 109E. The Messerschmitt was at 9,000 ft when Hussey attacked from astern, giving it a one-second burst. The Messerschmitt immediately turned and dived away, followed by Hussey, who fired more bursts at the fleeing German, whose aircraft lost pieces with each burst. Flg Off Cox observed Hussey's kill, watching the Messerschmitt diving vertically with showers of sparks and emitting white

A wrecked Spitfire Mk V at Souk el Arba following a German attack. (J. Lancaster)

Aircraft burning at Souk el Arba after a *Luftwaffe* attack. (J. Lancaster)

smoke, turning black, before it hit a hillside and exploded. The third success of the day went to Plt Off 'Jimmy' Corbin and Sgt P.E. Fowler during a mid-afternoon sweep south-west of Djedeida. Both pilots attacked and shared in the destruction of a Bf 109F, which was seen to dive into the ground. Jimmy Corbin noted the fight in his diary:

> Last patrol Pete, Robbie, Johnnie and self jumped two 109Fs. Pete shot at one and I got in a good deflection shot, strikes on engine and above fuselage, it then dived at about 40 degrees with glycol streaming from it. Pranged. Pete and I shared.

'Chas' Charnock added to his score on the 27th. Flying as Yellow 3 north-east of Djedeida, he got onto the tail of a Bf 109 and gave it a two-second burst. The aircraft was seen to crash by Flg Off Cox and Sgt Hussey. Charnock was not done for the day, though. Latching onto the tail of another Bf 109, he fired the remainder of his ammunition before observing the fighter diving very fast at a 70-degree angle. 'Chas' Charnock claimed this one as probably destroyed.

During the last sweep of the 27th around Djedeida, Tebourba and Tunis, Sgt Hussey and Flg Off Cox both claimed a Bf 109 probably destroyed, while Plt Off 'Robbie' Robertson (RN-H) destroyed another Bf 109. Unfortunately Plt Off J. Lowe, who shot down a Ju 88 on the 25th, failed to return.

By the 28th the shortage of serviceable aircraft forced the squadron to reduce its flying rate, and on the morning of the 29th, as British paratroops dropped south of Tunis, the squadron was only able to put up

Plt Off David Cox. (72 Sqn)

L to R: WO Weedon, Flt Sgt Mann, Unknown, Flg Off Roy Hussey. Rear right: Sgt Jack Lancaster. (J. Lancaster)

nine Spitfires for a sweep of the Mateur and Ferryville areas. Later, while on airfield patrol, Flt Lt Krohn and Flg Off Cox each destroyed a Ju 88. Laurie Frampton ((ER598) noted in his logbook:

Defensive sweep. 'Killer' Krohn and Coxy pranged Ju 88 each before breakfast.

Jimmy Corbin recorded:

Dawn patrol. Ju 88s – Krohn and Cox 1 each. No luck for me.

Jimmy Corbin had injured his hand two days previously, and noted of this sortie:

Flew at dawn after raiding 88s. Krohn and Cox got one but I had no luck. Had a hell of a job taking off and flying with hand. Doc put me off flying again as I opened cut. Still only four kites – no replacements. Bombed again at night, in trench four times.

At 1000 hrs a joint sweep was made by 72 and 93 Squadrons with the nine Spitfires that could be mustered, to escort two tactical recce (Tac R) Hurricanes to Mateur and Ferryville. At noon the squadron put up eight Spitfires for a strafing sortie in the Djedeida area, damaging a staff car and a truck. Rodney Scrase remembers the lack of serviceable aircraft during this period:

'Chas' Charnock. (72 Sqn)

The months of November and December 1942 were particularly difficult for 72, with incessant rain making taxiing something which required the weight of two men on the tailplane to counter the plane's readiness to kiss the ground. This, with the almost night-and-day visits of German aircraft, meant there were many ops on which of the four squadrons of 324 Wing we could only muster ten or twelve serviceable aircraft.

In the afternoon the squadron was led by Wg Cdr 'Sheep' Gilroy in an escort to fourteen paratroop-dropping Dakotas. The paratroopers dropped successfully in the Pont-du-Fahs area, and when the squadron returned to the airfield it was informed that the operation had been cancelled!

Nine days after they had arrived in Algiers the remainder of the squadron pilots arrived at Souk el Arba. Some flew in badly needed replacement Spitfires, while the remainder flew in a Dakota transport. Plt Off Greggs Farish also arrived with the squadron MT. Of the rest of the ground crew, though, there was no sign. They were still stranded in Algiers.

Souk el Arba was the most forward of the strips being used by the Allies, and operating conditions were difficult. Until the squadron ground crew arrived, all servicing was done by RAF Servicing Commandos who appeared to be able to fix almost anything with only a spanner and a screwdriver. Pilots had to refuel from four-gallon tins themselves, and cooking was done on borrowed equipment. The strip itself was Sommerfeld tracking laid by Royal Engineers. Most nights the Germans paid the strip a visit, liberally dropping anti-personnel 'butterfly bombs', and fighter-bombers regularly bombed and strafed during the day.

Flg Off D.G.S.R. Cox. (J. Corbin)

Having been reinforced, the squadron flew an afternoon sweep of the Tabourka area. Descending through cloud it came out below to find itself head on with five Italian Savoia bombers. Surprised by the suddenness of the encounter, the Spitfires missed the

Squadron engineering officer Greggs Farish on his motorcycle with squadron Spitfire behind. (T.B. Hughes)

chance of a head-on attack. They turned quickly and gave chase, but only Sqn Ldr Oxspring was able to damage one bomber. As they returned to the airfield, Canadian Plt Off H.S. Lewis spotted four Macchi MC202s attacking a Spitfire, and he quickly joined the fight. During the engagement his Spitfire was badly shot up, but he managed to damage an MC202 in return before having to crash-land his crippled Spitfire, which he did at 230 mph. Climbing out of the wreck, he hitch-hiked back to the airfield with nothing more than a sprained ankle.

There was more action for the squadron on a morning sweep over Tebourba on 1 December. Twelve Spitfires were airborne from Souk el Arba at 0945 hrs. They spotted six to eight enemy aircraft over Tebourba and Tunis, a mixed formation of Macchi MC202s and Bf 109s. Sqn Ldr Oxspring, flying as Red 1, climbed behind the Macchis, followed by his No. 2, WO Alan Gear. The Macchis became aware of Red section just as Sqn Ldr Oxspring opened fire, and then dived away towards Tunis. Oxspring and Gear followed them down but could not close the gap. Sqn Ldr Oxspring fired several bursts during the dive and followed the Macchis to ground level, chasing them over the Tunis War Memorial before breaking off. The rest of the squadron strafed tanks and armoured cars near Djedeida, and Sgt Hussey found himself crossing Djedeida airfield during the attack, where he strafed a parked Ju 87, causing it to collapse and catch fire. Laurie Frampton witnessed the forced landing of one of his compatriots, and logged:

Maison Blanche–Souk el Arba. 'Lew' beat up by four Macchi 202s. Force-landed south of Beja – badly cut head and damaged ankle.

Jimmy Corbin logged the day's effort:

To Souk el Arba. Lewis missing – injured, but turned up later. M202s got him. Shot up tanks around Djedeida. Bags of flak from tanks.

An early-morning recce of El Alouina airfield yielded results for a three-Spitfire section led by Flg Off Cox on the 2nd. Several anti-aircraft gun posts were attacked and silenced, and Cox strafed a Heinkel He 111, leaving it smoking with a collapsed undercarriage. The squadron ORB notes, 'One German fitter was seen to look unhappy!'

The second sortie of the day was a sweep of the Tebourba–Djedeida area, and the Spitfires soon spotted a formation of about twelve Bf 109s, as well as formations of Bostons, Lightnings and another Spitfire squadron from Bone. They quickly became embroiled in dogfights, and Plt Off le Cheminant was caught by four Fw 190s which had joined the fight. He was badly shot up by the *Luftwaffe 'Experte'*, *Oberleutnant* Kurt Buehlingen of *II/JG2*, and crash-landed at Tebourba. Luckily, he was uninjured, and French troops returned him to the squadron. Laurie Frampton (EP904) saw le Cheminant go down, and noted it in his logbook:

Sweep Mateur–Djedeida. 'Chem' beat up by 109s. Force lobbed near Tebourba unhurt.

Jimmy Corbin wrote in his diary:

Sweep in afternoon, met Bostons and Lightnings and more Spits – lots of 109s bounced us through cloud – terrific dogfight. Several of us squirted, no time for results.

The first sortie of the 3rd was a twelve-Spitfire sweep of the Tebourba–Djedeida area, with no combats. This was immediately followed by a four-aircraft strike against enemy troop concentrations east of Djedeida, during which the Spitfires knocked out three lorries. In mid-afternoon the squadron was up again with a twelve-aircraft patrol over Tebourba and Djedeida. Plt Off Malan recalled this sortie:

A rising column of heavy smoke was observed over Tebourba and the CO decided to investigate. 'Flintstone' had reported Bf 109s flying high in the area, so the CO asked a squadron of Lightnings, which had been observed in the area, to act as top cover. Yellow Section was sent down to recce below cloud. At about 6,000 ft Yellow Section encountered four Fw 190s, which they engaged. Red and Blue Sections on diving down were reported by the Lightnings as Bf 109s and promptly bounced. Blue 4, Plt Off Macdonald, turned tightly and saw tracers going past his tail. By the time Red and Blue Sections had disengaged themselves from the Lightnings, the engagement between Yellow Section and the Fw 190s had petered out. One Fw 190 destroyed was shared by Yellow 1, 3 and 4, Flg Off Hardy, Plt Off Robertson and Plt Off Malan respectively.

The action continued when Yellow 4, Plt Off Malan, reported further Focke-Wulfs at between 9 and 6 o'clock. Malan realized that Yellow 3's R/T had failed, and broke away to attack. Yellow 1 and 2 had already begun to attack the two Fw 190s, and on his way down Malan spotted a further Fw 190 engaged in dive-bombing. He dived down on this fighter and got onto its tail, giving it

Flg Off Owen Hardy. (J. Corbin)

a 1.5-second burst from fifty yards. Malan observed strikes around the cockpit, fuselage and wing root. Suddenly, he heard an explosion from his Spitfire, and pulled quickly away into the smoke pall rising from the town below. Emerging from the smoke at 500 ft, Malan saw his radiator temperature was rising rapidly and realized he would have to land quickly. He prepared to crash-land straight ahead, and put the crippled Spitfire down two miles inside friendly lines at Grich el Oued. Malan received only a slight graze on his shoulder from the crash, and he was well looked after by the American troops he had landed among. Plt Off Roberston (RN-C) had seen Malan diving down, and watched him close to a very tight line astern with the two Fw 190s. The No. 2 Fw 190 skidded wildly out of the way as Malan closed, and then dropped back behind him and opened fire. Robertson then manoeuvred into position astern of the No. 2 Fw 190 of II/JG2 and opened fire. The first Fw 190 (Malan's) was seen to crash into the hills north-east of Tebourba, and the second Fw 190 limped off with heavy white smoke trailing behind.

While the pilots were busy overhead more ground crew were arriving at Souk el Arba, among them Ben Hitt:

On 3 December 1942 another group, including myself, went to Maison Blanche (Algiers airport), where we were transported in an American Curtiss Commando to an airstrip by the village of Souk el Arba. Our pilots and aircraft were already there, with the servicing being done by a group of RAF Commandos, who were gradually withdrawn as our various sections arrived.

Souk el Arba was one of those desolate areas, the small village being deserted. There were three Spitfire squadrons, 72, 93 and 111, with the later addition of a squadron of Hurribombers. We spent time erecting tents, dispersed for safety reasons. The work was quite hectic, with the squadron doing an average of four operations daily. By 6 December the score was nineteen German aircraft destroyed.

The 3rd was also notable as the day that 72 Sqn and recently arrived 111 Sqn were advised that all of the equipment, which had been so carefully packed back in the UK, was lost at sea. All the kitbags and thirty tons of engineering stores were gone.

On the 4th the squadron had another good day. That day Tebourba had been captured by German forces in heavy fighting. Taking off from Souk el Arba at 1440 hrs, eight Spitfires were patrolling the Tebourba area at 12,000 ft when several Bf 109s marked with white eighteen-inch bands a foot from each wingtip and a similar white band around the rear fuselage were seen slightly above and up sun. The Spitfires turned toward the Germans, but the Bf 109s climbed above them before spiralling down in sections. The Spitfires quickly broke formation, and in the free-for-all that ensued Plt Off Le Cheminant claimed one Bf 109, watching its pilot bale out before the fighter crashed six miles west of Sidi Athman. Plt Off Cox watched his victim, another Bf 109, crash into a hillside, and also confirmed Plt Off Daniel's victory over a Bf 109F. The fight was not completely one sided, however, as Chas Charnock had to fight for his life. He heard someone call that a Bf 109 was on his tail, and quickly climbed down sun. Looking behind he could see about twenty Bf 109s in pairs. Above him, in the direction of Bizerta, were another twenty. Charnock opened up on one Bf 109 from 250 yards; closing to seventy yards, and saw the fighter burst into flames and go straight down. Unfortunately, the doomed fighter's No. 2 had crept in behind him, and he began to take hits in the port wing. Suddenly, the magazine in the wing exploded and blew the wing completely off. Charnock decided it was time to leave, baling out of the 'out of control Spitfire' at 5,000 ft. As he hung beneath the parachute canopy he was shot at by a German fighter, which luckily missed. Landing safely, Chas Charnock was returned to Souk el Arba by the Americans on the 5th.

By the 4th the pilots were becoming exhausted, as Jimmy Corbin noted in his diary:

> *Dawn patrol with Browne, saw flak over Beja but no enemy aircraft came near base. Our squadron supposed to be having a rest from sweeps today, just doing aerodrome patrols and standby – also chance to give kites a bit of servicing as they have had no form of inspection yet and some kites have done 60 hours. Some of the boys, including myself, are feeling a bit shagged. For the past two or three days tempers have been a bit short, but general spirits good. Army getting a bit of a pasting and complaining about support – we feel sorry but we are doing our best.*

An early patrol of the Medjez el Bab–Depienne area by Red Section on the 6th bore fruit. Led by Wg Cdr 'Sheep' Gilroy, Sgt Laurie Frampton and Plt Off Jimmy Corbin sighted two Bf 109s flying north at 6,000 ft. All three shared in damaging one of the German fighters before they escaped. Corbin noted:

> *Tried to jump 109s. W/C Gilroy, Frampton and self prob destroyed one.*

William James 'Jimmy' Corbin DFC.

24

Bomber escort was the order of the day on the 7th. The first at lunchtime was for eight Spitfires to escort six Bisleys, derivatives of the Bristol Blenheim, to bomb targets at Tebourba. This sortie went off without a hitch. The second escort sortie had a more exciting time of it later in the afternoon. Fourteen Spitfires took of to escort eight Bisleys to Djedeida. The escort went off without a hitch, but as they were landing at base the Germans decided to pay a visit. Two Fw 190s swept over the airfield strafing and bombing, while five Bf 109s provided cover above. Several aircraft were damaged but luckily there were no casualties among the squadron. Ben Hitt was among those on the ground taking cover:

In mid-afternoon, to prove that it was not all one sided; we were ground-strafed by five or six Fw 190s. We all hit the deck at high speed, and my mind went back to the old Western films with bullets flying and dust spurting, but this was for real. Two of our aircraft were on fire. One of the lads lying flat under a main plane when the plane was hit had a shower bath when the radiator was holed. A considerable amount of additional trench digging followed this introduction to our hostile enemy.

Jimmy Corbin recorded:

Within fifteen minutes of the boys landing, a terrific dogfight above the 'drome as 109s came over – aerodrome patrol did well against twelve 109s, then cunning buggers that they are, two 190s came at zero feet out of the sun and bombed and machine-gunned the 'drome in one run – wrote off about four kites. Aerodrome patrol got one 190 and a probable.

German forces had continued to arrive in Tunisia in the preceding days, and they quickly invested Bizerte before the weather intervened on the 8th. The pilots took a well-earned rest during the heavy rains while the ground crew worked hard to service the Spitfires. Ben Hitt wrote of the difficulties the change in the weather brought to the airfield:

The rains came. We had already encountered problems with the runway. With the help of Army Pioneers we laid layers of rushes, to no effect, then we tried layers of cork bark, which was no good, either, as the planes kept bouncing alarmingly when landing, and if the Spitfire had one weakness it was the narrow undercarriage. Finally we laid down metal strips, used by the Army for bridging, and this proved to be a big improvement. Of course the planes were well dispersed, and getting through the mud to the runway was not easy. Two of us on each tail to prevent them from rising up. The Germans did have a big advantage as they were operating from purpose-built airfields in Tunis.

The next contact with the enemy came on the 10th, when WO Alan Gear was patrolling over the airfield. He sighted an enemy aircraft and shadowed it in and

Ground crew on train at Phillipville *en route* to Souk el Arba. 2nd from left is Ron Gregory. (R.H. Gregory)

out of cloud for some time before getting into a position to head it off. The aircraft, a Ju 88, sighted Gear, but he closed to seventy-five yards and opened fire. His cannon jammed but he continued to fire with machine-guns, seeing hits around the Junkers' port engine. Black smoke began to stream from the bomber, but it side-slipped into cloud and disappeared. Alan Gear's victim may have been an aircraft of *KG60*, which failed to return. Enemy bombers and the weather played havoc with the airfield again on the 10th, as Jimmy Corbin noted:

Rained like hell again last night. Still cloudy and occasional drizzle this morning. Just been interrupted by a Ju 88. Bombed town, set fire to building, oil and petrol. Bombed again half an hour later. Drome nearly u/s. Can only get three of our kites out of the mud. We have moved back to the tents again – brassed off with moving about. Bags of mud that sticks like glue. Pushing kites for one and a half hours to clear the way for Beaufighters. Bloody tired – covered in mud. A little wine relieves no end.

On the 11th the remainder of the squadron began to arrive at Souk el Arba. They had left Algiers by destroyer on the 4th. Arriving in Phillipeville they had a six-day, 250-mile train journey to Souk el Arba. Ben Hitt remembered their arrival and life on a desert strip at that time:

A day or so later the remainder of our ground crew arrived. Their journey had been by train over several days, and they finally turned up in trucks. There had been numerous stoppages for engine breakdowns and lack of fuel. At least we were back to full strength. The only major disadvantage – we were now twelve to a tent, six sleeping each side like tightly packed sausages, as well as having to sleep in our clothes. Water was in short supply, with only four gallons a day between us. We had a mugful each for cleaning teeth and shaving, the remainder being poured into a cut-down can for washing. For the last man it must have been like washing in a bowl of soup. Some squadron cooks became operational, and tinned food was served regularly along with teeth-cracking biscuits. Arab salesmen who appeared with eggs and oranges augmented our diet. One of our group, a Cockney lad, disappeared into the night and reappeared later with a small petrol stove and tins of beans. No questions were asked, but there were suppers of eggs and beans.

There was a French gun emplacement sporting a rather ancient cannon. Our own anti-aircraft were Bofors rapid-fire guns with British crews. We realized that the French gun, if aimed upwards, was no danger, but on the level it would have given us a direct hit. We moved our tent. Our days were still long, the weather a little easier. Apart from fighter sweeps, the squadron was escorting American Fortresses and Liberators on bombing missions. We, of course, were receiving almost daily visits from Me 109s and Fw 190s, with a little night bombing.

Jack Lancaster also recalls life for the ground crew working in the adverse conditions at Souk el Arba at this time:

Food was supplied in boxes to cater for fourteen men per day. These were called Compo rations, and were excellent, including a few cigarettes and sweets as well as a bar of chocolate. As water was in short supply, and as yet we had no bowser or transport, I believe the Army supplied us, and so we were able to have our char [tea], although washing was not very prevalent until the rest of the squadron caught up with us.

Those early days in Tunisia were a bit hairy, but I don't remember seeing anybody who was scared. I suppose we were all too busy. Keeping the aircraft serviceable was quite difficult with our very limited resources. I remember one day well. We had no spare wheels and we had one aircraft with a badly scored tyre. However, there was a crashed Spit on the other side of the strip, and I took a gang to remove a wheel from it. We were just about ready to remove the wheel, having removed the nuts, etc. I gave the order to lift to the lads underneath the wing, but I had hardly got the wheel off when the wing was dropped and I was left with the wheel between my legs and trapped. I happened to look to my left and saw lots of small flashes on the ground coming towards me. I was intrigued and only realized what they were when a 109 passed within a few yards. I can still see the very wide smile on that pilot's face, and though another six 109s passed by I was fortunately left unscathed. I now understood where the lads had gone, but my comments were unprintable at the time.

The rest of the squadron eventually arrived, and our little advance party was given a few days' rest. We were put in a truck with some Compo rations and went off to Ain Draham in the hills to the north. Here Bill Mann lost a finger endeavouring to quieten some rather boisterous Marine Commandos who were breaking up gramophone records. In hospital in Algiers he was offered the Purple Heart by the Americans – big laughs!

The weather turned very bad in December, and we had at times to practically lift the aircraft out of the mud. Christmas was almost upon us, and although the Compo rations were excellent, there was no drink. So one day Flg Off 'Spanner' Farish, the engineering officer, called me to join him in his jeep to see if we could find out what was happening to the NAAFI rations. We found the site the Army was setting up for distributing these, but the SNCO i/c told us that the store would not be opened until after Christmas. Flg Off Farish was not having any of this, and demanded that we needed beer and spirits now, as he was not going to have 72 Squadron go without a drink at Christmas.

After a lot of palaver and form signing, we left the depot for our camp with a jeep full of booze. If anything contributed to our success as a squadron it was 'Spanner' Farish, a super guy.

We had a bit of scare when Rommel pushed through the Kasserine Pass, but we all knew what to do in the event of having to withdraw. I was one of the 'lucky' ones to stay and see the aircraft off, and was to sit on one of the pilot's knees or 'vice versa' when leaving. Thank goodness it didn't happen.

The heavy rains of December made life on the airstrip particularly difficult, but despite this the newer pilots on the squadron were learning what air fighting was all about, as Laurie Frampton recalls:

During December, heavy rains turned the airfield into a quagmire. The Summerfield track was laid to form a runway and taxi track. The mud came up through the mesh, and on take-off the radiator would sometimes become so clogged with the stuff that an immediate landing was necessary. The taxi track became very holey and rutted, and on occasion everyone would turn out at night to provide human jacks under Spitfire wings to lift an aircraft out of a hole and move it onto more solid ground. To stop our tents from falling down we had to drive pegs into the mud and lay sandbags on the guy ropes.

During this period we were involved with daily sorties involving offensive sweeps over the German-occupied territories from Mateur to Tunis, and to the south to the Kairouan area, escort to Hurricanes on bombing and reconnaissance, and defensive patrols over base, with the occasional scramble when air attack was imminent. While on a number of these sorties no contact was made with enemy aircraft, the squadron was still compiling a not inconsiderable score. Personally, I was learning what air fighting involved, with very little to show for my efforts. I had a few encounters, including diving after a 109, which was getting away; when I pulled out of the dive the reflector gunsight had gone blank, as the spring-clip holding the bulb in the base of the sight had been pulled out by the G.

When escorting Hurricanes on a recce near Mateur, we were told that in the event of any enemy action they were to return to base and not get in our way. During the resultant mêlée an aircraft with rounded wingtips was turning to port 150 yards ahead of me. I was about to open fire when it straightened up – it was a Hurricane which should have been back at base by then.

One sweep was to cover the Army advance through the Sedjenane valley; cloud base was level with the tops of the hills on either side. When we arrived the preceding squadron was still on patrol. Imagine twenty-four Spitfires milling around in a very restricted space. Two aircraft did collide; in the circumstances we got off lightly.

On the 12th two sorties against enemy road transport were flown. The wing leader, Wg Cdr Gilroy, flew on both, and on the first a light lorry was attacked between Djedeida and St Cyprien, crashing into a ditch in flames. No one got out. The second sortie, by six Spitfires, attacked transport on the Tebourba–Medjez road at zero feet, destroying several vehicles. By the 13th, Rommel was unable to hold his position at El Agheila and retreated. On the 15th the squadron provided a seven-Spitfire escort to twelve US B-17s bombing Bizerta. During the escort Plt Off Dalton Prytherch damaged a Bf 109. By the 15th, conditions were improving slightly, as Ben Hitt remembers:

Had first wash and shave for four days and received my first mail from home. Our plane RN:Q had crashed on take off – pilot OK. We took over a new plane, RN:Z. Two days later it was shot down, but the pilot baled out and duly returned.

Aircraft, of course, need petrol and oil, all contained in four-gallon cans. From time to time a party of us would board a large truck and head back, I know not where, to an Army depot containing, seemingly, thousands of cans. The roads were rough, with side ditches, and at the sign of any aircraft, theirs or ours, we were in the ditches. If our British workers were accused of slow working, then a visit to this vast petrol dump would prove the opposite. The big ambition was to get the hell out of it fast. The truck had hardly stopped when loading began at high speed and we were away, scanning the skies even more intently and then on our return to base we spread the fuel around the various dispersals. We felt sorry for the Army lads who had to stay and work in that fuel volcano.

Bomber escorts were the order of the day over the next few days. On the 17th Jimmy Corbin recorded of the previous night:

Very bad evening – blitzed by Ju 88s and Me 110 for about two hours, but eventually to bed at 11 p.m.

On the 18th, ten Spitfires were airborne from Souk el Arba at 1010 hrs to escort twelve Bostons attacking Mateur airfield. Twenty Bf 109s were waiting for the bombers over the airfield, and 72 Sqn was soon embroiled in numerous dogfights. Plt Off Robertson (RN-X) shot down a Bf 109, and Chas Charnock claimed a Bf 109 and an Fw 190. Having narrowly escaped death at the hands of the *Luftwaffe* on the 4th, Charnock was roughly handled by them again following his dogfight victories. Descending to ground level, he was followed and attacked by four Bf 109s and Fw 190s. As the rounds smashed into his Spitfire he was wounded in the head and arm by cannon splinters, and received burns to his waist and face. He bellied-in the crippled Spitfire and ran for cover as it burst into flames. The victorious pilot was *Leutnant* Erich Rudorffer of *II/JG2*. Laurie Frampton (ER962) returned early and noted in his logbook:

High cover escort 12 Bostons to bomb Mateur. Returned mag trouble. Robbie got 109. Chas got 2 –was shot down himself, wounded.

Jimmy Corbin was also involved in the fight, and noted:

Escort Bostons and Fortresses to Mateur sidings and aerodrome. Good job by Americans – Bounced by 109s. No luck – Robbie 109 dest. Chas missing – later safe– wounded. 2 109s destroyed.

He amplified his logbook note in his diary later:

Hell of a mist at first, but took off at 10 a.m. as top cover to Bostons and Fortresses, we were at 17,000 ft. They pranged railway sidings at Mateur and aerodrome with

109s on – a very good job by the Yanks. After they had bombed Mateur we were jumped by 109s, about six attacked and eighteen stayed above. I had no R/T, which made it a bit sticky, and my No. 2 went home earlier; two got behind and I had a dogfight; high pressure. So did Chumley. I shook mine off but could not get in a position to fire. On landing Robby had destroyed one and Chas was missing, he was last seen apparently climbing like hell towards the 109s. We hope he comes back; he should, being an expert Hun destroyer, baler-outer, etc. A great day – a gramophone has arrived – civilization has come to us at last, will these records be overused.

Charnock's danger was not entirely over, however. Coming across an Arab he asked for help, but the Arab was reluctant. An Arab dog attacked him and he was forced to pull out his revolver and shoot it. Following this, the Arab became more amenable to assisting the wounded pilot, and took him twelve miles to British troops, who transferred him to the aid of a field ambulance unit, from where he was taken to the military hospital in Bone.

On 20 December the airfield was attacked, and Sgt Roy Hussey increased his score again, shooting down a Messerschmitt Bf 109 and bringing his score to two destroyed, one probable and one Ju 87 ground victory. Robbie Robertson (RN-R) was shot down by a Bf 109G, but was later credited with shooting down a Bf 109 himself. Laurie Frampton (EP962) missed the excitement, but entered in his logbook:

Patrol base. Drome strafed by 109s. About to take off – missed the fun. Roy got a 109. Robbie shot down – crash-landed, wounded in head.

72 Sqn group inspecting a Bf 109G shot down near Mateur by the squadron. (T.B. Hughes)

On the 22nd, during an escort to two Tac R Hurricanes in the morning, Flt Lt Forde was able to attack a light tank south-east of Medjez, while in the afternoon two more Hurricanes were escorted to the Medjez and Pont-du-Fahs areas. During the second operation Sqn Ldr Oxspring destroyed an Fw 190, and Sgt Laurie Frampton (EP962) damaged another. Flg Off Hardy claimed a Ju 88 damaged. Laurie Frampton managed to become separated from the rest of the squadron, recording in his logbook:

Escort 2 Hurricane Recco Medjez el Bab – Pont-du-Fahs. No. 2 to CO; lost squadron chasing 88 in cloud. We bounced 109s near Medjez. CO got one, I damaged one.

Over this period the squadron was fully occupied in providing escorts to TAC R and fighter-bomber Hurricanes, and patrols over the airfield. The airfield patrols were not entirely effective, though, and several times the *Luftwaffe* managed to get through and make attacks. Ben Hitt remembers the preparation in the lead-up to Christmas in Tunisia:

Christmas was coming. We had a new RN:Q and regular pilot, Pete Fowler, flying it. Christmas Eve it was raining heavily. The plane's radiator developed a leak, and Jock and I spent a long time fitting a new one, finishing in darkness, soaking wet and covered in mud. So to Christmas Day, and it was still raining. A single Spitfire took off and never returned. We got extra rations and Jock made a Christmas cake from dry biscuits and some fruit. It was not appreciated. We were able to buy ten cigarettes and a bottle of beer each, and one of our pilots, Flt Lt Forde, gave us another ten cigarettes. That night Jock and I were on guard from 6.30 to 10.30, and then the rest of the night in a small marquee, ankle deep in mud and very wet. It was not a very happy Christmas.

A few days later we were working like the clappers. It was dawn-to-dusk stuff, a lot of air activity. We were in the middle of the airfield with petrol for a stranded aircraft, German bombers and fighters overhead. There was a bomb crater a couple of hundred yards away and we headed for it like Olympic sprint champions on the theory that lightning never strikes twice in the same place. That action overhead resulted in two Ju 88s shot down in flames and one Spitfire lost.

On Christmas Eve reinforcements for 72 Sqn were offshore in a convoy off Gibraltar. One of them was Rodney Scrase:

Tom Hughes and I spent Christmas Eve 1942 on board HMT Salacia. We were in the Bay of Gibraltar and awaiting disembarkation. All night long depth charges went off at frequent intervals, so it was a relief when we landed and were put up in a convent. I need hardly say there were no longer nuns on the premises.

Our first task was to test a number of tropicalized Spit Mk Vb and Vc aircraft which had been assembled at North Front and were ready to go out to Oran to make good losses we were suffering from the Luftwaffe.

There was little cheer on Christmas Eve at Souk el Arba, but the squadron made the most of what it had, as Jimmy Corbin noted in his diary:

Bags of panic last night. Allocation of two squadrons for strafing armoured vehicles, one for Tac R and one for aerodrome defence. Our day for aerodrome defence, they are expecting a blitz of 'dromes as Jerry has bags of reinforcements and he aims to knock out our 'dromes. I did a dawn patrol, but recalled as weather u/s. Rained like hell – with occasional patrols. I did one in the afternoon, raining like hell all afternoon, 'drome in a hell of a state. Hell of a do eating, sliding about in the mud – Gee what a Christmas Eve – wet-through up to ankles in mud. Saving grace, we have managed to get 48 halves of beer, six bottles of whisky and two of gin – drinking in a tent, raining like hell, closing down, making best of Christmas Eve. Share-out came to two bottles of whisky for our tent and two bottles of beer per man. Ten of us in small tent, raining like hell, fairly happy – few revolver shots and so to bed.

Christmas Day was little better, according to Jimmy Corbin:

Still raining like hell. Too lazy to go to breakfast, just as well as cookhouse flooded out. Rain stopped by lunchtime. Had a glorious Christmas dinner of stew; we only get stew every day. Still, it could be a lot worse. A Hurricane went off to look for the Army and has not returned, probably lost in cloud and rain, poor chap. Got more booze from the NAAFI and had a sing-song in a house in town, nearly everyone hey ho. Pryth very funny falling about in mud, and so to bed.

On the 30th ten aircraft dropped bombs on the airfield, damaging two aircraft on the field. On the 31st Ben Hitt and several others managed to escape from the endless work and the bombing to a rest camp in the hills:

New Year's Eve – A small rest camp had been set up in the hills in a place called Ghardimaou, and about eight of us, including Jock and myself, were to go there for three days – Shangri La. As we left, Souk el Arba was being bombed again. We did not stay up to see the New Year in, but retired to bed for a well-earned rest. New Year's Day we had a good wash and clean-up, writing letters, and walked to some hot springs where much time was spent on washing of feet. We then had our photograph taken by the squadron cameraman, known as 'Kodak'. Flg Off Tom Hughes in 1941. (T.B. Hughes)

The pilots were getting increasingly frustrated by the lack of flying due to the weather and the poor state of the airfield by the 30th, as Jimmy Corbin relates:

Rodney Diran Scrase. (R.D. Scrase)

Sweep cancelled – done very little for past few days. Jerry must be beginning to think that we have no Air Force – the Army must also think so. A few aerodrome patrols, I took off on panic with Dan, the Huns have been overhead three times today. The last time eight dive-bombed and gunned 'drome, damaged three kites, injured few people and scared most. The 'drome patrol probably got one. It is about time someone got their finger out, organized an offensive with more squadrons of fighters and bombers and gave Jerry something to think about. We still live on the 'drome; not a good thing for the nerves and comfort.

On New Year's Eve twelve Spitfires attacked the MT Repair Shop to the south-east of Pont-du-Fahs, bombing the building and strafing two lorries and a staff car on the return trip. Later five Spitfires were tasked to sweep the Medjez el Bab–St Cyprien road, but were quickly diverted to deal with seven Bf 109s bombing the airfield. The Messerschmitts destroyed a Beaufighter on the ground before escaping. The squadron suffered no casualties during the attack. Laurie Frampton (EP962) was among the pilots giving chase to the attackers:

Escort Hurricanes. Enemy aircraft reported five minutes after take-off. Strafed 'drome. We chased them without results.

Jimmy Corbin had more to say on the subject of lack of aircraft and operational capability in his diary entry for the 31st:

Boys came back after 190s that bombed and gunned the 'drome at 3.30 p.m. We wish we could take the offensive, but some stupid clots think that you can win a war by sitting on the 'drome and getting strafed. Eighteen aircraft to protect 'drome and Army and fight Luftwaffe with pilots somewhat shagged but in fairly good spirits. Eighteen aircraft against about 120 German aircraft within about eighty miles' radius, apart from dive-bombers, recce and heavy bombers. Alas alack, hey ho, we can't do anything, maybe someone will remove finger higher up.

There was no respite for the squadron on New Year's Day 1943. Twenty-nine patrols were flown over the airfield. There were several changes in the squadron,

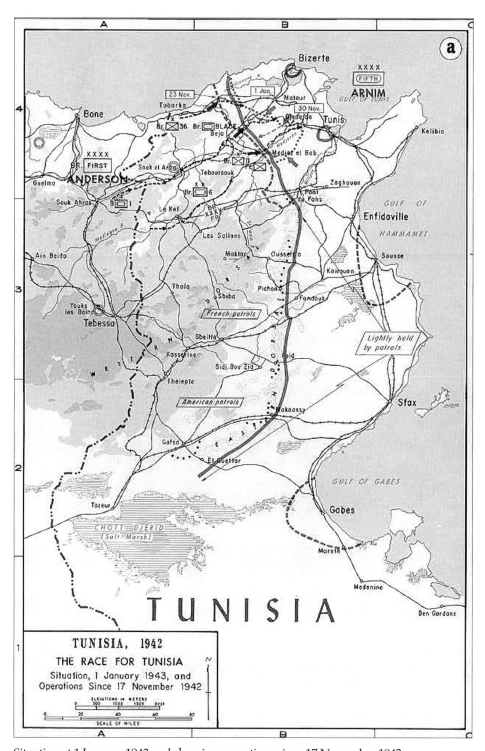

Situation at 1 January 1943 and showing operations since 17 November 1942.

though, with 'A' Flight commander, Flt Lt Krohn, posted, and Flg Off D.G.S.R. Cox taking his place. 'B' Flight also rang the changes, with Flt Lt Forde being promoted to squadron leader and posted to 152 Sqn. His replacement as flight commander was Plt Off S.W. Daniel.

On the afternoon of the 2nd twelve Spitfires took off to escort eight Hurri-bombers in an attack of an enemy strongpoint in a farmhouse just south-east of Medjez el Bab. The Hurri-bombers were very accurate in their attacks, and bombs were seen to go through the roof of the farm building. Overhead the Medjez–Massicault area, the Spitfire pilots sighted some Bf 109s, and in the ensuing battle Sqn Ldr Oxspring shot down a Bf 109F, while newly promoted Flt Lt Cox damaged another. Oxspring's victim was the Knight's Cross holder *Feldwebel* Anton Hafner of II/JG51, who was wounded.

Early on the 5th Wg Cdr Gilroy led eleven more 72 Sqn pilots in a Hurri-bomber escort. They were after an enemy road convoy lurking in a gorge. Blue Section was allowed to dive down and begin strafing runs, during which a light armoured car, a gun post and a house in the area were hit. Unfortunately, Sgt Dewar failed to return from the sortie. A few hours later Wg Cdr Gilroy led the squadron off again, and just west of Mateur they joined battle with a formation of Bf 109s. A wild mêlée commenced, and Flg Off Hardy and Plt Off Lewis both destroyed Fw 190s which had joined the battle.

The day's work was far from done, though, as Sheep Gilroy led the squadron again in the afternoon on a sortie to cover ground operations west of Mateur. On the way back to Souk el Arba they sighted twelve Junkers Ju 87s and six Fw 190s, all laden with bombs, at 5,000 ft. The Spitfires immediately waded in, and the Germans all jettisoned their bombs on sighting the attackers. Though the Stukas and Fw 190s tried to make good their escape, they left many of their number behind burning on the desert floor, as 72 Sqn had a field day. WO Alan Gear and WO Hunter shared a Ju 87 destroyed, Plt Off Stone and Plt Off Daniels both shot down Fw 190s, Flg Off Arthur Jupp and Plt Off Dalton Prytherch both damaged Fw 190s, and Sgt Griffiths shot down another Ju 87. To add to the victory celebrations on this day of success it was learned that Sqn Ldr Oxspring had been awarded a second Bar to his DFC and Flt Lt D.G.S.R. Cox had also been awarded the DFC, the citation recording his 'inspiring leadership'.

Wg Cdr Gilroy accompanied the Spitfires of 72 Sqn once more on a ten-aircraft escort to Hurri-bombers. The Hurri-bombers successfully attacked their target, enemy gun positions, and on the return a lone Fw 190 was sighted. Red Section dived after it, and Flg Off Hardy, Flg Off Arthur Jupp and Sgt Smith all shared in its destruction, watching as the German fighter rolled over and crashed into the ground upside-down. At 1200 hrs eight 72 Sqn Spitfires were airborne and soon mixing it with German fighters. The sole victory in the fight, a Bf 109F, went to Flt Lt Daniel. Later in the afternoon another formation of eight Spitfires were patrolling near Mateur when they sighted some enemy aircraft. The Spitfires found it difficult to engage the Germans as they were dodging in and out of cloud. During this game of tag, Plt Off Le Cheminant noticed that his cockpit canopy was coming loose, and he was forced to fly with one hand while holding on to it with the other to prevent its departure. He dived down to ground level to get out of the way of the impending fight, but was followed down by two Messerschmitts. Hoping to evade this difficult situation, he began dodging up and down valleys at low level, and with some luck he managed to come around behind the German fighters, where he opened fire on one of the unsuspecting aircraft with a long burst. The Messerschmitt was last seen heading east and descending. Le Cheminant claimed one damaged.

Ground targets came to the top of the list on the 9th, and eight Spitfires carried out a 'Rhubarb' in the Pont-du-Fahs area, where they shot-up two large armoured cars, a blue car which crashed into a ditch and a German truck carrying troops. Between the 11th and 15th the pilots were kept busy providing escorts to Hurri-bombers and Tac R Hurricanes, and though they saw no action themselves they were given a grandstand view of the large-scale ground fighting around Medjez el Bab. Jimmy Corbin flew one Hurricane escort on the 11th, and noted:

Bags of flak. Bombed ravine 15 miles south of Pont-du-Fahs. Landed Souk el Khemis as our 'drome u/s.

On his second escort sortie he noted:

Bags of flak at Medjez. Good battle on ground,

and he amplified on this in his diary:

Up at dawn, took off at 0745 to escort Hurri-bombers to ravine fifteen miles south of Pont-du-Fahs to bomb concentration of German troops and transports as Army wanted to advance. Shaky take-off after frightening job taxiing round track; almost a seaplane on take-off. Looked a good job by Hurris, but over target area too long for comfort. Landed at new base at Souk el Khemis, where 111 and 93 had moved to, a very good 'drome and near to one that we hope to take over in a few days' time. Fed with 111 who have a good setup in a farmhouse away from the 'drome. Tac R in afternoon, Medjez to Pont-du-Fahs area, bags of flak and good battle on ground, otherwise all quiet. 93 collected trouble that we stirred up, one boy down by flak, but Wg Cdr Gilroy got a 109 with his No. 2.

Among the forces involved in the struggle for North Africa were the Free French of General Leclerc, who had fought their way into Libya from Chad and by the 12th had chased the Germans out of the Fezzan in Southern Libya, assisting the British, who began another push in Libya on the 15th. The squadron ceased operations on the 15th to transfer to a new home on the airfield at Souk el Khemis, known by the codename Euston. The squadron HQ personnel had arrived at Euston the day before, having waited at Ghardimaou since 24 December for orders to move up. As he retreated, Rommel left a rearguard at Buerat in Libya, but this was defeated by the Eighth Army by the 16th, and the distance to the Tunisian border was now only 300 miles. That day the squadron settled in by flying twenty-four patrols over their new base. While Jimmy Corbin was airborne, Ben Hitt was on the move by road to Souk el Khemis:

A move to a new airstrip at Souk el Khemis, which was a much larger, flatter area with better drainage, and for the ground crew, better accommodation. Only eight to a tent and situated in the middle of an orange and lime grove, away from the airfield. Again a lot of time was spent digging trenches, setting up latrines and so on. There were moans about the food, a welfare committee was set up, not sure why, but the food improved. Rice, porridge and potatoes, but still dry biscuits! There was a slight disadvantage to the new campsite, and that was the occasional appearance of a snake. There was no way of knowing if they were venomous, so no chances were taken.

Jack Lancaster also remembers the move to Souk el Khemis:

We left Souk el Arba in January 1943 and went to Souk el Khemis, where the ground was much better (or was it?). It was sandy soil and therefore much drier. However, once the sun shone again it dried out, and the air was filled with dust when aircraft taxied or took off.

We changed our Spit Vbs for Spit IXs, and found they were not tropicalized, and therefore subject to problems from the sand. It became necessary to change the front four cylinder plugs after each flight, and dismantle and clean the automatic boost units every day at least. Flg Off Farish ingeniously designed a filter that could be hung over the air intake and then dropped off after take-off. This caused a tremendous amount of extra work, but it shows the kind of mechanics we had that we held the serviceability record in North Africa and the squadron accounted for fifty-three enemy aircraft destroyed, twenty probables and fifty damaged. I couldn't have wished to have been associated with a better team than those chaps on 72. They were the salt of the earth. I remember one day I was standing on one of the aircraft, had the automatic boost control in bits, and I was saying rather nasty things about the people who sent out Spit IXs without filters to a sandy Africa, and a voice over my shoulder said, 'Well, I can understand your feelings, lad, but it was the only thing we could do for the time being, and we shall get over it as soon as we can.' I turned round to find that he was an air vice-marshal, and he was the engineer for 242 Group. I was careful in the future not to express my feelings without knowing who was around.

A view of Souk el Khemis, looking down the taxiway to Spitfires parked beyond. (R.D. Scrase)

'Rio' Wright remembers Souk el Khemis for another reason:

Conditions at Souk el Khemis were so much improved, though my recollections of the effects of Mepacrin and Atabrin were that spades were kept handy for a few days in case it was not possible to reach the normal toilets.

Jimmy Corbin (ER812) flew a patrol off Cape Rosa and crashed on landing, noting in his logbook, 'Horrible prang on landing.' He expected to be in some trouble over the incident:

Patrolled Cape Rosa at 1.30 for 1½ hours, bags of activity but none near us. I had a horrible prang on landing, damaged my own kite and nearly wrote off a 'B' Flight aircraft. A damn poor show, expecting one hell of a strip. Can't figure out why or how I did it.

Souk el Khemis drowning in mud on Christmas Day 1942. (L. Frampton)

On the 18th the Germans launched a counter-attack, gaining ground against the Free French but being repulsed by the British forces they encountered. Six Spitfires escorted Hurri-bombers attacking enemy positions in a prison south-east of Pont-du-Fahs. The Germans attempted to get between the fighters and Hurri-bombers, but the British formation managed to turn away and the Germans flew into cloud. Four of the Bf 109s reappeared, and Sgt Pearson was able to pounce on one of them, sending it home damaged. Later that afternoon the six Spitfires were giving escort support to Hurricanes bombing tank formations east of Bou Arrada when they sighted the Bf 109s. A tail chase commenced, in and out of the clouds, with five of the six pilots opening fire on the fleeing Germans. The closest they were able to close the gap to was 350 yards, and one of the Messerschmitts was seen to slow down. Sensing the chance of a kill, the Spitfires continued to close, but just then a wall of intense light flak came up at them and they were forced to break formation and head for home individually, the Messerschmitts escaping in the process. The following day Jimmy Corbin (RN:D) was in action again, escorting Hurribombers to a tank depot near Pont-du-Fahs, where, as he noted in his logbook, he had head on poop at 109, no visible results. Later damaged by Sgt Pearson.

Tom Hughes and Rodney Scrase had yet to properly join the squadron, and they were still employed in ferrying aircraft from Gibraltar, as Rodney remembers:

A casual meal at Euston. (L. Frampton)

On 18th January we flew out as part of a balbo of twenty or so aircraft with a Beaufighter to guide us. My logbook shows 2 hrs flying time. But we were not to be sent forward. A C-47 Dakota took us back to Gibraltar.

Order, counter-order! The next day it was back to Maison Blanche, the airport for Algiers, and on from there on 28 January to Souk el Arba.

On the 19th the Eighth Army had captured Homs and Tarhuna, and was closing on Tripoli. By the 23rd Montgomery was in Tripoli and three days later had taken Zaula, less than 100 miles from the Tunisian border. Three days after that, the first Eighth Army troops crossed the border from Libya. Over the days that followed, the squadron busied itself with escort and ground-attack sorties, and then on the 26th disaster struck two of the pilots. Eight Spitfires left Euston at 1330 hrs to escort Hurri-bombers to the railway station at Jefna. Things began to go wrong, however, when the Hurricanes dropped their bombs several miles short of the target onto British troops displaying yellow flags. While the bombing was in progress, two of the Spitfires, Blue 2 (ER589) and 4 (ER678) collided in mid-air. Flg Off Jupp in Blue 3 observed the whole tragedy:

The sergeants' mess at Souk el Khemis. Horner, Tager, Hamilton, Unknown, Boakes, Charnock, Hogg, Frampton, Sollitt, Garland, Riddell, Hunter, Watkins, Field. (L. Frampton)

The whole flight turned starboard and I saw Blue 4, Plt Off Stone, turning on the inside, slightly ahead of me, and he continued to turn until it seemed as though he saw Blue 2, Sgt Smith. He tried to skid away, but both their starboard wings touched. Blue 2's starboard wing went through the roundel of Blue 4's starboard wing. They stayed together for a few seconds, then broke away. Blue 2 appeared to climb, and then commenced to spin, while Blue 4 did a gentle turn to the right, finally developing into a spin. I saw both aircraft hit the ground.

Laurie Frampton (ER808) recorded the sortie in his logbook:

Escort Hurri-bombers – Jefna. Bloody good bombing but wrong side of lines [comment about side of lines later deleted and replaced with 'turned out to be OK']. Plt Off Stone and Sgt Smith crashed and spun in.

Jimmy Corbin also recorded the sortie:

Hurri-bomber escort. Supposed to be to Jefna station, but they bombed our troops. Sgt Smith and Plt Off Stone collided, both killed.

The Spitfires had collided at 1,500 ft, and the pilots had little chance of escaping by parachute before they hit the ground. A pilot of 93 Sqn reported seeing one of the aircraft, minus a wing, burning at the foot of some hills. The bodies of Plt Off Stone and Sgt Smith were later found by the Army.

Ben Hitt remembered the 26th for an entirely different reason: 'A morning off, and had first bath since leaving Algiers.' After a day of rest on the 27th, escort sorties were flown on the 28th, during which the pilots shot-up ground targets. Replacement pilots also arrived on the 28th in the shape of Flg Off T.B. 'Tom' Hughes, Plt Off R.D. 'Rodney' Scrase, Sgt A.E. Passmore and Sgt J.B. King. The last few days of the month were filled with further escorts and ground-attack sorties, with many enemy gun positions and emplacements being attacked for no loss. Rodney Scrase found the arrival on the squadron to be something of an eye opener:

We were soon to realize that being on a squadron was not an easy break. Standing at dispersal to watch our colleagues who were flying in a two-squadron formation, we had the shock of seeing Flt Lt Mortimer Rose DFC crash into the wing leader – Wg Cdr 'Sheep' Gilroy. 'Sheep', who was probably no higher than 900 ft, managed to bale out, but Mortimer Rose crashed and was killed. I thought, 'What on earth is happening to us, here we are, green boys straight out from England.' The lost pilot was very experienced, with a DFC, and was lost on virtually the first operations in North Africa.

Following two and a half gruelling months of operations, which had commenced on 16 November, the squadron was finally rested and taken off operations on 1

February. The pilots were sent to Constantine, where the RAF had set up a rest-house, for a few days of rest before heading back to Gibraltar to pick up brand-new Spitfire Mk IX replacements. The battle-weary Mk Vs were dispersed to other units. Rodney Scrase went back to Gibraltar once more:

Plt Off Stone, killed in a collision on 26 January 1943. (72 Sqn)

For Tom and me it was a question of back and forth from Algeria to Gibraltar. The squadron was sent back to re-equip with Spit IXs. We spent most of the month in Gib, getting experience on type, and then returned to Tunisia – this time to a new airfield fifteen miles away at Souk el Khemis, which translates as Market Wednesday. The engineers had built four landing-strips on a sandy, fast-draining surface. These were named after the main London termini. Our strip was Euston – just over 1,000 metres in length, and happily a big improvement over Souk el Arba, the translation of which is Market Friday. The nearby railway halt became our Squadron HQ, and despite the frequent bombing by German aircraft – 109s and 190s – we were able to hold our own.

A small group of the squadron ground crew were also given a rest period, being sent to the 5 Corps rest camp at Ain Draham for three days. While the pilots were away from Souk el Khemis, the nearby airfield, codenamed Waterloo, was attacked by enemy fighter-bombers, and though the squadron's attached anti-aircraft flight would have dearly loved to engage them, they were too far away to open fire. Much damage and several casualties were left at Waterloo. On the 3rd, the fighter-bombers returned to Waterloo, causing more damage and casualties. On the 4th the Germans attempted to mete out the same punishment to Euston several times, but each time RAF fighters headed them off. That day a servicing party from the squadron set off for Le Khroub airfield at Constantine to meet the new Spitfire Mk IXs as they arrived from Gibraltar. Ben Hitt went with the detachment:

A small detachment, including John Dodds and myself, were going to a place called Constantine to meet the Spit IXs, a journey of approximately 160 miles. On arrival we had our first taste of bread since leaving the troopship. Constantine had a huge chasm right through the centre of the town. Very picturesque, with some old Roman baths – those Romans certainly got around. There was a forces canteen and a cinema with an English-speaking film. We visited a local hairdresser. John Dodds and Jock Turner were getting rather scarce of hair on top, and decided to have it all off so as to encourage luxurious growth. They sat side by side, and two Arab hair cutters started to cut simultaneously, so that neither could back out. Much laughter and wise-cracking from those of us who had hair, and of course the luxurious growth was all a dream.

On the 5th another party of ground crew left for well-deserved rest at Ain Draham, while the first party returned to Souk el Arba. Having been well rested at Constantine, the pilots left on the 7th for Telergma, where they boarded a Dakota for the trip to Gibraltar. The Dakota landed at Maison Blanche *en route*, but due to the urgent need for transport aircraft to fly supplies to the front, the pilots were offloaded and had to stay in Algiers.

The personnel at Souk el Khemis had some things to boost their morale over this period too; a large quantity of mail arrived on the 6th, and after seventy-seven days of biscuits the squadron had an issue of white bread on the 8th. While the pilots were stuck in Algiers the weather took a nasty turn, and those left at Souk el Khemis suffered severe thunderstorms, which left many of their tents flooded. The first party of pilots finally arrived in Gibraltar to collect their new charges on the 12th, followed the next day by the remainder. Rommel was determined not to give any more ground, and in fact hoped to throw the Allies back in a counter-offensive on the 12th. The attack against the US 2nd Corps in central Tunisia threw the Americans back in disarray, and this was followed by further success on the 14th, when Von Arnim's 5th *Panzerarmee* pushed 2nd Corps even further back, inflicting heavy losses in the battle at Kasserine Pass.

While the pilots flew familiarization sorties on their new mounts at Gibraltar, the ground crew had a little excitement at Euston on the 14th, when one of the tents caught fire, with the loss of most of the kit in it. Ben Hitt and the ground crew detachment returned to Souk el Khemis after two weeks' waiting for the new Spitfires:

After two weeks of the somewhat quieter life, we heard that our Spitfire IXs were not now coming to Constantine, after all, and that we had to return to Souk el Khemis. During this period the American forces had been pushed back, the Germans having advanced sixty miles. We had to take a different route because of armoured vehicles on the main roads. We stopped at night at a British Army camp. They were all away on patrol, so we borrowed their tents and bedding. About 3.00 a.m. they returned and were not amused to find the 'Brylcreem Boys' in residence. As we could hear heavy gunfire in the distance, there was no great ambition to leave. We passed through Souk Ahras and Le Kef. The roads were crowded with supplies and vehicles going in the opposite direction to assist the Americans. The weather was appalling, with rain and strong winds. We heard gunfire in the distance and we held our Sten guns at the ready. Dinner was one slice of bully beef and a dry biscuit. This was not the good life. Arrived back at Souk el Khemis at about 4.00 p.m. to be met with a fantastic thunderstorm, and the whole airfield looked like a lake. The Germans were still advancing in the south. There were rumours of us being cut off, as well as warning of possible German parachute landings, and still we had no Spitfire IXs.

Second Bar to DFC Citation

LONDON GAZETTE, 16TH FEBRUARY 1943

Squadron Leader Robert Wardlow Oxspring DFC*

During initial operations from forward airfields in North Africa Squadron Leader Oxspring led his formation on many sorties. He destroyed one enemy aircraft, bringing his total victories to eight. His outstanding devotion to duty and fine fighting qualities have been worthy of high praise.

Offensive operations recommenced on the 17th as the German advance beyond Kasserine was halted. The Germans suffered another reverse in the south as the Eighth Army captured Medenine. Over the days that followed the weather deteriorated and restricted training flights at Gibraltar and the ground crew had to suffer a tremendous gale followed by a huge thunderstorm on the 19th.

DFC Citation

LONDON GAZETTE, 16TH FEBRUARY 1943

Cox, David F/O

This officer has participated in many sorties including attacks on transport, troops and airfields. His inspiring leadership has won the confidence of his fellow pilots. Flying Officer Cox has destroyed six enemy aircraft, three of them in North Africa.

The attached flight of anti-aircraft guns and their crews left the squadron on the 20th as part of a general reorganization of ground defence, and was to become the nucleus of No. 4350 AA Flight, RAF Regiment. During their time attached to the squadron they had been called upon to defend the airfields many times, and were responsible for the destruction of at least one enemy aircraft. The squadron was sorry to see them leave. Fierce fighting continued in central Tunisia as the Germans attempted to exploit their advance following the breakout from the Kasserine Pass, but by the 20th offensive operations were halted and the Germans began a withdrawal toward the Mareth Line. On the 24th, while waiting for the new Spitfires, the ground crew were kept busy looking after some others flown by Americans, as Ben Hitt recalls:

An early morning start as an American fighter squadron arrived flying Spitfires. We refuelled and inspected them, and they took off to escort an American bomber force.

The pilots left Gibraltar on the 21st with their new Spitfires, and flew in to Maison Blanche where Plt Off H.S. Lewis had undercarriage trouble and was forced to crash-land, escaping uninjured. Over the next few days more familiarization sorties were flown at Maison Blanche before the Spitfires finally arrived at Souk el Khemis on the 25th. The arrival at Souk el Khemis was anything but routine, however. The weather when the seventeen-aircraft formation set off had been reported as cloudy inland but clear along the coast. The Spitfires flew along the coast before turning inland near the Tunisian border, passing through a tropical storm in the area. Before they could reach Euston the storm broke with full force over the airfield, and very quickly the runway became flooded and visibility lowered rapidly. It was then that things began to go awry. Two of the Spitfires made good landings at Tingley, while Sgt Hussey managed to make a very good wheels-down forced landing on a flat piece of land in very bad conditions, damaging the airscrew in the process. Plt Off Jimmy Corbin (EN198) tipped his Spitfire onto its nose trying to land on the runway, before the rest of the pilots, bar one, were able to make safe landings. Sgt Passmore (EN246) misjudged his landing speed, attempted to correct this, stalled and spun in. He was thrown clear of the aircraft in the crash and was killed. Jimmy Corbin wrote in his logbook:

Maison Blanche – Euston. Sgt Passmore spun in at Paddington. What an arrival, hail, rain and runway in six inches of water.

Amplifying this in his diary, he wrote:

Just past Souk el Arba ran into a terrific electric rainstorm. Complete shambles – visibility 3/5ths. No R/T reception with Chukka – eventually landed. Realized on touch down that I would nose over, tried to avoid by slight moving but no go. Very depressed, beautiful nine f***ed up. Told my No. 2 not to land. I found I was sixth to land. CO said 'drome was fairly dry when he landed. Chem, the fifth to land, said he almost nosed over. I landed five minutes

Oxspring and Cox congratulate each other on the award of their DFCs. (72 Sqn)

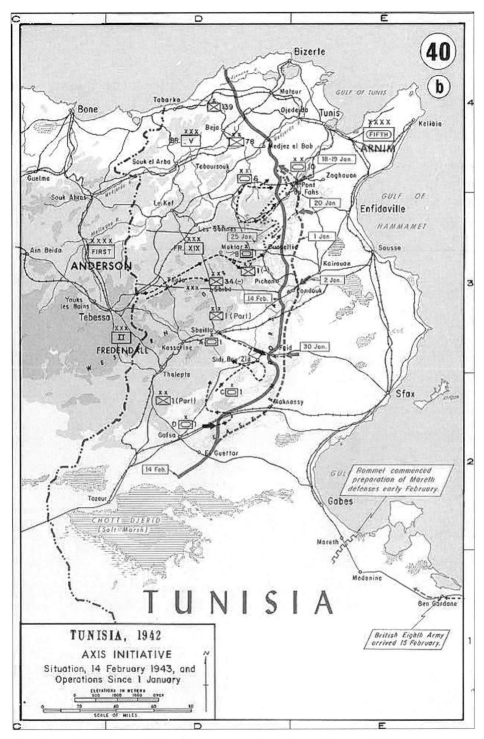

Situation at 14 February 1943, showing operations since 1 January 1943.

after him and wish I hadn't. Drome put u/s in about ten to fifteen, never seen so much rain. Two landed at Waterloo, five at Paddington. Sgt Passmore spun in on landing at Paddington and was killed. Sgt Hussey crash-landed at Ghard. Two more landed at Tingley. Everyone very brassed-off about bad luck and bad start. I have been told by the engineering officer that I had burst tailwheel, which did not make things easier.

Ben Hitt recalled the disastrous arrival:

Our own Spitfire IXs were due to arrive. During the afternoon they arrived, and along with them came another terrific thunderstorm. The first two or three managed to land, other turned back and we lost four aircraft and one pilot. The airfield was again like a lake. The gods were not smiling on us. The next day the rest of the aircraft arrived. Radiators and propellers damaged by hailstones and much paintwork removed from the main planes. During this period there was considerable air activity. Almost a non-stop flow of American bombers and P-38 Lightning fighters endeavouring to slow the German advance.

Rodney Scrase brought in one of the Spitfires from Gibraltar and witnessed the untidy arrivals:

In February we returned to Gibraltar to collect Mk IXs. On our return flight, six hours in all, in loose formation and with an overnight stop at Maison Blanche, we arrived at Souk el Khemis in the midst of a heavy rainstorm. Landing on a darkened airfield was no fun. No lights but I had the thrill of a safe landing. Such was not to be the case for all my colleagues. One fatal casualty and a number of damaged new Mk IXs did not speak well for our skill as pilots. The improved performance of the Mk IX spoke wonders in our efforts to combat the enemy. They were flying from concrete runways on the outskirts of Tunis and Bizerta; we from muddy 1,000 ft strips covered with Somerfield tracking. This resembled chicken wire and did give us some help in taking-off and landing, but many were the occasions when an airman sitting on your tail was a requirement when taxiing.

On the 25th the RAF began a round-the-clock bombing campaign in Tunisia, flying more than 2,000 raids in the next two days. On the 26th the aircraft which had landed at Tingley flew in and the squadron buried Sgt Passmore at Souk el Arba. Laurie Frampton (EN299) recorded the arrival in his logbook:

Maison Blanche–Euston. Arrived in terrific storm – Sammy Passmore stalled in at Paddington.

The squadron's first offensive sortie with the new Mk IXs was flown on the 27th, led by Sqn Ldr Oxspring. Six aircraft took off for an offensive sweep over

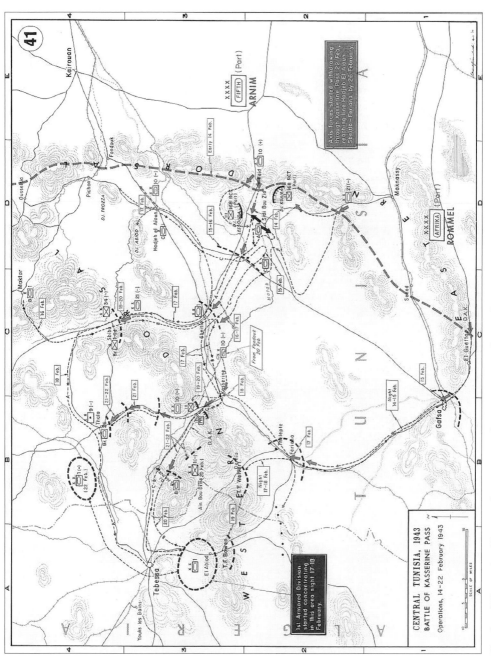

Battle of Kasserine Pass and operations between 14 and 22 February 1943.

Beja and Medjez el Bab. Shortly after take-off, Red 1 returned with radio failure and Red 2 with an engine problem. The four remaining Spitfires continued and were vectored to engage some Bf 109s near Taboursouk, but they were only able to get close enough to the enemy to note that they were marked with blue and white stripes on the rear fuselage forward of the tail. At this point Jimmy Corbin and the other pilots were somewhat concerned about the proximity of the Germans to the airfield:

Never seen so much air activity. Hurris over about four times. Mitchells and Spits in dozens giving cover and strafing Jerry in the Mateur–Beja valley. We can hear bombing from our 'drome and occasional gunfire. Jerry only about four miles from Beja. If he gets Beja will definitely get out. But we think with today's blasting the Army will hold OK.

TO/ O.C 72 SQUADRON
FROM/ 126536 P/O CORBIN
DATE/ 26/2/43

Accident Report to Spitfire EN198

Dear Sir,

I have the honour to report an accident to Spitfire EN198 on 25/2/43.

As Green 1 I was flying from Maison Blanche to Souk el Khemis (Euston) and on reaching my destination we ran into a very bad rain storm. As visibility was bad I went away from here to allow Red, Yellow and Blue Section to land. After some time I called up the aforementioned section to find out whether I could land but could get no reply. I asked my No. 2 to call up Chukka but I did not get any satisfactory response so decided to land, telling my No. 2 to remain airborne. Soon after touch down I realized that my tail would not stay down and thought that I might tip on my nose. Due to the amount of water on the runway I considered it inadvisable to go around again, thinking that the sudden acceleration would cause me to go over on my back. As the speed decreased the aircraft started a slight skid to the left. I checked this and immediately swung slightly and skidded to the right and after skidding some thirty yards tipped up on my nose. I immediately informed my No. 2 to land at another base.

After this accident I was told by the pilot who landed five minutes before me that his tail also came up quite a bit on landing, so the aerodrome had become u/s within five minutes.

I was also told by the Squadron Engineering Officer that my tailwheel had burst. This may have been done on take-off at Maison Blanche or on landing. The burst tailwheel would also cause the tail to bounce badly on landing.

The last day of February saw three sweeps. During the second, an escort to Hurri-bombers attacking tanks near Beja, the six Spitfires spotted an enemy fighter below. Sqn Ldr Oxspring led the headlong dive to catch it, and opened fire, seeing pieces flying off the Bf 109 from his fire. Several other fighters were inconclusively engaged, and the squadron returned with only Sqn Ldr Oxspring's damaged claim to show for the fight. Tom Hughes recorded the sortie in his logbook:

Hurribomber escort to Beja. Two bursts at 109 & 190. Stb'd mainplane holed.

The third sweep had slightly more success. Flt Lt S.W. Daniel led six Spitfires as high cover to Hurri-bombers, and on completion of this task continued to patrol the area. They soon sighted six Bf 109Fs north-east and slightly behind and below. The Spitfires turned, as did the Messerschmitts, which flew into the sun hoping to escape. The Germans then split their pairs, one fighter continuing to climb, while the other dived for the deck. Flt Lt Daniel, Red 1, was slowly overhauling one of the climbing fighters when it flicked over and dived for the ground. Daniel flicked into a dive and followed it down at full speed, opening fire on the German at 300 yards. He soon saw hits on the German fighter, but was forced to break away by anti-aircraft fire. Meanwhile, Plt Off G. Malan, Blue 2, was chasing another Bf 109F, which was last seen pouring out white glycol smoke and heading as fast as it could go for Bizerta.

Returning to report their successes, the pilots found that several promotions and awards had been announced that day. Flt Lt Forde, who had left the squadron for 152 Sqn, had been awarded the DFC and Mentioned in Dispatches. WO Chas Charnock also received the DFC, as did Plt Off R.J.H. Robertson, who had lost an eye in his crash-landing on 20 December. Promotions were announced for Plt Offs J. Le Cheminant and W.J. 'Jimmy' Corbin, both now flying officers.

As March opened, the Germans were desperately attempting to push through to Beja in a three-pronged assault. The Allied forces put up a stiff resistance, ably assisted by 324 Wing. 72 Squadron's new Spitfire Mk IXs gave the wing the added bonus of an aircraft which could engage the Focke-Wulfs and Messerschmitts at higher levels than their previous mounts. The opportunity to show this new ability came on 1 March, when a high-level Bf 109 was pursued by Wg Cdr Oxspring (EN116) and WO Hunter (EN135). Patrolling along the coast at 18,000 ft, six Spitfires sighted two Bf 109s above and to starboard, but were unable to engage them. However, shortly afterwards another four Messerschmitts were seen east of Beja heading westwards, skimming through the base of the clouds. The Messerschmitts bounced the airfield patrol Spitfires over base and in turn were engaged by Oxspring and his men. The wing commander and Hunter shared in the destruction of one Bf 109, whose pilot did not take any evasive action and appeared to be relying on his speed to evade the Spitfires. Having been badly hit, the Messerschmitt pilot baled out, but when he pulled his ripcord the parachute deployed then broke away, and he fell to his death. Plt Off Le Cheminant (EN242) also claimed a Bf 109 damaged. The new Spitfires had stood the test in the air, but on the ground it was a different picture, as Ben Hitt remembers:

Flt Lt S.W. Daniel. (J. Corbin)

I had a raging toothache, but we had all seen photographs of Arab dentists using pliers, so I had to travel to a small town controlled by the British Army, and the offending tooth was removed. The good news was that our pilot, Pete Fowler, was commissioned. There was a problem with the Spit IXs. The old Vbs had tropical air filters and the IXs did not. This led to dust and sand creating a problem with take-offs. Some of the more technical brains devised a cover that covered the intake and then released after take-off. We then collected the covers, and when the aircraft returned we replaced them and returned to dispersal perched on the tail.

The second mission on 2 March was an escort to B-17s attacking La Goulette. Eight Spitfires flew with the bombers to the target and as far as Beja on the return leg. Friendly fire was always a risk during these operations, particularly from the inexperienced USAAF units involved in the campaign, and on this mission the Spitfires were attacked by the B-17s' P-38 escort. Plt Off D.J. Prytherch (EN309) bore the brunt of the attack by three of the P-38s, but their fire was inaccurate and he escaped unscathed. Over Beja twenty Bf 109s were seen, but unable to climb fast enough to reach the Spitfires they turned away. Shortly

---

BRADFORD TELEGRAPH & ARGUS MARCH 1943

Bradford's 'Adopted' Fighter Squadron

I wonder how many Bradfordians know that this city officially adopted No. 72 (Fighter) Squadron of the Royal Air Force way back in May 1939.

They can be forgiven if they are unaware of this interesting fact, for inquiries I have made among Bradford's civic leaders reveal that, with one exception, they know nothing about it.

The scheme for the affiliation of RAF fighter and bomber squadrons to the principal cities and towns of the country was approved by Sir Kingsley Wood when he was Secretary of State for Air in April 1939.

Bradford was among the West Riding towns to which the squadrons were affiliated, having No. 72 Squadron, then stationed at Church Fenton, attached to them. Other allocations were as follows: Leeds, No. 609 (Auxiliary) Yeadon; Huddersfield, No. 166 (Bomber) Leconfield; Halifax, No. 97 (Bomber) Leconfield; Doncaster, No. 616 (Auxiliary) Doncaster; and Barnsley, No. 64 (Fighter) Church Fenton.

'NOBODY'S BABY'

Our report at that time stated that, 'Squadrons will be affiliated as a general rule to the town most conveniently situated, and it will fall to the municipal authorities and to the squadron commanders to maintain close co-operation. Each squadron will pay an annual ceremonial visit to the town to which it is affiliated, and will give demonstrations of formation flying. At other times the squadrons may participate in civic events and important local functions at the request of the municipal authority, when Service commitments permit.'

What has Bradford done about it since May 1939?

Official affiliation took place on 5 May 1939 but this fact was never made public. It was discussed by a sub-committee of the Corporation Finance Committee on that date and subsequently this squadron evidently became 'nobody's baby'.

Well, not quite. I mentioned this matter of the adoption to Alderman T.J. Robinson, who was Lord Mayor of Bradford in 1938–39. He recalled visiting Peel Park in June or July 1939 when five machines of No. 72 Squadron flew over from Church Fenton and gave an aerial exhibition.

CIVIC CONFESSION

But after that they must have flown, for no one in an official position, and much less the public of Bradford, has heard of this squadron and its exploits during the present war, or anything about its personnel and their achievements in battle.

Aldermen Titterington, Illingworth and Smith (Bradford's Lord Mayors since the war) and the present Lord Mayor (Mr. James Harrison) confessed that they had no knowledge of No. 72 (Fighter) Squadron, or even of the fact that it had ever been affiliated to Bradford.

We know this squadron is still operating, but details are not available about its members, and municipal Bradford doesn't seem to care!

afterwards four Bf 109s were sighted over Medjez el Bab and were engaged. Plt Off Arthur Jupp (EN292) and Sgt Hussey chased one Bf 109 to ground level and all the way to Pont-du-Fahs before their combined firepower shot it down. The pilot of the Bf 109 was *Oberfeldwebel* Herbert Rollwage of II/JG53. Rollwage, flying Messerschmitt Bf 109G-4 W.Nr.16067, was wounded in the engagement and force-landed his shot-up aircraft at Bou Arada.

The final sorties of the day were carried out by six Spitfires taking off from Souk el Khemis at 1600 hrs. Climbing to 12,000 ft over Beja they began to encounter anti-aircraft fire, and suddenly four Bf 109s appeared. After a brief mêlée the Bf 109s sped away at high speed, but not before Flg Off Le Cheminant (EN242) managed to get a few rounds into one Bf 109G, chasing it down to ground level. As they approached Pont-du-Fahs, the Messerschmitt flew headlong into the hillside at 380 mph. The remaining Spitfires continued to patrol following the engagement, and while near Tebersouk Flt Lt Tom Hughes (EN245) radioed that his engine had cut and that he was crash-landing. Tom recorded in his logbook:

Sweep at 15,000 to cover Hurri-bombers. Forced landing due to a 'missing link' in throttle. Walked home – 20 walking hours. Fired at 109 from below head on and vertically upwards.

Later he wrote a detailed account of his walk in the wilderness:

Six of the squadron were escorting a late-afternoon Hurri-bomber attack between Beja and Medjez el Bab. I was flying No. 2 to Plt Off Prytherch DFM. We suddenly met six Me 109s head on at 15,000 ft. They pulled up straight ahead of us and I fired

New Zealander Plt Off J.A.C. Pete Fowler on a motorcycle in North Africa. (72 Sqn)

at one's belly as it climbed. Eventually I seemed
to be shooting vertically upwards. I did not see a
single strike; I had not allowed enough deflection.
Then my engine failed! It simply throttled back to
tick-over speed with the throttle lever linkage loose
in my hand. I put on some steep gliding turns.
Fortunately 'Pryth' saw something was wrong and
followed me down. I had no idea where we were
in relation to the 'bomb line'. I felt we were over
the lines on the German side. I seemed quite clear
of all the other Spitfires and Me 109s, except for
Prytherch, who was circling, watching 500 ft above
me, good chap that he was.

I stretched my glide westwards towards home,
looking for somewhere to land. Then I saw a green
valley and picked on that. I saw smoke from a fire
somewhere and checked the wind direction. I made
a good wheels-up landing and stepped out unhurt.
The Spit looked sad with its Rotol prop snapped off

Oberfeldwebel Herbert Rollwage.
(via E.J. Mannings)

on all four blades, but it would fly again. I wondered whether to blow it up or not.
There was not a sound of gunfire from the battle on the ground.

I ran across the field to the hillside, which was covered with sand and scrub. In
no time I was well buried with just my face showing. I thought I would watch and
wait. Suddenly an Arab appeared and walked around the aeroplane, which was a
hundred yards from my hiding place. He may have been a farmer for all I knew.
There was still no clue as to whether I was on the German side of the lines.

It soon got dark and I thought I would head off west towards Souk el Khemis,
or at least friendly troops. The stars were out and there as no moon. There was
not a distant shot to be heard. The ground underfoot was very rough. Sand, rocks,
thorn, scrub and endless foothills were all very hard to see by starlight. I stumbled
once and put out my hand; there was a stout stake with a curved top almost like a
walking stick. It was quite miraculous, for it was suddenly there in my hand. The
North Star steered me westwards all that night. It was amazing how I could always
see hills ahead against the night sky. My flying-boots were warm and sloppy and
hell to walk in, as they did not fit well around the ankle. As the night wore on I
made good progress; although scratched by thorns, I had not fallen, thanks to my
stout stick. I thought that by dawn I should get up on a hilltop to see what I could.
I misjudged the dawn and got to a hilltop at least an hour too soon. It was freezing
cold and my teeth chattered as I waited – wondering.

As the new day dawned I could see some Spitfires circling one of the airstrips
in the valley near Souk el Khemis. I thought I only had about ten more miles to
go. I walked down into another valley past a sleeping shack where Arabs lived. A
few chickens scattered and a dog barked. I climbed more foothills and realized how

Tom Hughes's crashed Spitfire EN245. (G. Farish)

thirsty I was. I dropped into a little gorge where an Arab was loading a little donkey with sticks for a fire from the scrub and bushes. I asked him if he had any water, and he took me round a rock, where there was a crystal spring. I had my RAF-issue sunglasses on, and their tin with the strange domed lid was in my pocket. I had water-purifying tablets and dropped one in as I scooped up the welcome drink. The Arab thought me more than fussy, and drank with one hand to show me how. He looked at my revolver and wondered if he could win it from me, but we parted friends and I was refreshed by his cool spring water.

The heat of the day was terrible. I took off my thin jersey and hooked it over my forehead like a nurse's cap. By the afternoon I looked out over the wide valley with its five airfields and its muddy river. I saw two Spitfires, Dan and Pryth maybe, searching through the hills. I had two red flares, but why waste them if my legs were still working? I came to another Arab's hut, and he proudly showed me his First War Croix de Guerre and a photograph of when he served the French against the Boche. He offered me his donkey, but I proudly refused it for I was in sight of home.

I got back to the mess, pretty dehydrated, and told Greggs Farish, the engineer, that the throttle linkage had let me down. A split pin was left out and a cotter pin vibrated out. The aircraft thus had crashed but was subsequently salvaged.

On receipt of this news at base, the squadron engineering officer, Flg Off Greggs Farish, set off to locate the downed pilot, but he was unsuccessful in his first attempt. Later in the evening he set out again, this time on foot and accompanied by an airman. Farish returned at 0800 hrs on the 3rd, having searched unsuccessfully for over six hours in the area of the forced landing. Later in the day Tom Hughes turned up at the airfield in a semi-delirious state, from which he soon recovered. When he recounted his tale it transpired that the search party had, at one point, been within half a mile of the pilot. Hughes had been striking matches to help light his way, and one such light had been seen by Farish. An air search later discovered the downed Spitfire, and a ground party recovered any usable spares from it, as it was a write-off and not worth salvaging. The spares recovered from the wreck went some way to alleviating the desperate shortage of parts for the Mk IXs.

Rodney Scrase recalls the month of March for the low sortie rate and the opportunity to obtain some locally produced supplies to make life a little more bearable:

In the month of March I was to do just nine operational flights. Why so little? Our campsite had suffered from theft of parachutes by some baddies. When the police came to the camp they were able to converse only in French. Silly Scrase started talking to these guys in their own language. Well, that fixed things, and from then on I was seen as 'Squadron Interpreter'. Not only that, but some days later and greatly daring I chased some young lads who were wandering round our campsite. They were carrying some stolen goods, so I pulled out my .38 revolver and fired – admittedly in the air, but to good effect, as the boys stopped and I was able to hand them over to the burly gendarmes for appropriate attention.

Another diversion was our wine-collection run. Some twelve miles away was the village of Thibar. During the latter part of the 19th century the White Fathers had come out from France – originally with the intention of proselytizing the local population. But the Fathers soon realized the best way to achieve their object was by example, so they set about cultivating the land in that area, which benefits from the waters of the ever-flowing Medjerda river.

The rich red soil was cultivated to produce wheat, fruit, vegetable and vines. As well as the Church, a seminary, a hospital and a school were set up in the village. Houses were built for the local population. To find more work for the locals they also began the production of fine carpets. But for us there was the opportunity to buy wine and also the thick sticky liqueur Thibarene. So, at the end of most days, there was a queue of Army and RAF vehicles waiting to purchase wine and also collect supplies of beer. On many occasions I was called on to make the purchases for 72 Sqn.

The first sweep on the 3rd produced no reaction from the enemy. However, Flt Lt Cox (EN298) did return with intelligence information that the airfield at Mateur appeared to be abandoned by the enemy.

Squadron engineering officer Greggs Farish at rest. (T.B. Hughes)

Ground crew at Souk el Khemis, Spring 1943. (J. Lancaster)

The Germans made a thrust westwards from Sedjenane on the 4th, which was countered by the Allies moving reinforcements forward to meet the attack. 72 Sqn provided top cover for this movement, and in the afternoon escorted Flying Fortresses to Bizerta to bomb military camps and shipping in the Lac Bizerta. The *Luftwaffe* did not contest the attack. The day ended with information from 324 Wing that 72 Sqn was top of the wing victories list, with thirty-one destroyed, eight-and-two-thirds probably destroyed and twenty-one damaged.

There were no operations on the 5th, which was just as well, as there were major serviceability problems with the squadron's Mk IXs. The Merlin 61 was having major problems with sand ingress, and the Vokes air filter used by the Spitfire Mk V was unsuitable for use on the Mk IX. The Spitfires had to be kept flying, and as a temporary solution scavenged waste oil was being spread on the runways to reduce the dust levels.

The 6th was filled with escorts to Hurri-bombers and recce aircraft, and with darkness falling early in the region the final sorties of the day saw the Spitfires making dusk landings. The most notable incident of the day was a new order from the AOC that pilots should pay more attention to their dress standards, which had given him cause for complaint, following his recent visits to the squadrons. This order came after the squadrons had been operating in the field in poor conditions for some five months.

On the 7th the squadron was tasked to escort B-17s to Bizerta, but once again the Flying Fortresses failed to make the rendezvous, and the Spitfires had to be content with a sweep instead. The weather worsened later in the day and no more flying took place. However, welcome news arrived to the effect that the Allied armies had defeated the Axis attacks in the battles around Beja, and that the success was in no small measure due to the efforts of the RAF squadrons involved. Once again, on the 8th, the B-17s failed to turn up at the rendezvous with the squadron's Spitfires, and the pilots had to content themselves with an escort to Hurri-bombers attacking targets in the Sedjenane area after lunch in support of efforts to stall a thrust by Von Arnim's forces attacking from the north. The squadron also received some welcome reinforcement on the 8th in the guise of Australian Sgt K.E. Clarkson and Canadian Plt Off G.N. Keith.

By the 9th the Allied forces were successfully pushing back the Axis at both ends of the Tunisian front, and the Eighth Army had been particularly successful in smashing a strong tank attack by the Germans. The squadron was heartened by this news.

The problem of sand ingress in the Merlin engines continued to give trouble, and in the absence of an official solution Greggs Farish and Plt Off Fowler had been giving much thought to the problem. Between them they came up with a design for a filter for use while taxiing, which could be jettisoned after take-off and recovered for reuse. The experimental filter proved a success, and mass production commenced.

On 12 March the squadron area of operations was temporarily switched, and in company with Spitfires of 93 Sqn they strafed targets around the Pichon–Fonduk area. A recce was also made of the Kairouan airfield, which appeared to be obstructed but otherwise abandoned. The *Luftwaffe* was once again conspicuous by its absence in the air as well as on the ground. The day was rounded out with the news that WO Norton, the NCO i/c the Squadron Armoury, had been mentioned in dispatches for meritorious service while at Biggin Hill.

By mid-March the Axis forces were being squeezed into a reducing enclave and were forced to attempt supply by air, with *Luftwaffe* transport aircraft dropping large bomb-shaped containers to the beleaguered troops below. The supply drops would have little effect on the outcome of the campaign; however, 72 Squadron and the rest of 324 Wing were kept busy intercepting the transport sorties. Unsuccessful interception sorties were flown between the 13th and 15th, and then, on the 16th, the Spitfires returned to mixing it with the *Luftwaffe* fighters. Late in the afternoon five Spitfires scrambled to intercept an enemy formation near Tabarka, but were unsuccessful, and one of the Spitfires was damaged on landing. This was quickly followed by a high-cover escort to intercept bandits, again over Tabarka. This time the Spitfires sighted five or six enemy aircraft diving down north-east of Souk el Arba, and gave chase. The enemy fighters were lost in cloud near base.

The squadron flew four sorties on the 17th, sighting Stukas on the second near Souk el Arba, but were unable to give chase due to fuel shortage. On the final sweep of the day a Spitfire in US marking was sighted. The Spitfire was behaving unusually, and this drew the pilots' attention to it. As it flew towards Bizerta, one of the Spitfires drew into a firing position behind it. At this point a voice on the R/T was heard to say, 'OK American', and it was last seen heading towards Mateur. The squadron pilots had previously been briefed on the possibility that the *Luftwaffe* were operating captured Spitfires in the area; however, they were unable to investigate more closely as they were vectored to further enemy aircraft reported near Beja and Cap Serrat. On return to base, Rodney Scrase had a close thing on landing in Spitfire EN259:RN-K, and noted in his logbook, 'Patrol – Cape Serrat, Medjez. Damaged pitot-head in a very ropey landing!'

Meanwhile, in North Africa the Eighth Army had begun its offensive on the 19th against the Mareth Line in southern Tunisia, and by the 26th had won the battle, pushing the Axis troops north. One of the biggest explosions ever witnessed by the pilots of 72 Sqn was observed on the 24th during an escort to B-17s bombing Ferryville. Meeting the Fortresses at Souk el Arba, the Spitfires flew to the target at 26,500 ft. As the bombs fell on the target there was a huge explosion throwing up a column of smoke to a height of 12,000 ft. The raid did not go uncontested, and the *Luftwaffe* tried to reach the bombers, using their vapour trails as cover. However, the Spitfires did a good job keeping them away, though during one dogfight Flt Lt Cox (EN298) was robbed of a certain kill by a cannon stoppage

On 25 March the squadron changed its mode of operation and began operating by day from an airfield at Thelepte, returning each night to Souk el Khemis. To facilitate these operations a skeleton ground crew moved in a convoy of six lorries to Thelepte. The convoy travelled through the recent battlegrounds around Thala, where the German thrust through the Kasserine Pass had been checked in February 1943. The roads along their route were lined with wrecked tanks and debris. The detritus of war did not impede their progress, though, and coming through the Kasserine Pass on the morning of the 26th they halted for breakfast. A dead donkey at the roadside drew AC Ben Hitt to inspect it, and in doing so he stepped on a concealed landmine. Besides AC Hitt, seven others were wounded. The timely arrival of personnel from an American first-aid post who gave AC Hitt expert attention probably saved his life. The casualties were transferred to Feriana general hospital, while the remainder of the ground crew party arrived at Thelepte as the squadron's Spitfires began landing. Ben Hitt recalled his untimely departure from the squadron:

Four from our tent were told to pack up their kit and be ready to move by 9.00 p.m. We were going south to support the Americans. The journey was uncomfortable, to say the least, in the back of a 3-tonner. In early morning we arrived at the Kasserine Pass. It was a bleak area and many ground battles had been fought here. The road was pock-marked with shell holes, and landmines had been laid in profusion. We crawled from the back of the 3-tonner, all covered in white dust, and there was an urgent need to answer the call of nature. Off the side of the road there was a nasty anti-personnel landmine. I found it, together with John Dodds, with whom I had shared so much of my service in the great 72 Squadron. We also shared the shrapnel. The good news was that we were close to an American Field Hospital (48th Surgical), and an American ambulance transported us there. After four days we were passed fit to travel, and we had a long journey back over some very rough terrain to an American Evacuation Hospital at Tebessa.

In the north the British First Army went on the offensive on the 26th, and by the 30th the Eighth Army in the south had broken through at the Gabes Pass, 100 miles inside Tunisia. The squadron discovered that the airfield at Thelepte was much larger than Euston, and allowed a full squadron to take off simultaneously. However, the sandy and stony ground produced more sand ingress problems in the engines due to the lack of available filters at the new airfield. Arriving at Thelepte, Jimmy Corbin noted in his logbook: 'Largest 'drome I've seen. Three Yank squadrons.'

The first offensive sortie from Thelepte saw the squadron acting as withdrawal cover to a formation of Douglas A-20s attacking the airfield at Djebel Tebaga. The close escort flying 5,000ft below at 17,000 ft began mixing it with fifteen Fw 190s and Bf 109s and 72 Sqn dived to join the fight. Two sections bounced the surprised Germans and Flt Lt Daniel (EN351) destroyed one Bf 109 and damaged a second, while Flg Off Hardy (BS558) shot down a Bf 109 and Flt Lt Cox (EN298) damaged another. Plt Off Fowler (EN251), suspecting he had been

Spitfire Mk IX EN351, still to have its individual code applied, at Souk el Khemis. (R.D. Scrase)

hit by flak, returned to Souk el Khemis and Sgt Hussey (EN291) landed, short of fuel, at Sbeitla. Thelepte was home to the US 31st Fighter Group (FG), and both pilots and ground crew were provided with excellent food by the Americans during their stay. The Americans, in turn, were much impressed with the Spitfire Mk IXs ability to deal with the Fw 190s and Bf 109Gs which had been causing them problems when encountered at high altitude. Tom Hughes wrote of this sortie:

> *Scramble to 29,000 ft, Pont-du-Fahs. Withdrawal cover for Fortresses and Bostons with Lightning escort. Four 109s seen and lost. Cloud base 32,000 ft.*

Jimmy Corbin wrote:

> *Sweep Maknassy area as top cover to bombers and P-39s. Jumped 109s. Yellow Section stayed up and frightened 109s that tried to climb. Dan and Owen 109s destroyed. Dan and Chum 109s damaged.*

He wrote in his diary for that day:

> *Fourteen of us took off for Thelepte at 0800. Made very welcome by the Yanks who were all ears and praises for the IXs. Met McDonald and McAbie who were in 309. Did one sweep to Maknassy area as top cover to P-39s and bombers. Jumped 109s who were about to bounce P-39s. Yellow Section stayed up. Dan, Owen each destroyed one. Dan and Chem damaged two others. Chumley's damaged a 109 that tried to climb up and he was taught that he could not outclimb a IX. Tight turns were plentiful, Chumley led very well. Yanks very excited about us jumping 109s as they and P-39s had been bounced rather a lot.*

After the detachment to Thelepte, the ground crew returned to Euston on the 27th in time to give the pilots a thrashing on the football field, winning 5–3. Notwithstanding the ongoing sand filter problem, the squadron also had a severe shortage of tents and was preparing for the imminent onset of the malarial mosquito season. The following day the squadron was informed that it should no longer destroy its aircraft in the event of a forced landing in enemy territory, but only disable them. The enemy apparently rarely attempted to salvage them. It is likely that destroying the aircraft would be the last thing on the mind of a pilot just down in enemy territory and thinking of escape and survival in inhospitable conditions; in any case the forced landing would probably have done a fairly good job of disabling it.

On the 30th Flt Lt Daniel, Plt Off Prytherch and Plt Off Fowler provided a demonstration of the Spitfire Mk IX's capabilities to a visiting Turkish Mission, and then on the last day of the month the squadron flew in support of an Army push towards Sedjenane. As French and British troops moved forward, the squadron provided some timely intelligence to the Army on enemy dispositions. By lunchtime the troops were in contact with the enemy to the north and south of Sedjenane, but were temporarily held up by the blowing-up of the road bridge by the Germans, all of which was observed by the pilots patrolling overhead. The squadron ended the month with a score of four destroyed, three damaged and no losses.

DFC Citation

LONDON GAZETTE, 30 MARCH 1943

Daniel, Stephen Walter Acting Flight Lieutenant

Before going overseas Flight Lieutenant Daniel participated in some 60 operational sorties over Northern France. Since his posting overseas, he has been engaged in many operational sorties and has destroyed at least four enemy aircraft. In addition, this officer has destroyed and damaged several enemy transports during low-level machine-gun attacks. Flight Lieutenant Daniel has given outstanding service and has always shown exceptional keenness to engage the enemy.

Turkish Mission visits 72 Sqn at Souk el Khemis, 1943. Rear: RAF conducting officers. Front, L to R: Flt Lt Cox, OC 'A' Flt; Turkish officer; Sqn Ldr Oxspring, OC 72 Sqn; Turkish officer; Turkish officer. (72 Sqn)

Squadron dispatch rider Darryl Briggs passed through Sedjanane on the way to Cap Serrat shortly after the battle:

I met a solitary Arab 'going my way', and so against rules and regulations I gave him a lift. After many miles and somewhat near to my destination I told him as best I could he was on his own, and this was true. It was a bleak landscape, no signs of life. He was OK though, but it did puzzle me as to how he had endured the ride: no footrest, only a carrier instead of a seat and a hot exhaust pipe – the blighter was also barefoot!

Coming to Sedjenane, I saw signs of a recent battle, dozens of Italian sun helmets with feathers as decorations were strewn around; I believe they were a Bersagliari unit. German tanks, half-tracks and trucks were burnt out – courtesy of 72?

I again disregarded the rules and decided to inspect a half-track which looked like an old charabanc as regards seating; it was also very badly burnt out. Inside the driver's side was a type of slit pocket from which I got a huge revolver, a knife, fork and spoon in a neat metal holder which incorporated a bottle opener (think of everything, these Germans) which was much more practical than our loose 'irons', and two pay books. One of these was for Paul Wiegers, who was my age, but born the month previous.

Well, I got to Cap Serrat, but they were not a very hospitable lot, and I was glad to shake the dust off and ride into the sunset. About half way back disaster struck; a flat rear tyre. With no grass to stuff in the tyre I did attempt to carry on, but in the end could go no further. The tyre shredded, and as I had not been issued with a carrier pigeon I was really 'up the creek'.

After an hour, smoking and thinking, an American jeep pulled up. 'What's up, buddy?' They hoisted the bike on the jeep and took me to their camp. 'Go get some chow, buddy. One of our guys seen a French bike down a ravine, we'll go take a look.'

What a meal, loads of coffee, food as you only dreamed of, not a sign of bully beef and biscuits. If there had been a recruiting officer there I would have been a GI. Well, they got the wheel, and luckily it was the right size. They even fitted it; great guys. I cannot remember if I told Chiefy Arthur or Sgt Calver of my journey, but much sand and mud has passed since then!

The first days of April 1943 saw the squadron grounded due to poor weather, and the opportunity was taken to reorganize the living arrangements of both air and ground crew. Operations recommenced on the 3rd with a high-cover escort to Mitchells attacking enemy airfields in the Tunis area and north of Enfidaville. The possibility of good hunting among the bombers brought the *Luftwaffe* up, but 72 Sqn was a match for them. On the return trip several Bf 109s were encountered in the Medjez el Bab area, and Flt Lt Cox (EN298) shot one down and damaged another. Plt Off Keith (EN351) was also successful, shooting down a Bf 109 for his first victory. Unfortunately, Australian Sgt K.E.

German soldier Paul Wiegers' pay book. (D. Briggs)

'Keith' Clarkson (EN250) was shot down, having damaged a Bf 109. He was heard on the R/T calling that he was baling out. While attempting to bale out he became caught in the cockpit, and only managed to extricate himself as the Spitfire descended through 1,000 ft. The *Luftwaffe*, stung into action, attempted two raids on the Allied airfields, but lost at least seven aircraft in the attacks. The squadron ground crew, directed by Flg Off Farish, were able to bring machine-guns to bear on some of them.

During this period the Axis troops had been receiving active support from Junkers Ju 87 Stukas in the battle area. The Stuka pilots, using cloud cover in an attempt to shield their slow and vulnerable mounts from marauding fighters, had some success, and their tactics made them difficult to intercept. It was decided to hit them at home, and on the 4th 72 Sqn provided escort to eighteen Hurri-bombers attacking the Ju 87 base at St Marie du Zitt just after dawn. The attack was successful and no enemy fighters attempted to intervene.

Sgt Clarkson returned to the squadron that morning with a Bf 109 damaged to his credit prior to his bale-out. In the days that followed the squadron was kept busy providing escorts to B-17s and B-25s attacking Tunis, Bizerta and Enfidaville, and working with Hurri-bombers close to the front around Enfidaville and Medjez el Bab. On the 6th British and US forces launched attacks against 5th *Panzerarmee,* and by the 7th US 2nd Corps had joined up with the British Eighth

Army in central Tunisia. The British First Army meanwhile was making good progress in the north. By the 9th the weather was restricting operations and allowing the hard-pressed Axis forces an opportunity to withdraw under heavy pressure from the Eighth Army.

The squadron was able to increase its score once more on the 10th, when twelve Spitfires escorted others bombing German motor transport on the Pont-du-Fahs–Enfidaville road. As the bombs fell on the targets below, seven Bf 109s were sighted to the north. The squadron immediately attacked the intruders and Flg Off Hardy (EN291) and Sgt Hussey (EN292) each damaged Bf 109G-4s. Rodney Scrase (EN259:RN-K) took part in the sortie, writing in his logbook:

> Close escort, Spit bombers near Enfidaville. Ended up as R[ed] 3 due to 'fall outs'. Hardy damaged 1 Me 109, Hussey damaged 1 Me 109.

The next day brought celebration to the squadron when Plt Off Malan (EN301) brought down the squadron's 150th enemy aircraft while escorting Hurri-bombers of 241 Sqn. On the return leg the squadron was vectored to the north-west of Medjez el Bab and ten Bf 109s. The Germans were caught by surprise, and as well as Malan's victory, Sqn Ldr Oxspring (EN303), Sgt Shaw (EN309) and WO Alan Gear (EN135) all damaged Bf 109s in a fight which stretched from 20,000 ft to ground level. 72 Sqn lost one pilot, Sgt Sollitt (EN292), who was last seen with two Bf 109s on his tail, while 241 Sqn lost three aircraft to flak during the ground attack. During the second sweep of the day the pilots searched for Sollitt but had no success. As the Germans were pushed into a smaller area and desperately attempted to maintain their supply routes, the anti-aircraft guns around Tunis were reinforced, as the squadron noted on the third sortie of the day, an escort to B-17s bombing the docks. The fourth sortie of the day was another Hurri-bomber escort, and on returning from this the pilots were heartened to hear that Sgt Sollitt had survived his encounter with the *Luftwaffe* and was in hospital, though not badly injured.

By the 10th, Sfax, 150 miles south of Tunis, had been captured, and Kairouan fell the following day, bringing the Allies fifty miles closer. On 12 April the Eighth Army took Sousse, and the focus moved to attacks on the few airfields left to the enemy. The first sorties were escort high cover to eighteen Mitchells bombing Oudna. Returning from the sortie, 72 Sqn was diverted to Le Kef to intercept an enemy formation, but it was unable to intercept. In the afternoon 72, 93 and 111 Squadrons escorted twelve Bostons, again to Oudna airfield. Numerous enemy fighters were seen and the squadron engaged three Bf 109s north-east of Medjez el Bab. Flt Lt Daniel (EN309) fell upon one and last saw it at 1,000 ft over the Goubellat Plain belching black and white smoke and with a windmilling propeller. Plt Off Dalton Prytherch (EN301) also damaged a Bf 109, leaving it trailing white smoke.

At 1730 hrs that evening Wg Cdr Gilroy led all three squadrons of the wing off in a sweep of the Kairouan area and straight into a hornets' nest of enemy aircraft. Flt Lt Cox was leading twelve 72 Sqn Spitfires as top cover when twenty-five Bf 109s and Fw 190s escorting six Ju 88s south of Djebebina were spotted. Gilroy immediately led the wing into battle, and the squadron noted that the Bf 109s were marked with yellow crescents and white wingtips – they had last encountered this unit in March. Flt Lt Cox (EN298) probably destroyed an Fw 190, while Flg Off Rodney Scrase (EN259:RN-K) damaged a Bf 109G. Scrase noted his seventeenth operation in his logbook:

Sweep Kairouan area. (In our hands). One 109G damaged. Next to Plt Off Lewis. Quite hectic. Flg Off Walker Sgt Griffiths 109s damaged. Flt Lt Cox 109 probable.

Flg Off Walker (EN135) damaged another Fw 190, and Sgt Griffiths (BS553) damaged a Bf 109. 93 Sqn also managed to damage a Bf 109. The day's success brought congratulatory messages from the AOC, AM Coningham, and 242 Group HQ.

The squadron flew several inconclusive sweeps over the days that followed, and in line with other units in the area of operations painted their spinners red as a recognition feature. On the 15th, Plt Off Prytherch chased a Bf 109 from Medjez el Bab to Mateur in an attempt to bring it down, but he was forced to break off the chase by heavy flak. Later in the day the wing was scrambled to intercept fifty enemy aircraft reported in the Medjez area, but the only interception was an inconclusive one by Flt Lt Cox (EN298), who had spotted a Bf 109 attempting to get into a position to bounce 81 Sqn.

In mid-April all ranks on the squadron were ordered to take a hitherto untried anti-malarial tablet called Atabrin, developed by the Americans. By the next morning more than half the squadron was laid low and unfit for duty. The dosage was reduced, and with no further problems encountered the squadron returned to normal. The Atabrin worked, and there were few cases of malaria at Souk el Khemis.

Mid-morning on the 16th saw the squadron escorting A-20s to bomb Djebel el Rass. Returning from the bombing it was diverted to Medjez el Bab, whereit encountered nine Messerschmitts. Sgt Hussey (EN291) tore into the formation, attacking five altogether and damaging two, while Plt Off Lewis (EN368) also claimed one Bf 109 damaged. At 1715 hrs 72 Sqn was in the air again, escorting two 225 Sqn aircraft on a combined shipping recce and fighter sweep. On the way back it ran into twelve enemy aircraft near Beja. 72 Sqn bounced these and came away with one Bf 109G-4 damaged by Flg Off Hardy (EN309). This brought some compensation, as the enemy formation had been attacking 72's airfield, though little damage was caused. Further damage was caused to this formation by Flt Lt Cox, who had been on an air test over the airfield at the time of the attack. Sighting three Fw 190s lagging behind, he closed to 200 yards and opened fire. He scored hits on the starboard wing of one fighter but then spotted more fighters above and broke off the attack before he became a potential victim himself. Rodney Scrase (EN259:RN-K) had returned early from a sortie and wrote in his logbook:

Sweep to Bizerta (24,000 ft). Returned early with Flg Off Walker to find the 'fields' being bombed!

Jimmy Corbin (EN303) flew on this operation:

Sweep – Medjez el Bab. About twenty Huns about – bounced by five 109s but foxed them. Hussey two damaged – 'drome bombed 1800 hrs twenty 109s.

The Germans came back to attack the airfield again on the 17th, and their bombs fell on the 243 Sqn dispersal, though they caused little damage. Jimmy Corbin noted:

Bombed at night by 88s. Quite an interesting show, flak very attractive, trying to put out flares. They put 'T' out of commission.

The large-scale attacks by the Allied light and medium bombers over the preceding week had stung the *Luftwaffe* into responding, and the attacks were the result. The enemy situation was so desperate that they even flung Ju 88s into the attack, and these had not been seen in the battle area since January. Jimmy Corbin recorded the return of the Germans on the 18th:

190s bombed us at 1645 in two waves, they damaged my F model and pranged some of 243s who intercepted them, and shot down two and four probables. Flak did well.

Axis airfields were heavily attacked on the 19th, and Wg Cdr Gilroy led 72, 93, 154 and 81 Squadrons on a freelance sweep of the Tunis area. About nine Bf 109s were spotted, and 72 Sqn engaged them. During the fight Flt Lt Daniel (EN116) destroyed a Bf 109 but then collided with a second Messerschmitt. Daniel managed to force-land his crippled Spitfire at Oued Zarga and returned to the squadron later in the day. Flt Lt Cox (EN298), Flg Off Corbin (EN30) and Flg Off Hardy (EN292) all damaged Bf 109s. Rodney Scrase (EN259:RN-K) added the following to his logbook:

Offensive patrol (10,000 ft) Tunis–Bizerta raid. 5 Free Lance Squadrons, 48 Bombers with 3 Squadrons close escort bombing La Sebala, Protville. Very hectic; Danny shot down (safe) after getting a probable (later 109 destroyed), Jimmy a 109 damaged. Wg Cdr Gilroy 109 destroyed.

Later he wrote:

On the 19th of the month we were one of five squadrons providing freelance cover to forty-eight Bostons and Mitchells. A further three squadrons flew as close escort. We ran into some 109s and 72 Sqn claimed two enemy aircraft destroyed and one damaged. This was the biggest show in which I had taken part. There was a similar operation the following day, but then we met much less enemy opposition. The drier weather, the better flying conditions and improved serviceability of our aircraft meant we were really getting on better terms against the enemy. One could see that in North Africa the end was in sight.

In the evening it was the turn of the ground crew to be in the firing line. AC Pratt, who had just returned from hospital, had the very bad luck to be struck by a spent 0.5 in. bullet fired by a bomber gunner and ended up back in hospital, though not seriously injured. News also came to the squadron that the victims of the land mine explosion at Kasserine Pass in March were all on the mend.

During this period there was great rivalry between 324 and 322 Wings in the race to have a squadron be the first to score fifty victories in the campaign. 72 Sqn had been leading by a comfortable margin, but in the preceding days this had been reduced and 81 Sqn was close behind, and 111 Sqn was in the running, too. The days that followed would settle the matter.

The First Army was being reinforced at this point with the intention of launching large-scale attacks in all sectors, and the enemy, having anticipated this, launched their own counter-offensive on the 21st. Their effort was repelled, but the weather did not bode well for the First Army's assault on the 22nd.

The pilots returning from sweeps reported clouds of dust as forces manoeuvred, burning tanks and shell fire falling all over the Goubellat Plain. The squadron lost its first pilot since January in a late-afternoon sweep. The Spitfires met twelve Bf 109s at 22,000 ft over Djedeida, and WO Alan Gear (EN135) destroyed one. WO W.H. 'Red' Hunter (EN311), a Canadian, was last seen chasing a Bf 109, with two others

Rearming a Spitfire at Souk el Khemis, 1943. (J. Lancaster)

Plt Off Jupp and ground crew with Spitfire Mk IX at Souk el Khemis, spring 1943. (J. Lancaster)

on his tail. He did not return. Hunter had been one of the original party to arrive in North Africa. Rodney Scrase wrote in his log:

Sweep Mateur–Tebourba (22,000) Huns below. Yellow Section down. WO Gear 109 destroyed. WO Hunter missing.

On the 23rd the squadron received news that Sqn Ldr Oxspring and the very experienced and successful Flt Lt Cox were to be posted away, both now tour expired. The squadron flew a twelve-aircraft sweep of the Tebersouk Bou Arada–Medjez el Bab area in the evening at 20,000 ft. North of Bon Arrada it bounced four Bf 109s, and WO Alan Gear (EN135) damaged one.

The weather had not improved by the 24th, and a sweep of the Pont-du-Fahs area by six Spitfires had to be flown at 1,500 ft. The patrol was uneventful for a time, then four Bf 109s made the mistake of diving down to attack ground troops directly in front of the 72 Sqn flight. Flt Lt Daniel (EN359) and Sqn Ldr Forde (DN:F) fell upon two of the Messerchmitts, damaging both. On a second sortie in the same area Sqn Ldr Forde (DN:F) was successful again, damaging a Bf 109 with his machine-guns. The success of these two sorties caused a third to be mounted. It appeared that the *Luftwaffe* was using the poor weather to sneak their fighter-bombers into the battle area. The third sweep was even more successful, with Flg Off Le Cheminant (EN250) blowing one Bf 109 in half, the fuselage separating behind the cockpit. The tailless Bf 109 climbed briefly before falling away. Sgt Hussey (EN291) destroyed another Bf 109, while Flg Off Rodney Scrase (EN259:RN-K) and Sgt Griffiths (EN292) both damaged one each. Wg Cdr Gilroy (GK:G) also scored, destroying a Bf 109. The debit score was only slight damage to Plt Off Keith's Spitfire, but he returned safely to base. Rodney Scrase flew as Red 2, and noted the fight in his logbook:

> *Sweep – Salt Lakes–Pont-du-Fahs (8,000) 109G damaged. Flg Off Le Cheminant, Sgt Hussey 109Gs destroyed. Sgt Griffiths 109G damaged. Wg Cdr Gilroy 109G dest. In a fantastic doggers-ho!*

Having heard of the departure of the CO and Flt Lt Cox, the squadron was pleased to be informed that their replacements would be Flt Lt Daniel, promoted to squadron leaderr, and Plt Off Prytherch, who would take over as 'B' Flight commander. In addition, two replacement pilots, Sgt H.B. Smith and Sgt J.T. Connolly, arrived.

On the 25th twelve Spitfires flew as high cover to six of 152 Sqn, who had a successful sortie, meeting six enemy fighters and damaging two. 72 Sqn met a further eight Bf 109s, but only Flt Lt Dalton Prytherch made an attack, but with no claim, as the enemy made good their escape toward Tunis. The squadron was about to lose another very experienced pilot when news arrived that Flg Off Le Cheminant was to be posted to 232 Sqn as a flight commander.

The *Luftwaffe* put its bombers into the battle area around Pont-du-Fahs on the 26th in a desperate venture, and 72 Sqn was there to meet them at 8,000 ft. The Spitfires turned and climbed to 12,000 ft to intercept the bombers, six Bf 110s and six Ju 88s, escorted by Bf 109s and Fw 190s. The enemy formation was coming at the squadron head on, and the pilots were only able to fire short bursts before the bombers and escort broke through. Flt Lt Prytherch (EN301) scored hits on one already flak-damaged Bf 110, by which time the enemy formation was diving away at speed and rapidly getting out of range. Plt Off Malan (EN294) and Flg Off Tom Hughes (EN292) gave chase to one Bf 110 at 1,000 ft. Tom Hughes saw Malan weaving frantically to avoid flak before he too was forced to take evasive action and lost sight of him. Malan failed to return. Tom Hughes wrote in his logbook:

> *Patrol Medjez–Bou Arada. Head-on attack on Me 110s with top cover of Me 109s. Followed Plt Off Malan after Me 110 down from 8,000 ft. Intense A/A. Believe Malan shot down by own A/A (News on 1 Jun 43: Died of wounds).*

Rodney Scrase was flying EN259:RN-K as Yellow 2, and wrote of the battle in his logbook:

Sweep – Salt Lakes–Pont-du-Fahs (8,000). Met about eight Ju 88s and eight Me 110s escorted by 109s and 190s. Everyone fired – with no result. Plt Off Malan missing.

Laurie Frampton (EN148) noted:

Sweep Medjez–Pont-du-Fahs–Bou Arrada. Met Jerry bombers head on just after they bombed Bou Arrada. Complete shambles, George Malan missing.

Laurie later wrote of the events of the 26th:

The Army was advancing and being attacked by enemy aircraft, and all Spitfires were scrambled to go to their aid. Over the target area the enemy aircraft had departed and the sky was full of Spits, all trying to avoid each other. It was dusk by this time, and on returning to base the ground staff had set out two rows of goose-neck flares to mark the runway. The landing area was approximately 900 yards long and 20 yards wide, with a taxi strip 15 yards wide alongside. The other squadron sharing Euston had Mk V aircraft, the exhaust ports of which had three pairs of stubs each side directly at eye level. Our Mk IXs had individual stubs, six per side. At night the flare from the exhausts cut off all forward view. In the failing light our CO asked the other squadron leader to allow 72 to land first, in view of the greater restricted view with our aircraft, with which he agreed. When it was my turn to land, one of the Mk Vs cut in front of me as I was levelling-off for touch-down. At about twenty feet I hit his slipstream, my right wing dropped; I picked it up and landed. Out of the corner of my eye I saw two rows of flares – I was on the taxi strip. Kick the rudder hard left, hard right, a quick chicane between two flares, lined up on the runway as the boss taxied past.

Flt Lt Cox's replacement arrived on the 26th in the shape of Flt Lt R.A. Hagger, ex-81 Sqn and taking over 'A' Flight. Sgts Scott and Condon also arrived as replacements. On the ground the offensive had made little progress during the five days of battle, and the Axis forces were still putting up a fierce resistance. The enemy were being squeezed but were not yet defeated. By this point the Axis in North Africa had lost 66,000 troops killed, wounded or captured in the first three and half months of 1943.

The squadron had a strange encounter on the 27th when a formation of aircraft was sighted bombing well behind the Allied front line, and it flew to intercept them. As they closed, one pilot fired a short burst before it was realized that they were in fact P-40s of the US 12th Air Force. The pilot was Jimmy Corbin (EN303), who noted the incident in his logbook:

Freelance patrol Lake area. Bumped into P-40s. Pooped at Yanks who asked for trouble.

The squadron had a more successful encounter on the following day when Flt Lt Hagger (EN250) and Wg Cdr Gilroy (GK:G) intercepted two Bf 109s near Tunis. Hagger shot one down, believed to be the Bf 109G of *Stab/JG53* pilot *Leutnant* Johannes Boehm, who baled out. The Wing Commander had the bad luck to have his engine cowling come loose just as he as about to open fire, and he had to break off. Meanwhile, the rest of the squadron was climbing in an attempt to intercept fifteen more enemy fighters at 16,000 ft, but they did not stay to fight, and dived away.

In the afternoon Sqn Ldr Daniel led twelve Spitfires on a sweep over Pont-du-Fahs and Tebourba, during which they encountered six Messerschmitts cloud-hopping below. As they watched, an Fw 190 dived in behind them and Sqn Ldr Daniel (EN359) rolled over and dived down, scoring hits on it. The rest of the squadron dived on the Bf 109s and one Spitfire was observed in a vertical dive streaming glycol, plummeting down to crash south of Tebourba. The pilot was Sgt H.B. Smith (EN368), who had only been with the squadron for five days. Rodney Scrase was flying as Yellow 4 (EN461:RN-A), and recorded Smith's loss in his logbook:

Sweep – Medjez–Tebourba (8,000). Some excitement. Saw 109s and 190s. Sgt Smith crashed S of Tebourba.

Sgt Sollitt, who had survived being brought down on the 10th, was posted away from the squadron on the 29th. The Axis made a last desperate attempt at an armoured counter-blow on the 28th, but this was repulsed by the British troops. By the end of the month the ground offensive appeared to be running out of steam, and though advances had been made, not all of the objectives had been reached. To the squadron's credit it had come out as the top-scoring unit for the month, with eleven destroyed, three probably destroyed and twenty-one damaged.

Throughout this period of the Tunisian campaign the superiority in numbers of the Allies in terms of aircraft and warships was such that the interdiction of Axis supply ships was highly successful. This in turn forced the Germans to attempt resupply of their forces by air. To do this they used a fleet of Junkers Ju 52 and Messerschmitt Me 323 transport aircraft, both of which were slow, cumbersome and poorly defended. Several Allied air units had run up high scores in the preceding weeks intercepting these flights. On 1 May 1943 72 Sqn would attempt to get in on the hunt. Overnight the ground crew worked to fit long-range tanks to the Spitfires, to enable them to have the range to sweep into the Gulf of Tunis. In order to surprise the Germans, the squadron's twelve Spitfires, in company with those of 111 Sqn, took off and flew at zero feet to the

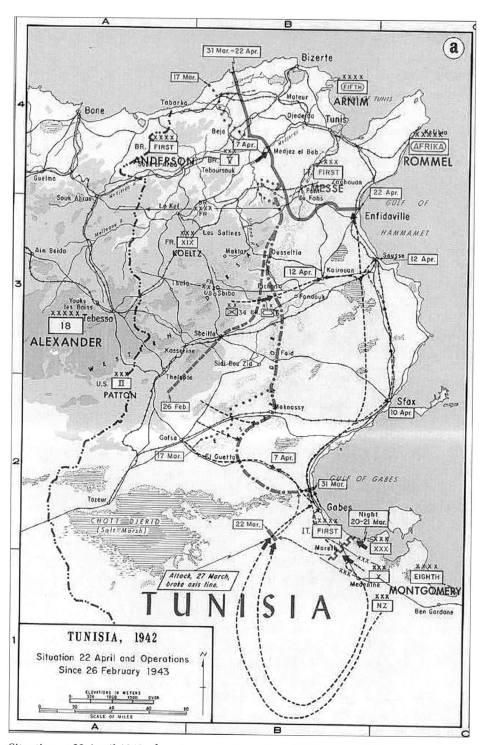

Situation at 22 April 1943, showing operations since 26 February 1943.

north of Tabarka before turning east to begin the patrol of the coast between Bizerta and Tunis. The hoped-for transports did not appear, but a lone He 111, escorted by six Bf 109s, was sighted, and Wg Cdr Gilroy led 111 Sqn into the attack, shooting down the He 111. The Messerschmitts promptly fled.

The competition to be the first squadron to reach fifty victories in the campaign was becoming fierce, and for the first time 72 Sqn lost its lead when 111 Sqn brought down six Bf 110s and one Bf 109 in a single day. 111 Sqn was now leading the pack, with the respective scores – 111 Sqn 48^4/$_5$ths kills, 72 Sqn 48½ kills. The ground fighting began to peter off during this period, too, with the First Army taking time to reorganize its units for further attacks. The effort in the air, however, continued at high intensity, with 324 Wing flying 239 sorties on the first day of the month.

Despite the need to keep the pressure up, the welfare of the troops had not been entirely forgotten, and a rest camp for aircrew had been set up in Tabarka. The first from the squadron to be sent for a well-earned rest were Plt Off Fowler and WO Gear. The squadron also received news that Flg Off Hardy and Flt Lt le Cheminant, now with 232 Sqn, had been awarded the DFC.

During the lull in fighting on the 2nd, the squadron was warned of an impending move to Djebel Abiode, but in the event only 93 and 111 Sqns moved out. The *Luftwaffe* and its attendant anti-aircraft batteries was conspicuous by its absence, and numerous Tac R and recce sorties were flown to establish enemy movements. 72 Sqn provided cover for several of these. The US ground forces also captured Mateur at this point. Over the days that followed the squadron was kept busy providing escorts to bombers, fighter-bombers and Tac R aircraft as the ground forces gathered strength for the final push. The absent *Luftwaffe* was encountered again on the 5th as British troops broke through the defences of 5th *Panzerarmee* to the south of Tunis. South-east of Mateur eight Bf 109s were engaged at 15,000 ft, and Wg Cdr Gilroy (GK-G) and Flg Off Hardy (EN258) damaged one each. North-west of Tebourba the squadron ran into heavy and accurate flak, and Sgt M.R. Jacobs' Spitfire (RN-F) was damaged and he received a splinter wound to his eye.

In the evening the CO attended a briefing where the plan for the final offensive was revealed. The planned breakthrough would be made on a line between Medjez el Bab and Tunis on a narrow front supported by intense artillery and air attack, followed by armoured thrusts. It was estimated that Tunis could be in Allied hands in forty-eight hours if all went to plan. Australian Flg Off Gordon C. Sharp from Broadmeadow in New South Wales and Flg Off R.R. Barnfather both arrived on the squadron just in time to take part in the new assault.

Sqn Ldr Stephen Daniel. (T.B. Hughes)

72 Sqn joined the battle at 0740 hrs on the morning of the 6th, and later in the day discovered it had been pipped at the post in the race to fifty victories by 111 Sqn, which destroyed two Bf 109s before breakfast. On the first sortie of the day the squadron had some success, but Rodney Scrase recorded his disgust at not being involved in the fight. Those involved were using the callsign 'Fetters', and Rodney's section was 'Poppet'. Rodney was Poppet Red 2:

> *Scramble – Patrol Tunis, Mateur, Medjez (4,000–18,000). R2 Poppet. Fetters – Wg Cdr Gilroy, Flg Off Hardy 109s damaged. Poppets saw F.A. [Fanny Adams – nothing.]*

Wg Cdr Gilroy led the squadron off at 1400 hrs for a sortie over Tunis. As it flew north toward Bizerta at least fifteen Bf 109s were sighted flying south, staggered between 10,000 and 16,000 ft. The Germans fled northwards on sighting the approaching Gilroy and his section of Spitfires. The Messerschmitts' luck ran out, though, as the other sections were in a very favourable position below the Germans. The Spitfires climbed rapidly and got inside the Bf 109s, and a terrific dogfight began. Despite their superior numbers the Messerschmitts were routed, and the squadron shot down at least five of them for no loss. Flt Lt Hagger (EN250) shot one down and damaged another, Plt Off Keith (EN518) downed two and probably destroyed a third. Plt Off K.R. Shaw (EN309) and Flt Lt Dalton Prytherch (EN301) destroyed one each. Flg Off Jimmy Corbin (EN303) and Sgt J.T. 'John' Connolly (EN311) each damaged a Bf 109. Jimmy Corbin wrote:

> *Sweep – area cover – bomber ops. 18+ 109s over Tunis. Terrific doggers. Played looping with one 109 and damaged it. Squadron got five destroyed and three damaged.*

Only three of the enemy escaped unscathed. 72 Sqn returned to base with its tail up as it had broken the fifty-aircraft-destroyed barrier in this fight. Once again Rodney Scrase, flying in the Yellow 2 position (EN259:RN-K), was involved, but again he had little luck:

> *Patrol Djedeida Tunis area (10,000). A glorious mix-up with twenty 109s and 190s. I fired – cannons jammed. Little to show although within 25 yards. Flt Lt Hagger 109 dest[royed] 190 dam[aged]. Plt Off Keith two 109s one prob[able]. F/L Prytherch, Plt Off Shaw 109s dest[royed].*

The next sortie was in the early evening, once again over Tunis. Four Macchi MC202s and two Fw 190s dived out of a solid overcast at 10,000 ft west of Tunis and were immediately engaged by the Spitfires. Once again Flt Lt Hagger (EN358) was successful, shooting down an Fw 190. As the squadron fought overhead, Massicault fell into Allied hands. The Germans fought harder along

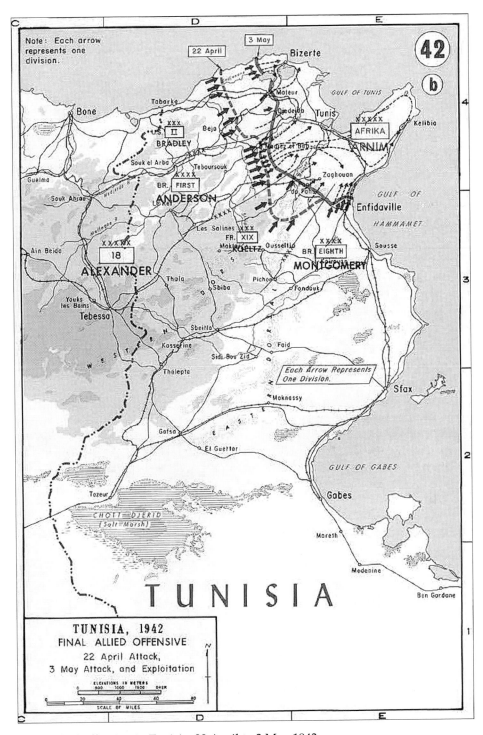

Final Allied offensive in Tunisia, 22 April to 3 May 1943.

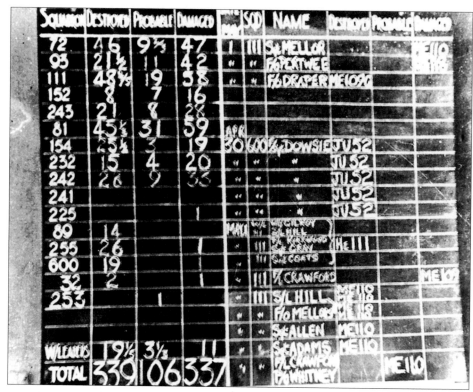

Scoreboard on 1 May 1943, showing 72 Sqn in second place to 111 Sqn in numbers of enemy aircraft destroyed. (72 Sqn)

the line between Tebourba and St Cyprien, where a night attack was planned to force an opening for the Allied armour.

Overnight the weather worsened and the squadron was forced to sit on the ground waiting for a clearance, and did not get off until 0905 hrs for an uneventful sortie, during which the pilots observed a tank battle and numerous enemy MT fleeing toward Tunis. The Allied advance continued throughout the morning, and by mid-morning units had taken Tebourba and were also on the outskirts of Tunis. By now the *Luftwaffe* had been withdrawn to Sicily and Italy in an attempt to conserve its dwindling numbers and escape the inevitable collapse and capture. The Protville–Tunis road was packed with fleeing enemy MT, and the squadron took the opportunity to strafe some of them in a lunchtime sortie, leaving four lorries smoking on the road. Tunis had fallen.

In the mid-afternoon the squadron had the unusual pleasure of flying over Tunis at 5,000 ft with no flak coming up. Later in the evening news was received that Ferryville had also fallen into Allied hands. As the evening wore on and land targets became impossible to find, the Allied fighters and bombers turned to shipping attacks. Sqn Ldr Daniel (EN258) led twelve Spitfires off at 1805 hrs looking for shipping near Tunis. A destroyer and eleven small craft were sighted off Sidi Bou Said and attacked. The destroyer was set on fire and one small craft was also left burning. Two other small craft were sunk. In return Flg Off Keith (EN518) returned with damage to his radiator, making a forced landing, unhurt, at the landing-ground at Medjez el Bab. More shipping targets were found a little further south, and the squadron sank an MTB and left four barges on fire. Rodney Scrase returned from this sortie with damage to his port wing caused by a large part of the exploding MTB. During the day's ground-attack sorties, numerous and varied enemy targets were destroyed by the squadron and are listed in the table below:

DESTROYED	PROBABLY DESTROYED	DAMAGED
5 Aircraft	1 Me323	Several Me 323s
26 MT	4 MT	2 Ju 52s
1 Barge	1 Pinnace	12 MT
3 Troop-carrying launches	4 Barges	7 Bf 109
5 Small craft		1 Destroyer
2 E-boats		8 Tanks
1 MTB		1 Trawler
		1 Small craft

The table lists only the confirmed targets destroyed or damaged as many other attacks were made, but the results could not be confirmed. Jimmy Corbin wrote in his diary of the days strafing attacks:

First show at 0900, nothing doing. Learnt later that we had captured or rather entered Tunis. Next show we patrolled area and did a bit of strafing up road between Tunis and Bizerta. Next show at 1500 was rather useless as weather bad. Had to take off at 1818 to strafe, reversing the Dunkirk. Started at Carthage and fired at ships, three pranged, two seriously, flak terrifying. Then attended to MTB-type vessel and six of us set fire and it later sank. Then west to five barges and damaged one. Had a terrifying experience on way home across land. La Sebala area in and out of 109s and 190s, on ground flak very intense from Jerries later Yanks, green and red golf balls. Landed at dusk.

Rodney Scrase wrote of the operations in May:

A lot of strafing, little opposition. I claimed an SM79 destroyed on the ground and a 109 damaged. Always a price to pay for low-level attacks, as when attacking some barges off the port of Tunis, I was hit in the port wing by part of one of the barges at which I had been firing. Happily just a dent in the wing.

As the campaign in Tunisia was nearing the end, the squadron, in line with other squadrons of the wing, was ordered to withdraw all surplus equipment to a central depository in a move designed to make the squadrons fully mobile. The squadrons of the wing were also ordered to be ready to move at short notice. These changes did not affect the daily routeing of flying operations, and on the 8th twelve Spitfires were airborne at 0710 hrs for a fighter sweep over Tunis at 10,000 ft. The enemy were seen to be fleeing toward Cap Bon in a desperate attempt to escape, and the Spitfires had numerous targets to engage, leaving two trucks and a gun limber smoking in one strafing run. No shipping to rescue the retreating Axis forces was sighted during the sweep. On return to base the pilots found that limits on the areas they could strafe had been set as Allied forces became entangled with the retreating enemy.

The 'Turkey Shoot' now began in earnest as the enemy were squeezed into a tiny area, abandoning aircraft, tanks, trucks and equipment as they fled. The second twelve-Spitfire sweep took off at 0950 hrs and soon found ground targets near Korba, leaving four vehicles destroyed and several damaged. The *Luftwaffe* was conspicuous by its absence in the air, but it had left rich pickings for the squadron on the ground. North of Korba a landing-ground was found with at least sixty aircraft scattered and abandoned over it. Flt Lt Hagger (EN461) destroyed a He 111 and a Bf 109, Sgt Keith Clarkson (EN135) damaged two aircraft and Flg Off Tom Hughes (EN357) damaged another, while many others were hit. Tom Hughes recorded:

Ground strafing Cap Bon peninsula. Beat up trucks and Hun aerodrome (Korba). Damaged Savoia SM79, destroyed later by Flg Off Scrase.

Rodney Scrase noted:

Strafing Korba airfield. Poppet Red 2 (EN259:RN-K). One SM79 destroyed (flamer). 109 damaged. Strikes on 3 M[C]202s. 6 other 202s destroyed. 190s and 202s damaged.

There was only light flak to contend with. The landing-ground still offered rich pickings, so a further sweep was laid on and the twelve Spitfires took off at 1305 hrs to return there. This time they were able to spend more time over the target, and the score amounted to one SM79, five Macchi MC202s, one Fw 190 and one Bf 109 destroyed, and five MC202s and several other types damaged. For good measure the administration buildings and a flak tower were given a going-over, and a lone German soldier, brave enough to raise his rifle, quickly dived for shelter as the Spitfires opened up on him. The pilots returned to base in time to hear a piano recital by the celebrated pianist Reginald Forsythe. The operations record book noted that it was a 'novelty to hear a piano trying to make itself heard against the continuous stream of aircraft overhead'! The day was brought to a close with an uneventful sweep of the Cap Bon area in the evening

By the end of the day it was obvious that there was little chance of escape for the surrounded enemy troops as Allied forces closed in on Cap Bon. The sea between Tunisia and Italy was being patrolled constantly by the Royal Navy, and there was no hope of rescue from the sea. Against this background the squadron began preparing to move forward. At this time rumours were spreading in the wing that a return to the UK was in the offing with the successful conclusion of the campaign, but these were quickly scotched by a signal from 242 Group.

By the 9th the sweeps by the squadron were taking on an air of futility, as the *Luftwaffe* was long gone and ground targets had all but dried up. Sqn Ldr Daniel was asked to recce a landing-ground believed to be used to fly out high-ranking enemy officers and officials, but there was no indication that this was the case other than two wrecked Ju 52s on the landing-ground. The only incident of note during the morning was when Sgt Griffiths (EN368) had his undercarriage break up on landing short of fuel at Paddington landing-ground. The aircraft was a write-off, but Griffiths escaped unhurt.

The day ended with the welcome arrival of 316 bottles of beer! This as an initial issue based on one bottle of beer per pilot per day. Reports from squadron personnel visiting Souk el Khemis indicated that a huge number of enemy POWs were being held there and that many POWs were driving their own transport from the front to captivity! Finally, the squadron was placed on one hour's notice to move to a new base.

By the 10th the squadron had run out of targets. Allied forces had reached Cap Bon and the only Axis stronghold still holding out was a small enclave north of Enfidaville. The advance party was brought to immediate readiness to move, and orders were received that the Spitfires were to move to La Sebala on the 11th to provide cover to convoys approaching Bizerta. During the journey to La Sebala by the advance party they found every road crammed with abandoned enemy equipment and vehicles, and huge numbers of enemy troops marching into captivity. Arriving in Tunis one section of the convoy became separated and was quickly mobbed by cheering men, women and children throwing flowers as the truck passed by. Tom Hughes noted the situation in North Africa at this time in his logbook:

The last few days have seen complete disappearance of Axis aircraft from N. African sky. 72 Squadron operates from Hun aerodrome. Me 109Gs in good condition on aerodrome.

Arriving at La Sebala, the party quickly began a tour of the airfield, avoiding mined areas, and scavenging enough German solar topees to equip everyone with good protection against the sun. This was most welcome, as the airfield was completely devoid of shade, with the exception of an olive grove on the eastern side. Only four aircraft remained on the airfield. One of these, a Ju 52, contained thousands of undelivered letters to the enemy from Germany and Italy. On the 12th all of the German and Italian forces in Tunisia surrendered. Among the 130,000 German and 120,000 Italian prisoners were General Von Arnim and twenty-five other Axis generals.

The Spitfires arrived from Souk el Khemis on the 13th, and with the arrival of the rear party construction of the campsite began in earnest. Several parties went out on inspection tours and returned favourably impressed by the quality of the abandoned enemy equipment, among which were a large number of tent pegs of far superior quality to the British issue, which soon broke in the hard Tunisian ground.

With the immediate fighting over, the squadron settled down to a routine of convoy patrols and visits to places of interest on the battlefield. Even as victory in North Africa was being celebrated, the Allies were looking forward to the next campaign, and the Royal Navy began bombardment of the island of Pantelleria, half way between Sicily and Tunisia, in preparation for its eventual invasion. A victory parade was to be held on the 20th, and from the 16th the squadron began practice for this, selecting thirty-two men over 5 ft 8 in. tall to be led by Flg Off G.C. Sharp and Flg Off G.N. Keith. Rodney Scrase wrote of the last days of the campaign in Tunisia:

With the end of the campaign we were called upon to carry out sundry duties such as escorting convoys bringing supplies into Bizerta and Tunis. Shown as half-ops time! On 12 May we moved from our base at Souk el Khemis. Other flights that month were few. Bringing repaired kites back to our new location at La Sebala just north of Tunis was one such task.

The Axis forces surrendered on the 13th of the month. Next day I was one of a group of chaps who drove out in our 15 cwt truck to the Cap Bon peninsula, where the enemy troops, now disarmed, were marching back towards their POW camps. Revolvers and binoculars were being thrown into the bushes – available for one to pick up. I got a pair of super binoculars.

I had learnt something about operational flying, but I was still a 'new boy' and I felt my shooting had to improve. At the same time I had fitted into the team and could be relied on to carry out instructions I was given.

Patrols continued on the 17th, and news reached the squadron of the loss of Cpl Southwick, a fitter, who had been previously admitted to hospital with acute appendicitis. In an unusual change of role, some of the squadron pilots became infantry for the day when they captured five German soldiers, all armed with

Flg Off R. Rayner, Flg Off J.J. McNair and Flg Off J.M. Eyles discuss an air combat in North Africa. (72 Sqn)

machine-guns, in a wood near Korba. On the 18th the squadron was released from operations and spent the day swimming and taking in the sights of Tunis. News was also received of the award of a DFM to Sgt Roy Hussey.

The Tunis victory parade took place on the 20th as planned, and No. 72 Squadron led the RAF contingent. The parade took three hours to pass the saluting dais as nineteen squadrons flew overhead in a flypast representing all of the various commands involved in the campaign. 72 Sqn did not take part in the flypast, instead providing top cover off Cap Bon to dissuade any enemy attempt to interfere with the proceedings.

On the 21st four Spitfires were scrambled to intercept an enemy plot, and by dint of some good vectoring by the radar controller at 'Mixture' Control, contact was soon made with the target, a Messerschmitt Me 210. The Me 210 took no evasive action, and WO Alan Gear (EN298) was able to position above it and open fire. Gear fired two bursts and the Messerschmitt's port engine caught fire. It then spun down, hitting the sea, and leaving only a pool of oil to mark its watery grave. Rodney Scrase flying EN259:RN-K as Blue 2 recorded:

Patrol Convoy 'H' off Bizerta going E. WO Gear Me 210 destroyed. Scrambled to Tabarka.

72 Sqn at Souk el Khemis. Standing, L to R: Jupp, Corbin, Gear, Smith, Walker, Le Cheminant, Daniels, Pearson, Hussey, King, Griffiths, Hughes, Prytherch. Seated, L to R: Scrase, Clarkson, Hunter, Sollitt, Malan, Hardy, Frampton, Fowler. (72 Sqn)

DFC Citation

LONDON GAZETTE, 21ST MAY 1943

Flying Officer Owen Leslie Hardy, Royal New Zealand Air Force

This officer has completed 70 sorties, including a number in the campaign in North Africa, where he has rendered excellent service. In air combat he has destroyed 3 enemy aircraft, while in low-level machine-gun attacks on enemy transport he has achieved success. Flying Officer Hardy is a keen and skilful section leader.

On the 22nd the squadron was ordered to move to Utique, but the move was postponed till the 23rd. The move would be temporary, as the squadron's new base was to be at Mateur. Relieved of all operational flying by USAAF units, the move of aircraft and ground parties commenced. By the 25th most of the ground crew had arrived at Mateur along with those of the other squadrons of the wing, and by the afternoon of the 26th the Spitfires had arrived from Utique. Preparations began immediately for the squadron's involvement in Operation Husky, and the enemy, though ousted from Tunisia, still took an interest in Allied activity, sending over aircraft at night to carry out reconnaissance and to harass. The flak batteries at Ferryville, close by, were kept busy.

DFC Citation

LONDON GAZETTE, 21ST MAY 1943

Flying Officer Jerrold Le Cheminant

This officer has a fine operational record. He fought in the Battle of Britain and afterwards took part in many sorties over Northern France. In operations in North Africa he has proved himself to be an excellent section leader and has contributed materially to the successes obtained. He has destroyed 6 enemy aircraft.

As operations were limited, the opportunity was taken to send ground crew on leave to Ferryville and pilots to Tunis and Tabarka. On the 28th the squadron was treated to a veritable fireworks display as thousands of shells and tracers burst over Ferryville and Bizerta in attempts to shoot down enemy aircraft. Four new pilots arrived to strengthen the squadron for the next operation: Flg Off King and Sgts Piper, 'Red' Weller and Morris. On the 30th the squadron received sad news. Plt Off Malan, who had gone missing on 26 April and had subsequently been located, badly wounded, by elements of HQ 7 Brigade, had died of his wounds on the same day.

John King, Sgt Pearson and Sgt Griffiths with a captured German *Kubelwagen*. (T.B. Hughes)

Pilots inspecting a downed Messerschmitt Bf 109. (72 Sqn)

On the 31st four pilots were detached to Kalas Djerda to ferry Spitfires to Souk el Khemis, otherwise the month ended quietly. During the Tunisian campaign the squadron had scored fifty-three and one-sixth destroyed, twelve and two-thirds probably destroyed and fifty damaged, making them the highest-scoring RAF squadron of the campaign.

With the fighting over, the pilots spent a few well-earned days resting and sightseeing in Tabarka and Tunis. The ground crew, by 1 June, however, were working flat out to prepare the aircraft and pack equipment for the next move of base. The aircraft, which had been painted in desert camouflage of dark earth and mid-stone upper surfaces and azure blue undersurfaces, were repainted in the European scheme pf dark green and ocean grey on top and light grey beneath. The lack of proper spray paint made this a difficult task. As well as painting aircraft, the ground crew were busy painting identification numbers onto all of the squadron transport and packing their own kit. As the scale of personal equipment had been changed, this meant that much of their equipment was handed back or sent to the 242 Group Depository.

While the squadron was busy preparing to move, a signal arrived ordering as many personnel as possible be sent to Carthage to listen to an address by a VVIP. In the event the pressure of work only allowed five airmen to attend and listen to a speech given by none other than the Prime Minister, Winston Churchill.

The following day the squadron began to say farewell to some of its members who were tour expired. Four were in the original party to land in North Africa: Flg Off O.L. Hardy DFC, Flg Off W.J. 'Jimmy' Corbin, Plt Off P.R. Fowler and Plt Off H.S. Lewis. Flt Lt R.A. Hagger and Flg Off N.W. Walker made up the remainder of the departing party. Jack Lancaster noted:

We were not at Mateur very long, and we were then given instructions to move to Sfax, where we were to get on a boat and go to Malta. It was very interesting coming towards the Tunis road because we came across hundreds, thousands of German and Italian prisoners of war walking along toward the big cages that they built to keep these prisoners in. There were a few unruly comments made from both sides while we passed.

DFC Citation

LONDON GAZETTE, 1ST JUNE 1943

Hussey, Roy Jack Hubert, 1312369, Sergeant, RAFVR

In operations in North Africa, this airman took part in a very large number of sorties, including attacks on airfields and road transport. He has invariably displayed fine leadership and great tenacity and has destroyed at least four enemy aircraft in combat.

Tunis beach, 1943. L to R: Flt Sgt Griffiths, Dalton Prytherch, Plt Off Eric ?, George ?. (T.B. Hughes)

Loading of the squadron transport onto LST *403* began on the 7th. The LST had a capacity of fifty vehicles and 250 men, and the embarkation began on the morning of the 8th. Two hours later the bow doors closed and 72 Sqn sailed for adventures new.

Sgt 'Red' Weller. (R.D. Scrase)

72 Sqn Spitfire Mk Vc over Tunisia in 1943. (K.C. Weller)

CHAPTER TWO

Malta

No. 72 Squadron had had a busy and eventful war up to mid-1943. Re-forming on Gladiators at Tangmere in 1937, they replaced the antiquated biplanes with Spitfires just before the outbreak of the war. Action in the 'Phoney War' was followed by fighting over Dunkirk, the Battle of Britain and offensive sweeps over Occupied France, before decamping to North Africa and the successful Tunisian campaign. Following the end of this campaign the squadron was to move once more to a new base, there to re-equip with replacement aircraft and reinforcements.

LST *403* was one of three in convoy, escorted by a corvette, HMS *Roxinia*. It was a fine day and the sunset at sea caused much comment among those on board. An uneventful night passed, and by dawn the airmen could see land. This was their new home – Malta. Saying their farewell to the navy crew of the LST, the ground crew disembarked at noon and began the journey to Hal Far airfield. They were gratified to find that, for the first time in seven months, they would not have to live under canvas but were billeted in empty houses in the small, picturesque village of Birsebbuggia. After settling in, the evening was spent in bathing in the sea. Jack Lancaster remembered the arrival on Malta:

We were posted to Hal Far. It was a stony old landing-ground and Malta is just a rock, no doubt about that. We had no billets up at the aerodrome and we were billeted in a little village just down at the bottom of the lane not far from Hal Far, and we had our sergeants' mess in a pre-war restaurant. Malta was a hive of activity, there were aircraft flying all over the place. Sgt Ernie Pointer was in charge of the electrics and WO 'Choter' Weedon was in charge of all the wireless repairs. They were both very nice chaps, and 'Choter' went to Sicily with us. Ernie Pointer was replaced by Flt Sgt Archie Bibby, and Weedon was replaced by Flt Sgt Doug Harris.

All good things come to an end, though, and on the 10th the Spitfires arrived from Mateur and everyone buckled down to preparing the new base, unpacking stores and servicing the aircraft. Malta may have been picturesque, but it was still a dangerous place to be. The Germans and Italians were still sent over on regular bombing raids, and a delayed-action bomb from one of these was responsible for injuring one of the squadron's airmen, AC1 Bucksey, when it exploded.

The pilots began flying practice on the 11th, and the ground crew was forced to take some of the squadron transport off the road when it was discovered that there was a dire shortage of motor fuel on the island and that only essential journeys were to be made. The squadron also heard the wail of air raid sirens for the first time in seven months; the enemy declined to come over and drop any bombs though. As the squadron prepared for its next phase of operations, Operation Corkscrew was launched to capture Pantelleria, which, due to the preceding twenty-day bombardment, fell with little resistance. On the 12th the squadron was pleased to receive news that Sgts Hussey and Laurie Frampton had been commissioned and that they would remain with the squadron. While on Malta Tom Hughes and Greggs Farish discussed the skills and qualities required of a fighter pilot, and many years later Farish wrote:

Tom Hughes and I talked of shooting Huns down. We discussed it and he said that some people like Danny (Sqn Ldr Daniel) and George Keith were fitted by character to be fighter pilots. Even 'Joe' Scrase, with his boyish ways, would fight like a demon when in a tight corner. There seemed to be a certain absoluteness or concentration about it, besides the ability to shoot straight, to watch your own tail, to watch tactical enemy traps and not to follow a Hun down.

The squadron flew its first operation from Malta on the 15th as part of a wing sweep south-east of Sicily. The sortie was uneventful apart from some flak near Comiso airfield. Wg Cdr H.S.L. 'Cocky' Dundas flew with the wing but returned early with engine trouble. He had taken over as Wing Leader from Wg Cdr Gilroy, who was now promoted group captain and OC 324 Wing. Sgt Griffiths crashed his Spitfire (EN394) on landing but escaped unhurt. Later that day the squadron planned to ambush the regular *Luftwaffe* recce aircraft which approached the island every evening. But the plan was undone by the lack of IFF ('identification, friend or foe') in the Spitfires. The IFF arrived that day and work commenced in fitting it. The ambush would have to wait.

With IFF now fitted, the squadron flew on another wing sweep of southern Sicily on the 16th, but once again the only activity was flak coming up around Comiso airfield. The 17th saw a third sweep, but once again the *Luftwaffe* failed to react to a pure fighter sweep; they were waiting for the bombers.

The squadron's first success operating from Malta came on the 18th, but it was tinged with sadness. Despite Plt Off Keith (EN429) shooting down his fourth Bf 109, the mood on the squadron was lowered by the loss of Flt Lt Prytherch (EN301) on the same sortie. Prytherch's engine failed just off the Sicilian coast and he called that he would have to bale out. He lost height over the coast and jumped at 4,000 ft ten miles south of Marina Di Regusa. He was seen to bale out successfully; however, he was then seen being dragged along the surface by his parachute, apparently lifeless

Malta 1943. Front: Sgt Lancaster, Sgt Cousins. Rear: Sgt Wright, WO J. Norton MBE. (J. Lancaster)

or unconscious. WO Alan 'Sexton' Gear (EN135) descended to 50 ft and flew over the area of the sighting but could find no trace of Prytherch. Malta was informed, and they immediately sent out Air-Sea Rescue launches and search Spitfires. The search continued till dusk and recommenced the next morning but no sign of the missing pilot was found. Prytherch had been with 72 Sqn for over two years, latterly as a flight commander, and his leadership and experience would be greatly missed. Rodney Scrase (EN259:RN-K) was involved in the fight, flying in the Red 4 position, and recorded the events in his logbook:

Sweep to Comiso (27,000). 20+ Me 109s in three groups below. Nothing much done. Flg Off Keith Me 109 dest. Flt Lt Prytherch baled out. In dinghy but missing.

He later added:

We saw some twenty Me 109s in three groups but did not engage. Meanwhile one of our team, Flt Lt Prytherch, reported engine failure and that he would have to bale out. This was ten miles south of Ragusa. Two of our squadron went down to observe and fix the spot. His parachute was seen to be dragging him along the sea. Despite Air-Sea Rescue efforts, sadly he was drowned.

As the search commenced, the remainder of the squadron were flying inland as far as Ragusa, where at least twelve enemy aircraft were sighted. Flg Off Keith had become separated from the formation and was crossing the coast at 10,000 ft on the way back to Malta when he saw a Bf 109 attacking two Spitfires circling at 5,000 ft. He dived down to attack the Bf 109, which immediately broke away, diving to ground level before he had a chance to open fire. Keith followed the Bf 109 for two minutes and closed to 300 yards before opening fire with a two-second burst. He saw strikes on the port wing root, and glycol began to stream from the Messerschmitt's radiators. Closing in to 200 yards, he fired again, once more scoring hits on the port wing root. The German pilot tried to escape by climbing, but Keith followed, and at 800 ft and a range of only fifty yards fired a deflection shot which blew the cockpit canopy off. Plt Off Keith broke away to avoid a collision, and a moment later observed a parachute and the black puff of the Bf 109 exploding as it hit the ground. The German pilot was the commander of *II/JG53, Major* Michalski, who baled out over land with a wounded leg and broken ankle. He was quickly picked up and taken to hospital.

Tom Hughes at Hal Far in Malta, 1943. (T.B. Hughes)

A search was carried out for both Prytherch and Flt Sgt Brown of 43 Sqn, who was also missing, and a report produced by the Air-Sea Rescue Service had some telling points to make:

Appendix B

MOST SECRET

Air/Sea Rescue Report

The Malta Air/Sea rescue service failed to locate and recover F/Lt Prytherch (72 squadron) and F/Sgt brown (43 squadron) on 18th. June, because:

1. Crews did not carry out Standard Distress Procedure. They did not go over to Channel 'D' and give 'May Day'. There was far too much nattering over Channel 'B' and it was over Channel 'B' that the Controller first learnt that

---

crews were in distress. (All aircrew with R/T are reminded that Channel 'D' is reserved as an exclusive medium for fixing a position and for dealing with distressed aircraft. Any messages relating to distress procedure transmitted over any channel other than 'D' may not only occasion waste of precious time for fixing but is also liable to be jammed by simultaneous transmissions of an operational nature).

2. Until last light several squadrons of operational aircraft carried out a deck-level search for the missing crews. This took place very close to the enemy coast and in consequence R/T was used as little as possible. At one stage a sighting was made of a dinghy (there is no evidence that the other pilot got into his dinghy), but the orbiting aircraft, owing to misunderstanding, left the position before the relief aircraft had actually sighted the dinghy. (This emphasizes the facility with which a sighting once made can be lost again.)

3. The rescue was further hampered by the limited number of pyrotechnics the pilot was carrying.

4. The Rescue Launch, though able to reach the given position, had no field of view as the seas were breaking solid over her.

DO YOU KNOW YOUR AIR/SEA RESCUE STUFF?
DIS 730.
REBR.

20 June 1943 was an important day for Malta. The King made the first visit to the island by a British monarch for over thirty years, arriving on HMS *Aurora* with a destroyer escort. The squadron was kept at readiness throughout the day and was visited in the morning by ACM Tedder, AOC-in-C Mediterranean Air Command, and AVM Park, AOC Malta. The squadron only had the briefest of glimpses of the King as he passed by on the way to Kalafrana. During the readiness period it was scrambled five times, but only one of these produced a result. At 1830 Wg Cdr Dundas (EN358) led three Spitfires of Red Section flown by Flg Off C.C. Sharp (EN298), WO Alan Gear (EN144) and Sgt Keith Clarkson (EN461) off to investigate hostile plots in the Malta Channel. Climbing to 26,000 ft and flying toward the Sicilian coast, they sighted two enemy aircraft flying toward Gela. Dundas split his formation in two, with one pair providing top cover for the other two who set off in pursuit. Crossing the coast, the enemy sighted the Spitfires and turned around in an attempt to escape. While in a left-hand turn the lead enemy pilot fired a wide deflection shot and succeeded in hitting Flg Off Sharp's Spitfire just as Alan Gear called out a warning. Clarkson's Spitfire turned over on its back and dived into the ground near Biscari. Alan

72 Sqn at Hal Far, Malta, June 1943. (T.B. Hughes)

Gear latched onto the enemy leader and closed to fifty yards. He fired a three-second burst, blowing the cockpit canopy off. The enemy fighter turned onto its back and also crashed near Biscari. Clarkson had been avenged. Rodney Scrase (JK429:RN:N), flying as Blue 2, logged the fight:

> *Scramble, patrol Grand Harbour (28,000). Yellow section vectored on two 109s out to Sicily. Flg Off Sharp shot down by 109 – later shot down by WO Gear.*

Also on the 20th the squadron discovered that it was to lose some of its Spitfire Mk IXs. This was to bring the squadrons of 324 and 322 Wings into line with the other squadrons of the Desert Air Force, now operating alongside them, where only the most-experienced pilots would fly the Mk IXs with their superior engines, and the less-experienced pilots would fly the Spitfire Mk Vs. The change was made on the 21st, with the squadron handing over ten Spitfire Mk IXs in exchange for ten Spitfire Mk Vs. The squadron also introduced a new method of organization, requiring the unit to be split into three fully mobile, self-supporting parties in preparation for the invasion of Sicily. Some good news was received from the military hospital where AC1 Bucksey, who had been blown up by a delayed-action bomb shortly after the squadron arrived on the island, was taken off the dangerously ill list and placed on the serious list. The pilots were not impressed with their change of mount, as Rodney Scrase recorded:

> We had been one of the first squadrons in Tunisia to be equipped with the Mk IX. Now, in what we saw to be a retrograde step, we had to give up our exclusive use of that fine mark to share the planes we had with other squadrons in the wing – it was to be six Mk IXs for each, and we collected clapped-out Mk Vs to make up our establishment.

The decision to invade Sicily had been made in July 1943 by Churchill and Roosevelt, and was made in part to appease Stalin, who continuously clamoured for a second front to draw German divisions away from the Eastern Front and in equal parts to satisfy Churchill's ambitions in the region and to forestall American demands for a cross-Channel invasion in 1943. The operation was codenamed Husky, and the date was fixed for 10 July 1943. Prior to the invasion, the North African Tactical Air Force (NATAF) was disbanded and 324 Wing became part of the famous Desert Air Force (DAF). 324 Wing at this point comprised five squadrons: 43, 72, 93, 111 and 243, each with eighteen Spitfires. The squadrons of the wing were tasked with establishing air superiority over Sicily prior to and during the invasion.

While the Spitfires of the wing carried out an uneventful sweep over Sicily on the 22nd, the ground crews were busy preparing the squadron transport and equipment for embarkation on invasion shipping. This included waterproofing all of the vehicles with the help of REME engineers. The following day four Spitfires were allocated to a top-cover sortie for Spit-bombers planning to attack Comiso airfield. The weather forced a change of target, and two Bf 109s were sighted nearby. Flg Off Tom Hughes (EN144) chased one and fired on it, without result, recording the attack in his logbook:

> Sweep – S. Sicily. 90 deg deflection shots. Fired 120 rounds at two 109s before they half-rolled.

The squadron was stood down, for the first time since arriving on Malta, on the 25th, giving the ground crew the opportunity to take in the sights of Valletta. The squadron was further heartened by the arrival of a large quantity of mail, its first since 5 June. Laurie Frampton discovered he was being posted away, and two new arrivals turned up. Both were ex-43 Sqn men: WO T.R. Caldwell and Flt Sgt K. Hermiston. During this period the numbers attending sick parade had been climbing steadily, and by 27 June the wing had seventeen cases of malaria. In an attempt to stem this outbreak the issue of Atabrine recommenced, as it was believed it would help keep the disease under control. Orders were received on

Roy Hussey, Tom Hughes and Ken Smith in Valetta, June 1943. (T.B. Hughes)

the 27th for final preparations for embarkation, with all surplus equipment and stored to be handed in by 1 July. The opportunity for sightseeing on Malta was also taken, as Rodney Scrase recalled:

During the six weeks we spent on Malta, our non-flying activity was limited to looking at historic buildings, drinking – plenty of beer, joining the evening throng in the crowded Main Street, and swimming and sailing. One challenging swim was out to Kalafrana Bay, where lay the remains of one of our merchant ships, SS Breconshire. She had been in a March 1942 convoy and was so badly damaged that she had to be beached there. It was a good half-mile swim out to reach the rusting sides of the ship, and then after resting and sunbathing there was the race back to shore.

July brought us back to full operational state. There were now six wings of Spitfire aircraft, a total of twenty-three fighter squadrons, of which three were USAAC. Numerically this force, over 400 aircraft, was substantially in excess of the Luftwaffe and the Italian Air Force, but in terms of individual performance the Me 109G remained much superior to the Spit V.

On the 29th the squadron received further news on the fate of Plt Off G. Malan, who had been posted missing on 26 April in Tunisia. His Spitfire had disintegrated in mid-air and he died a few minutes after being rescued by personnel from 15th Light Field Ambulance. The last day of the month found the squadron stood down again, and once again the men made their way into Valletta for some well-earned rest and entertainment. Once again the squadron ended the month as the wing's top-scoring squadron.

Laurie Frampton with WAAF Rebecca Donnell after he left the squadron, tour expired. (L. Frampton)

By July 1943 the air battles over Italy were increasing in tempo with daily raids by strategic and tactical bombers, as well as fighter-bomber attacks on Sicily preparatory to the invasion of the island. On 1 July Sqn Ldr Daniel (EN309) led eleven Spitfires, four Mk IXs and seven Mk Vs, as escort to eight Spitfire fighter-bombers of No. 1435 Sqn. The Spit-bombers attacked Biscari airfield, but their bombs were observed to fall to the north of the field. On the return leg Sqn Ldr Daniel sighted four Bf 109Gs at 18,000 ft, flying east to west. Daniel turned and climbed in pursuit, closing on the Germans from the port side. The lower pair of Bf 109s turned to port and were followed by Black 5 and 6. Daniel, Black 1, continued after the starboard pair, and a dogfight ensued during which Daniel fired a three-second burst at one Bf 109, observing a series of strikes at the wing root, and white smoke began to stream from the aircraft radiator. The Bf 109 entered a steep dive, escaping to the north, and Daniel claimed it as damaged. Tom Hughes, flying a Spitfire Mk V, recorded his part in the action:

Sweep – Escort to Spit-bombers Biscari – Bounced by Me 109s, Macchi 202s, etc. Spun in off steep turn – quite successful though unintentional.

On the 4th the squadron was tasked for the first time to provide escort to bombers of the strategic air forces, escorting B-17s attacking Catania airfield. The following day the squadron found itself transferred from the control of the North-West African Air Force (NWAAF) Command to Middle East Command, and Tom Hughes recorded more action in his logbook:

Sweep to cover Fortresses. Dogfight at 25,000 ft. Damaged an Me 109.

On the 6th an escort was flown for three squadrons of P-40s bombing Biscari. It was apparent to the squadron that the full weight of the Allied air forces was being used to wreck the enemy installations and airfields on Sicily prior to the landings. Further bomber escorts followed, and it was apparent by the 8th that the Allies had gained almost complete air superiority over Sicily. While acting as withdrawal cover to B-17s over Comiso airfield, Plt Off Hussey (ES281) leading Blue Section reported three enemy aircraft circling to land at Comiso. Hussey dived down and attacked one white-wingtipped Bf 109G, which had one wheel down, offering an easy target. The Messerschmitt was quickly destroyed. Sqn

Ldr Daniel (JG793) pounced on a second Messerschmitt and opened fire at short range with his cannon. The Bf 109 fell from 1,000 ft and crashed. Sgt C.M. Scott (JK372) and Flt Sgt K. Hermiston (JK771) shared in shooting down a further Bf 109G and damaging two others. Tom Hughes watched the fight:

Squadron shot down two 109s in circuit. I gave top cover 4,000 ft.

Following the dogfight the squadron took the opportunity to strafe the airfield, and damaged a Ju 52, an Fw 190 and a Henschel Hs 129, as well as administration buildings and a wireless station.

On the 9th the squadron commanders were called to a conference where the plans for the invasion of Sicily were revealed. The assault would come from air and sea landings, with the British forces landing on the south-east coast, while the Americans would land in the south-west. Paratroops would be dropped to capture strategic positions in the path of the planned advance, and continuous air cover would be provided by Malta-based Spitfires. Losses were expected to be heavy.

The paratroops from the US 82nd and British 1st Airborne Divisions went in around 0200 hrs on the 10th, and heavy losses were suffered, many due to their aircraft and gliders being shot down by anti-aircraft fire from Allied ships below their flight-path. Hundreds were dropped into the sea and drowned, while others were dropped widely scattered and many miles from their objectives. The seaborne invasion followed at dawn and made good progress. 160,000 troops and 600 tanks were put ashore from 3,000 landing-craft, 200 of which

---

DFC Citation

LONDON GAZETTE, 9TH JULY 1943

Cox, David George Samuel Richardson, Acting Flight Lieutenant

Since taking over command of a flight this officer has shown outstanding leadership, which has been responsible for a large proportion of the successes attained by the squadron. He has taken part in a large number of sweeps and patrols and 40 sorties as escort to bombers. During this period he has personally destroyed four enemy aircraft, bringing his total victories to seven destroyed. Flight Lieutenant Cox has maintained a very high standard of enthusiasm and efficiency among the pilots of his flight and by his courage and devotion to duty has set a splendid example to all.

sank in rough seas. The British found little resistance approaching Syracuse, but it was a different tale on the American beaches, where they were held back by stiff resistance and strong counter-attacks by the German Hermann Goering and Italian Livorno Divisions. 72 Sqn stood by for action all day until 1545 hrs, when they provided escort to a bomber raid without incident.

The squadron saw its first conclusive action of the invasion on the 11th, when it encountered a formation of Italian fighters. Fifteen Macchi MC200s were engaged at 7,000 ft, and Sqn Ldr Daniel (JK173) and Flt Lt M.V. Christopherson (JG793) shared one destroyed. Plt Off Keith (JK637) destroyed two aircraft, and Plt Off Hussey (EN358) and Sgt Pearson (EN258) shared an MC200 damaged. Following the dogfight 72 Sqn became the first squadron to land an aircraft on Sicily when Plt Off Keith landed at Pachino, refuelled and took off from a road to return safely to Malta. Prior to his unplanned arrival at Pachino he had shot down an MC200 and a Ju 88. By the end of the day the invasion appeared to be progressing satisfactorily, with the enemy falling back everywhere except in the Comiso and Gela areas.

The squadron had a record day on the 12th. Three sorties were flown between Syracuse and Augusta and resulted in a score of thirteen destroyed, three probably destroyed and ten damaged. On the debit side two Spitfires were lost, Sgt King and Sgt Morris, and two others were damaged. Sgt Morris was picked up by the Royal Navy. The first patrol was over the invasion beaches at 0523 hrs and quickly in combat with German fighters contesting the landings. Sgt Keith Clarkson (EN309) destroyed a Bf 109 which dived into the sea, and damaged another, while Plt Off Keith (JK429) shot down a Ju 88 attempting to reach the invasion ships. Clarkson's victim was probably WNr 5522 'Yellow 6' of 7/JG53 flown by *Unteroffizier* Heinz-August Barth. Flt Lt Arthur Jupp (JG746) dealt with another Bf 109, sending it down to destruction. Sgt Morris (JK771) was attacked and crash-landed near Pachino, being returned to Malta by a Royal Navy LST. On his return he put in a claim for a Bf 109 probably destroyed.

The second patrol of the day by thirteen Spitfires at 1100 hrs turned into a terrific dogfight. A mixed formation of over thirty enemy fighters, Messerchmitts, Focke-Wulfs and Macchis, and bizarrely a lone Ju 52, was encountered over the beachhead. In the whirling maelstrom of the dogfight Flt Lt Johnston (JK990) and Sgt Scott (JK372) shared in the probable destruction on one Macchi MC200. Flg Off Tom Hughes (JG746) and Flg Off King (JK468) both destroyed MC200s, and Sgt Griffiths (EN309) had a field day, destroying two MC200s and damaging a third. Sqn Ldr Daniel (JK429) shot down a Bf 109G and Flg Off Rodney Scrase (JK275) sent one Macchi crashing down and damaged another (these were claimed as Macchis but were actually Fiat G.50bis fighter-bombers). Canadian Plt Off Bruce Ingalls (EN358) dealt with the lone Ju 52 and damaged a Bf 109G. WO Caldwell (JK637) and Sgt Scott both damaged Macchis, and Flg Off Cameron (JK429) damaged a Bf 109G and an Fw 190. Flt Lt Johnston and

Flg Off Smith (ES281) shared in the destruction of another MC200. Tom Hughes wrote of his part in the fight in his logbook:

Dogfight after bouncing Macchis. Mine baled out. Destroyed Macchi 200. Chased 109s. Dogfight with Macchis.

Rodney Scrase, flying as Yellow 3 and later as Red 4, recorded the dogfights:

Sgt Morris flying 'K' crash-landed. Picked up by Navy. Macchi 200 dest. And 1 Macchi 200 damaged in mass slaughter. 8 destroyed, 1 probable, 7 damaged. Doggers-ho with 109s. Squirted a little damage. Squadron destroyed 3, 1 probable, 2 damaged. Total Squadron score today 14 destroyed, 2 probable, 11 damaged. Sgt King missing.

He later wrote:

On 9 July I wrote 'a truly wonderful sight; the invasion starts tonight'. For the next few days we were patrolling 'Acid' beaches. On the 12th of the month occurred one of those extraordinary clashes. 72 in full squadron strength encountered what we took to be Macchi 200s. The squadron claimed a total of seven destroyed, one probable and seven damaged. My bag was one destroyed and one damaged. I chased two aircraft from the Italian formation. They kept on flying in echelon – a spick-and-span air show formation. My two guys just kept on straight and level. I lined up behind the No. 2 and fired. He fell away, smoke billowing from his fuselage. His leader continued, and in my excitement I kept my finger on the gun button for much longer than necessary. The plane was damaged, with bits flying off the wing. All I could do was watch and hope he would have to bale out. No such luck. Just one destroyed. I returned to base to be greeted by my ground crew and to have to confess twelve or thirteen seconds' firing time was nowhere long enough for me. It was only later that we learnt our opponents were Fiat G50 fighter-bombers and very likely moving out of the immediate combat area.

Tom Hughes also wrote of the great air battle of that day:

I was leading eight aircraft over Sicily in the Syracuse area. Suddenly I spotted a tight formation at the same height to the east, and they looked hostile. Opening up I gained a little height, and the 'bandits' started to dive to the northwards. The ten-mile gap closed quickly and they appeared to be the slow but very manoeuvrable Macchi 200 of the Regia Aeronautica. There were just six of them. I saw my seven Spitfires were nicely spaced astern, but there seemed nothing hostile above or behind. [Fifty years later the Italians confirmed that they had been Fiat G.50s.]
I closed extraordinarily quickly now and had to throttle right back. It seemed amazing that they had not seen me and had taken no evasive action. I gave one long

burst from line astern but saw no hits. I was now 200 yards behind another and I fired again. No luck. I dived below them and turned. My friends were in line abreast having good shooting practice above me. Suddenly the Italians broke formation. An amazing wheeling mêlée followed. Cameron, the Canadian, was turning tightly with an aerobatic Wop. I joined him, and in two turns was right on the tail of the Fiat. A one-second burst from my cannons set him ablaze. It was fearful to see. But there was a parachute near Melilli so I think the pilot got out. I hope he wasn't scorched too much.

I climbed up, and all seven other Spitfires soon joined up on me. I set course for the southern tip of Sicily and then home to Malta. On the way we were attacked by a Macchi 202 and two Me 109s, but they dived away, although I shot at the Macchi, without success.

We got back to Hal Far in good spirits. I knew there were only six Fiats in that formation because I had counted them carefully – we got the lot. My bag was just the ONE DESTROYED. Cameron was disappointed. I offered to credit him with half of mine, he would not hear of it.

The final patrol of the day saw the squadron up in strength, with nineteen Spitfires patrolling between Noto and Carlentini. The *Luftwaffe* and *Regia Aeronautica* were also putting up a strong showing, and a large number of Bf 109Gs and MC202s were sighted north-east of Carlentini. Once again the squadron was quickly embroiled in a dogfight and very clearly coming out on top. Flg Off Shaw (JK450) destroyed an MC202, Plt Off Hussey (EN258) and Sgt Scott (JK372) both destroyed Bf 109s, Flt Lt Jupp (JK429) and Plt Off Keith (JK637) each probably destroyed Bf 109s and Sgt Clarkson (EN358), Sgt Pearson (JK275) and Flg Off King (JK468) all damaged Bf 109s. Sgt King was missing following the dogfight, while Sgt Griffiths (EN309) returned in a damaged Spitfire, as did Plt Off Hussey. Griffiths' Spitfire was written off but Hussey's tail damage was quickly repaired.

While the squadron pilots were patrolling and giving the enemy some rough handling, the move of 324 Wing from Hal Far to Sicily commenced with the departure of the Wing HQ party. The successes of the day also brought a congratulatory signal from the AOC Malta.

There was no let-up in the pace of operations on the 13th, with four sorties being flown over Sicily as British forces captured Augusta and Ragusa. The progress of the invasion was going well, and with the capture of Comiso airfield plans to move the squadron ground personnel were set in motion. A technical party, led by the engineering officer Flg Off Greggs Farish, with reinforcement by a party of RAF Servicing Commandos, was ordered to stand by for movement by sea the following day.

The only successes of the day came on the second sortie, when Sqn Ldr Daniel led thirteen Spitfires over Sicily. From their lofty perch they observed great destruction at Catania airfield, and a few miles west of Augusta they bounced an enemy formation. Plt Off Hussey (EN258) shot down a Macchi and shared a Bf 109 destroyed with Sgt Griffiths (EN144). It was becoming a regular occurrence by now for fighters short of fuel to land at Pachino and refuel. Three of the formation did this and returned later to Hal Far.

Flg Off Greggs Farish led the technical party from Hal Far the following morning onto an LCT, and they landed on a beachhead in Sicily at 1900 hrs. By dint of marching and hitch-hiking they arrived at Comiso at 2230 hrs, where they met up with the 324 Wing main party which had been flown in by Dakota earlier in the day. The squadron's Spitfires

Flg Off Smith. (72 Sqn)

continued to operate from Hal Far, flying three sorties during the day. Action came on the first sortie when eleven Spitfires patrolled Augusta and Catania. The Spitfires became embroiled with a formation of Bf 109Gs, three of which were shot down. Plt Off Keith (JK637) claimed one, Flg Off Smith (EN258) a second, and the third was shared between Keith and Plt Off Hussey (JK372).

CHAPTER THREE

Sicily

The 14th saw British and German paratroops hotly contesting ownership of the key Primosole Bridge, and by the following day Canadian troops had taken Caltagirone, forty miles inland from Syracuse. The paratroops won the battle for Primosole Bridge and Montgomery began a drive toward Catania, while the Americans took Agrigento on the way to Palermo. On the 15th the squadron moved its base of operations from Hal Far to Comiso, with the first thirteen Spitfires flying in during the afternoon. The rear party remained at Hal Far awaiting the call forward. Arriving at Comiso on the 15th,

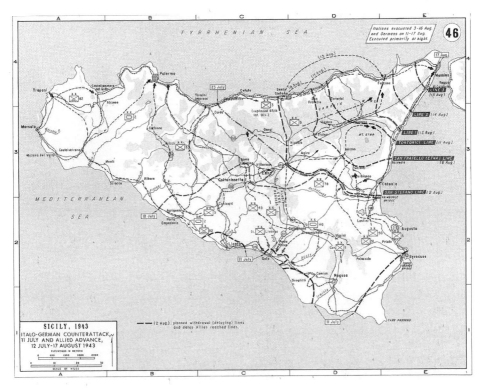

Allied invasion plans and Axis dispositions at 10 July 1943.

Tom Hughes wrote in his logbook, 'A beautiful aerodrome. Many serviceable Axis fighters.' Tom would have the chance to inspect one more closely quite soon. Comiso had been evacuated very quickly by the *Luftwaffe*, and in their wake they had left many anti-personnel bombs strewn around and a few booby traps. On the plus side, the bread was still warm in the cookhouse oven! Two more Spitfires and pilots arrived at Comiso on the 16th, and the squadron flew its first offensive sorties from the base and scored its first victories – and its first loss. Nine Spitfires patrolled the area north of Catania and sighted ten aircraft bombing the harbour. Shortly afterwards another formation of fifteen Bf 109s was sighted west of Augusta. The Spitfires dived on them and Sgt AM Griffiths (EN309) attacked and destroyed one Bf 109. Unfortunately pieces of flying debris from the doomed Messerschmitt flew back and struck Griffiths' Spitfire, which hurtled down alongside his victim. A parachute was seen to open, but it was not clear whether this was Griffiths or the German pilot. A second Bf 109 was shot down by Sgt John Connolly (JK826).

Four more pilots arrived at Comiso on the 17th, three by Dakota and one by Spitfire, while the rear party still waited at Hal Far. The final Spitfire arrived on the 18th, flown in by Plt Off Alan Gear. Rodney Scrase was one of those flown in by Dakota:

At the end of the week and in company with other pilots and ground crew, we were taken by Dakota first to Pachino and then to Comiso in southern Sicily. It was a regular air force base with a 2,000-metre runway. Imagine our surprise, not only were there a number of unserviceable aircraft lying about, but also cases of wine and Asti Spumante, which presumably the Luftwaffe had been unable to load onto their last departing transport plane. But very welcome to us!

On the 18th eight Spitfires flew a sweep to the west of Mount Etna, where they encountered eight Bf 110s bombing Catania. Plt Off Hussey (ES107) and Sgt C.R. Piper (JK786) chased one of the Messerschmitts for about ten miles, and then saw it crash into the ground and break up.

The rear party finally left Hal Far on the 19th, embarking on LST *65* at Valetta for the crossing to Sicily. It landed at Cap Passero early on the 20th in a bay full of shipping and a beach full of equipment all shrouded in sand and dust clouds. On reaching the town of Comiso they met some squadron pilots who led them to the airfield and their campsite hidden in the shade of some trees. As the squadron moved in, the Italian forces in the western half of Sicily surrendered *en masse* to the Americans. In the east, though, the drive on Catania was faltering as Canadian troops approached the slopes of Mount Etna.

While the ground party began the task of settling in at the new camp and making it habitable, disturbed only by a lone raider which bombed and strafed the airfield in the early hours of the 22nd, the pilots continued to fly sorties. The 22nd also found Gen Patton in Palermo and 45,000 Italians surrounded in

Tom Hughes, Greggs Farish, F. King and Rodney Scrase inspecting a Messerschmitt Bf 109 abandoned at Comiso. (R.D. Scrase)

the west. The pilots flew their first bomber escort to twenty-three Baltimores bombing Adrano, but did not encounter any opposition other than heavy and accurate flak over the target. Soon after arriving at Comiso, one of the ground crew, Alex McMillan, heard cries of distress from an area where 'S' mines had been laid. With a minimum of hesitation he reversed a 5-ton Thorneycroft lorry so that, with the help of another airman, they could recover the casualty.

Captured Messerschmitt Bf 109Gs at Comiso. (T.B. Hughes)

Unfortunately the casualty, who was a local civilian and should have heeded the warning notices, did not survive. Alex McMillan was awarded a Mention in Dispatches.

Palermo fell on the 24th, and the whole island except for an enclave in the north-east of the island, along a line stretching from north of Palermo to Catania, was now in Allied hands. The heavily outnumbered *Luftwaffe* was forced to resort to hit-and-run raids by lone bombers at night, and on the 25th one bomber dropped bombs in the Comiso area in the early hours. The raids were of little more than nuisance value, and little damage was caused. News of Mussolini's fall from power reached the squadron on the 26th, but any pleasure derived from this was countered by the loss of Flg Off Cameron (EN358) on a shipping recce.

Cpl Alex McMillan. (J. Lancaster)

Over the preceding days the squadron had been busy flying shipping recces observing the withdrawal of enemy forces across the straits to Italy. Cameron was leading four Spitfires off the north-east of Sicily when he disappeared, last seen near Messina. Throughout the sortie the flak on both sides of the straits was heavy and continuous as the Germans tried to keep Allied aircraft clear of their escaping forces. Tom Hughes took part in this sortie and wrote later:

Shipping recce Messina Straits. Dived to 5,000 ft over Messina. Acc[urate] flak. Intense and deadly flak. Flg Off Cameron shot down. Several A/C damaged.

Rodney Scrase flew as Black 4 (EN553:RN-K) and logged the sortie:

Shipping patrol Messina Straits (10,000). Flg Off Cameron, Black 3, missing in very accurate intense flak. Hit in tailplane.

On the 26th Tom Hughes flew a captured Caproni Saiman 200 biplane trainer, taking the Squadron engineering officer, Flg Off 'Spanner' Farish, with him, and judged it to be 'a pleasant light biplane with a powerful engine'. The squadron kept it as a war prize. The change of Italian government was swiftly countered by Hitler, who ordered German divisions to be rushed south into Italy to disarm the Italian army. On Sicily the Allies began to face stiffer resistance as they closed on Messina, bottling up the remaining Axis forces.

The heavy ground fighting continued, and on the 27th Kesselring ordered preparations to be made for the evacuation of the island. The squadron learned on the 27th that Sgt Griffiths, missing since the 16th, had indeed been killed, and he was buried in Melilli military cemetery. The pace of operations reduced somewhat on the following days, and on the 29th the squadron was warned to prepare a party for a move to a satellite airfield near Pachino. The move commenced on the 30th, and twelve Spitfires landed there that evening. In the preceding days the squadron had 'liberated' a Bf 109 and a Caproni biplane abandoned at Comiso, and following much work by Flg Off Greggs Farish the Bf 109 was made airworthy and flown up to Pachino by the CO, Sqn Ldr Daniel. Greggs Farish wrote of this captured biplane:

After North Africa we were relieved and spent some time on Malta prior to moving on to Sicily where we were stationed at a malaria-ridden place called Pachino. At least 75% of the squadron personnel came down with the disease at the same time so we weren't very operational!

While we were at Pachino we 'found' in an adjacent field a small Italian Caproni Saiman 200 dual-control 'flying machine'; it was a biplane very similar to a Tiger Moth and of course wizard for aerobatics. It seemed to be in perfect condition, and after a complete inspection and run-up, we turned it into wind and Tom Hughes (my best friend on 72 Sqn) carefully took off in it and flew it to our dispersal area. Apart from official duties, such as carrying messages and spare parts for the Spitfires, it was lovely to fly on a hot Sicilian afternoon.

Tom used to take me up in this 'pisser', as we called it, as often as he could, and sneaked some flying training into our schedule, although he never let me go solo in it.

A GI inspecting the wrecked aircraft and hangars at Comiso. (72 Sqn)

Squadron personnel throng around a captured defecting Caproni Saiman 200. (72 Sqn)

Entertainment for the airmen on active service was at a premium, and mostly they had to make their own. Jack Lancaster recalls one attempt to bring some entertainment to Comiso:

As there was not much air activity and the Army was moving forward, we were given a day off. So we decided we'd have a look around and see what we could find in the way of a piano. We had no entertainment on the squadron whatsoever and so we thought a piano would be a good thing. So off we went in a 5-ton Thorneycroft with Flg Off Farish driving. WO Weedon, Flg Off Hussey and Bill Mann were with us. We went to Augusta and the guard on the gate said we'd got to see the Town Major, so we dropped Flg Off Farish off and we went off with the wagon down a street with small houses. Bill Mann and I got out and were walking down this road when we heard someone in a house in an upper room. We went into this house and up the stairs and found two Military Policemen inspecting or looking for something. I said to one of them, 'Do you know where there is a piano?' He said, 'Oh, yes, I know where there's a piano.' I said 'Well, our engineering officer has gone to the Town Major to get a chitty for it so we'd like to collect it.' He said, 'Well, it's just across the road.' We came out of the house, crossed the road and found the piano in an upstairs room. They helped us downstairs with it and I put a couple of cushions inside the piano. I thought they would do for a pillow – I hadn't had a pillow for almost a year. We got the piano onto the back of the wagon and then we heard Flg Off Farish shouting, 'Hey, come on, we've got to get out of here.' So we picked him up and we just about flew out of the gates, and he said the Town Major had told him to get out, we'd no business there and we weren't to touch anything. It was a bit late for that, wasn't it?

On the way back to Comiso Jack Lancaster and the 'piano thieves' came a little too close to the enemy for comfort:

We made our way towards Catania, not knowing what the situation was at all, and on the way we saw and passed a bulldozer that had been bulldozing out the ground. He'd dug out a trench about 100 yards long and about 6 ft deep and they were already laying dead soldiers in the bottom of this great big trench. We suddenly realized that we couldn't be too far away from where the front line was. We continued and we were getting into a bit of a convoy, and then someone noticed that there were white lines on the side of the track that we were on and obviously this had been cleared of mines. We started going up a hill, and when we got to the top the Military Police said, 'What the devil are you doing here? Get over there, take your wagon and get over there and stay there until I tell you to move.' It appeared that the Germans were

Ground crew manoeuvring the captured Caproni Saiman. (72 Sqn)

just around the corner at the top and the wagons going up were support troops that were just going into the line. We'd had lots of cracks with them on the way up the hill, being asked, 'What are you doing here?' and we replied, 'Well, we've come to just help you out, you know, we've nothing much to do upstairs.'

However, we were called to go back down this road and told to clear off altogether, otherwise we were not likely to live very much longer. We came down the track along with more vehicles that were coming out, and as we got to the bottom the vehicle about three behind us blew up. We'd been over that mine twice but fortunately didn't set it off. We were very lucky. We set off then back to Comiso and the Squadron.

By the beginning of August the desperate Germans were fighting a ferocious rearguard action, and by the 3rd the evacuation had begun. August 1943 opened with good news for the squadron: Plt Off Alan Gear and two tour-expired pilots, Flt Lt Hagger and Plt Off Jimmy Corbin, were all awarded the DFC. Tom Hughes flew the captured Messerschmitt Bf 109G-6 (12.30.1160) on the 2nd on a local flight from Pachino to Comiso. He noted in his logbook, 'An excellent aeroplane but heavy on elevators.' Tom wrote a set of pilot's notes following his experience, and they are reproduced in Appendix 5. Two days later tour-expired Alan Gear also flew the Messerschmitt and almost came to grief. Tom was scrambled to escort him in safely:

Scramble! Squadron's Me 109 being fired at. Plt Off Gear avoided fire of all aerodrome's AA but landed 109 with one leg down.

Tom Hughes later wrote of these captured aircraft in greater detail:

In the summer of 1943 when 72 Sqn landed at Comiso in southern Sicily following the invasion there, they found devastation of the buildings, but dispersed among the

---

DFC Citation

LONDON GAZETTE, 27TH JULY 1943

Gear, Alan Walter, Warrant Officer

Warrant Officer Gear, who is now on his second tour of operational duty, participated while still in England in numerous sweeps over the Channel, including several to the Brest peninsula. During the campaign in Africa, he has destroyed two enemy aircraft and damaged several more. He has an exceptional influence among the pilots of his squadron which has undoubtedly had an effect upon the success achieved.

72 Squadron's captured Caproni Saiman 200, now coded RN-1. (R.D. Scrase)

trees and vineyards a few serviceable and many damaged aircraft of both German and Italian make. A Caproni Saiman biplane was flown out of a field nearby and soon painted anew with 72 Sqn markings. Another aircraft, which appeared to be in flying condition, was an Me 109G6. This was one of the Luftwaffe's favourite fighters and probably more of the type were built than any aircraft ever.

Although we suspected a booby trap, we eventually approached it, filled it up with 100 octane and started it. It fired first time. Sqn Ldr Daniel flew it first, and then I

72 Sqn pilots pose with the Caproni Saiman 200 captured by the squadron. (J. Lancaster)

L to R: Jock King, Jeep Jupp, Geoff Leach, Red Weller, Hoot Connolly with Caproni Saiman 200 and Spitfire Mk IX behind. (R.D. Scrase.)

did. Shortly afterwards the whole squadron was moved eastwards to a landing-strip on the coast called Pachino. There, too, was another abandoned Me 109G4. This was not in such good condition as the one we had left at Comiso. It was said that the Americans were to get all the enemy aircraft left there. We immediately planned an excursion to 'hijack' our enemy aircraft for further sporting flying. I went by road and Fergus King took a Spitfire IX to escort me back. Fergus flew in close formation and was a little concerned by a slow roll I did with the Me 109 without warning him. However, I did a fair landing at Pachino and taxied in safely.

After flying this machine I spent a lot of time writing flying notes [see Appendix 5], having explored the cockpit layout. I found that one wheel did not always lock down satisfactorily in flight. However, if the manual release was pulled, the undercarriage dropped down and locked under gravity. Flg Off Gear was a very experienced pilot, also one-time instructor from Training Command. He was anxious to fly our squadron's Me 109, and I spent some time showing him my notes. I also told him the trouble I had with the reluctant starboard wheel lock. He decided to take a trip in the machine one hot Sicilian afternoon. Somehow the warning message did not get through to the Army gunners who infested the local vineyards with light machine-guns to ward off low-flying attacks on our landing-strip.

Flg Off Gear flew straight out to sea, and a trigger-happy Navy boat took a shot at him, recognizing the characteristic profile of an enemy fighter, but not being too bothered with the RAF markings crudely painted over the German crosses and swastika. He turned back to the shore and the Army now let loose with everything they had got at him. The bullets whistled across the landing-strip from all sides. I was not far away from my own Spitfire, and I jumped into it after a fine hundred-

yard sprint. It started first time on the internal batteries and I took off as smartly as possible straight down the runway at full boost. Although it was said that I had neither parachute nor straps fastened, that was certainly not correct. I quickly found Flg Off Gear in the Me 109 being skilfully flown among the treetops amid a barrage of anti-aircraft fire from our own troops.

I was terrified by the tracer but managed to get fairly close behind the 'friendly' enemy, waggling my wings violently and hoping the Army would be kind enough not to hit me in the Spitfire or my friend in the Messerschmitt. By then all Flg Off Gear wanted to do was get his mount back to our landing-strip as quickly as could be. Unfortunately he forgot my careful briefing about the starboard undercarriage. It simply did not lock down, and although I was still behind him I was helpless for there was no chance of a radio message as we never got round to studying the German radio frequencies, or their equipment, in any case.

He did a fair landing on one wheel with the other leg still tucked up. I am not sure if the shooting had stopped by then. The Me 109 swerved as it slowed down and ran off the runway into the vines, but Gear stepped out rather smartly with a smile on his face.

The squadron was kept busy providing escort to bombers attacking Randazzo and Adrano for the first few days, and suffered its first loss of the month on the 4th. While escorting twelve Bostons attacking ground targets in the Catania area, Plt Off Keith's Spitfire (JK637) was hit by flak. The escort was returning from the target when enemy aircraft were reported north of Mount Etna. 72 Sqn descended to investigate and found the aircraft to be friendly fighters. Turning south, the squadron strafed a blockhouse at Miscali and left it on fire, and it was here that Keith's Spitfire was hit at 100 ft. He managed to climb to 2,000 ft but could not maintain height. He baled out at 800 ft over the sea, but unfortunately smashed his leg against the tailplane as he left the aircraft. Keith was quickly picked up by an Air-Sea Rescue Walrus and rushed to No. 25 Mobile Field Hospital. The surgeons operated on his injuries, but he sadly died the same day. US troops were brought to a halt by the fierce defence of the Furiano river and Troina on the 4th; however, the Germans withdrew from Troina on the 5th, having held on to it during six days of bitter fighting. Catania fell the same day.

As German troops poured into Italy on the 6th, the CO, Sqn Ldr Daniel, accompanied by Flt Lt Jupp, took a trip to view the Army at work at the front. They spent an hour under mortar fire north of Catania, and observed bombers escorted by 72 Sqn bombing Adrano. Another target, Randazzo, was the focus of operation on the 7th, with twelve-aircraft formations attacking the town every twenty minutes from dawn to dusk. 72 Sqn provided the escort for four of these 'very unsocial calls'. Over the next week the squadron visited Randazzo several times, as well as Fiumefreddo, Falcone, Oliviari, Navarro, Mascali, and Piedmonte.

The Germans were determined to get as many troops out of Sicily as possible, and covered by a defensive ring of over 500 anti-aircraft guns they began a night evacuation using 134 small craft during the night of the 11th. Rodney Scrase recorded a dogfight over 'Peaches' beaches on the 12th, in which the pilots flying the Spitfire Mk IXs engaged enemy fighters, with Plt Off Bruce Ingalls (MA637) and Sgt Connolly scoring two destroyed and two damaged between them. Rodney (JK430(RN-K), flying a Mk V as Yellow 3, saw seven Bf 109s, but they dived away and escaped combat. He noted that his aircraft was withdrawn from operations following this sortie with the note: 'K Sacked'.

By the 14th the Eighth Army was only twenty-nine miles from Messina, and the fighting was hard. On the 14th the squadron had a more personal indication of the difficulties being encountered by the invading Allies when German forces infiltrated to within two miles of the airfield.

Flg Off Tom Hughes caused a bit of a stir on the squadron on the 15th. He was flying the squadron's other captured Messerschmitt, a Bf 109G-4 version, when it developed a glycol leak and he was forced to bale out. Unperturbed he returned to the squadron to report a comfortable landing in a vineyard not far from Pachino. In his logbook he noted:

Speed trial with Spitfire IX. Rather disappointing. Not such a good specimen as the G6 flown on 2 Aug. Engine very rough. Spitfire had no difficulty in keeping up. Glycol leak into cockpit caused regrettable abandonment at 5,000 ft.

He gave more detail later:

Following Flg Off Gear wrecking our best Me 109, we were left with a rather decrepit G4 model. This sounded very rough when I started it up, but nevertheless we thought it would be interesting to compare its speed with the Spitfire in level flight. So one fine afternoon, with some trepidation and sitting on my RAF parachute, which did not properly match the German fighter's seat, I taxied out. Flt Lt Jupp taxied his Spitfire IX out to accompany me. This time we had alerted all the Army units in the vicinity, following their unprovoked attack on Gear the previous week.

As I got to the end of the runway I found that only one brake was working, and I wondered how I should manage to do a successful landing. However, the 109 had a lockable tailwheel, and as soon as I was rolling straight I engaged the lock, which at least kept me straight for take-off. We climbed together to 6,000 ft and I flew westwards at cruising speed. As I opened the throttle to maximum and increased the revs, the engine sounded horrible. I thought it would be sensible to return and land at once, and turned back eastwards to Pachino; Jupp was slightly behind. Suddenly there was a fearful escape of steam from under the instrument panel; some sort of leak in the coolant system had developed, and I found it not only hot but choking to breathe. I immediately jettisoned the hood and was pleasantly surprised with the excellent arrangement of it, which allowed quite an easy escape. I realized, however, that there was so much steam around my legs that it would be better to abandon ship.

At this point I should say that the RAF stopped their parachute training early in 1939, and apart from precise briefing to aircrew on how to escape from each particular aircraft no actual parachute drops were made during training. I think the incidence of broken ankles simply made such training uneconomic.

I had come to a point of decision, and may I say my last thought was to preserve a captured aircraft. It had already been examined a score of times by Air Ministry experts, and this made my decision a little easier. I undid my straps and started to climb out. I had a sudden change of mind: were my parachute straps tight? I tried to climb back in and somehow knocked the control column. In a trice I was catapulted straight up and clear of the cockpit

Tom Hughes on HMS *Nelson* in Malta, 1943. (T.B. Hughes)

and somersaulted over and over. I pulled the D-ring without bothering to count to three, which was part of the training advice. As the parachute opened I was startled by the shock from dropping freely. I was now supported underneath the canopy and saw galaxies of stars before my eyes, but what joy it is to be safely lowered to the ground on a silken thread.

I drifted down in the summer sunshine with a relief approaching ecstasy. I saw the German fighter crashing and exploding in a vineyard down below. Jupp was circling around me and I waved cheerily to him. Curses, I had dropped the D-ring. This with its Bowden cable always came out in your hand, and the packers always liked it returned. It seemed to take an age to do this 5,000 ft, but suddenly the vineyard seemed to be getting closer. I remembered the instructions about correcting for drifting. I found it facing the direction precisely, but for some odd reason I thought I should turn about, and reached for the webbing straps over my head with crossed hands, but it was too late and I landed perfectly in soft volcanic soil up to my ankles in the vineyard. I pulled on the lines and collapsed the canopy quite easily.

Two Sicilians appeared by magic. How could they tell if I was German, American or British, at least they knew I was not Italian. They took me to a little shack nearby and I was introduced to a tiny,

Tom Hughes on HMS *Nelson* on the return trip with the reason for the trip – bottles of whisky concealed in a Lux soap box! (T.B. Hughes)

ancient, shrivelled woman who must have been their grandmother. They gave me a glass of wonderful red wine and soon I was as cheerful as they were. With my parachute rolled up I got on their donkey-cart and headed for the main road back to Pachino. A jeep driven by Greggs Farish with Pearson on board rounded the corner and I was trans-shipped and returned to base, but only after we had all been back and had another drink of their famous wine.

That night the three of us, with our largest wooden keg, returned to the vineyard to try and buy as much of the red wine as we could. They took us to the outhouse of the nearby mansion, which seemed quite deserted, and from four great tuns siphoned several glasses. We eventually filled our cask with one of them, but all agreed it was not the same brew as I had that afternoon. I paid the packer of the parachute ten shillings (50p), which I was told was the traditional price for a repacking job.

Rodney Scrase received a new Spitfire Mk Vc on the 15th, EE799 coded RN:K and named 'Kalamity Kate IV', which he judged following an air test to be 'OK'.

By the 16th it was becoming clear that enemy resistance was failing and that the Sicilian campaign was nearing its end. As the Americans entered Messina on the 16th it was already too late, as the Germans had managed to evacuate some 100,000 troops to the Italian mainland to fight on. To keep the pressure up the squadron began forward-basing aircraft at Lentini, with fourteen Spitfires deploying there on the 17th as Allied troops entered Messina. From Lentini it flew five patrols providing escort to naval vessels and to Kittyhawk fighter-bombers attacking Palmi. During one of these sorties Rodney Scrase was flying Spitfire Mk IX ES107:RN-C as Black 2 when Smith and Pearson brought the squadron score to 201 aircraft shot down. Sgt Piper went missing in the newly arrived EE799:RN-K, Kalamity Kate IV. Scrase was flying a pair with Plt Off Hussey, and saw him get two Do 217s as he was forced, in his words to 'stooge around with a u/s engine'. Of the bomber crews, believed to be attempting to drop radio-controlled bombs on the invasion fleet, seven baled out and one unfortunately had his parachute snag on the tail as the bomber went down. Resistance on Sicily ceased on the 18th and the focus of operations turned to the heel of Italy on the 20th with a bomber escort.

Alan Gear, who had been awarded the DFC at the beginning of August, left the squadron, tour expired, on the 21st, and over the next few days the squadron was stood down from operations. Sgt Piper, who had been shot down on the 17th, made a welcome return to the squadron on the 21st, having walked back forty miles through enemy lines. Irvine Wright recalled his return to the squadron:

We were all pleased to have Pip back with us. He had not had much in the way of food since he was shot down, and the 'Doc' looked after him very well, to avoid him eating too much, too soon.

During a patrol of the Salerno–Nocera area on the 24th, the wing leader, Wg Cdr Dundas, and Flt Sgt Larlee destroyed a reconnaissance Ju 88 as the rest of the squadron climbed desperately to 30,000 ft to get involved in the scrap. On the 26th, operations recommenced with fifteen Spitfires flying to Agnovi airfield to operate from there in support of bombers attacking Bianco in southern Italy. The following day the squadron was on the move again with an advance party of ground crew setting off for Panebianco. The remainder of the squadron, less a small rear party, set off on the 29th, and on arrival had to contend with a tremendous thunderstorm while attempting to pitch camp. Nevertheless, by nightfall the squadron was, more or less, settled in. It had hardly had time to settle in, though, when rumours surfaced on the last day of the month of a move further north in preparation for operations over Italy.

For once the rumours were sound, and the squadron began another move, to Cassala, on 1 September. Once there it would come under the control of the 12th Air Force Air Support Command (12th AFASC). Cassala was an improvement on Panebianco and was much less likely to be affected by wet weather. The CO, Sqn Ldr Daniel, and the engineering officer, Flg Off Greggs Farish, flew over in the squadron's captured Caproni biplane. Unfortunately, when they were preparing to return to Panebianco, Greggs Farish was struck by the propeller while swinging it to start the engine and was seriously injured. He was evacuated to hospital and the next day was replaced temporarily by WO Price. Greggs Farish tells the tale of his unfortunate accident:

Then at last came the day when the troops on the Messina front had moved far enough forward for us to make a move up to Lentini, not far from Syracuse. By this time our CO, Bobby Oxspring, had been sent back for a well-earned rest, and Danny Daniels had taken over. On 1 September 1943 Danny and I decided to steal a march on the rest of the squadrons in 324 Wing by flying up to Lentini in the 'pisser' in order to pick out the best dispersal area. After we had decided on the best spot, Danny climbed into the front cockpit to come home. I was to start the 'pisser' by swinging the prop, which was the only way to get her started, and a procedure with which I was only too familiar. 'Contact', shouts I, and the engine starts first time, and then Danny couldn't see me anywhere! So he jammed on the brakes and climbed out again, leaving the engine running, as he had to, where he found me lying on the ground more or less under the prop. He dumped me into the back seat and flew me back to Pachino, where I was transferred to a field hospital in a hurry, and unconscious for two days.

While I was in hospital an enquiry into the incident was held within the squadron, at which time it was established that Danny had failed to apply the brakes before I shouted contact, a standard procedure when chocks were not available. I also think that we were on a slight incline and that the aircraft had simply rolled forward under starting power, which was sufficient to mow me down, like some massive lawnmower. My right hand, pipe (which I invariably smoked) and left front tooth were broken by one or other of the turns of the propeller, but the worst damage was a severe blow to the right of my forehead, where I still carry a scar.

The invasion of Italy, Operation Baytown, commenced on the 3rd, with the British Eighth Army crossing the Strait of Messina unopposed, and while keeping up a steady stream of patrols the squadron was once again ordered to move base, this time to Falcone on the north coast of Sicily. Packing began immediately and the advance party set off on the 4th. The move did not hinder operations, and the squadron flew escort to Kittyhawks striking targets in the invasion area, and provided beachhead cover over the south-west 'toe' of Italy. During this frantic activity Flt Lt Tom Hughes was posted to 43 Sqn as a flight commander. Patrolling continued, and the advance party arrived at Falcone on the 5th, by which time the Eighth Army had advanced ten miles into Calabria and captured San Stefano. The rear party left on the 6th, with the Spitfires taking off shortly afterwards. The ground crew followed a tortuous route through the mountains to Falcone, but was treated to magnificent views on the way, as well as first-hand viewing of the havoc wrought on the enemy, amply demonstrated by the wreckage they passed. They passed a chilly night and arrived on the 7th, with a few stragglers arriving the next day. Flg Off Rodney Scrase (MA520:RN-B) was not as happy about operating from Cassala, as he crashed on landing; however, he was only slightly injured, as he recalls:

One black mark was my hitting a tree on final approach at Cassala. I had a ninety-gallon overload tank and just did not allow sufficient height over the airfield boundary. The undercarriage collapsed and the propeller blades were broken off. The aircraft, MA520 'Sunshine', was a 'Gift of War' with only a few hours' flying time and was declared Cat 3. Yes, I did feel I had let the plane and its donor down. For me – a bruised forehead and a bloody nose, but I was back flying the next day.

Jack Lancaster recalled the period of operations from Lentini as relatively quiet:

At Comiso our tents were in a vineyard and it was nice to waken up in a morning, just lay your hand out and pick a bunch of grapes for breakfast. However, that didn't last for long, and eventually we moved up to Lentini, where we didn't do a great deal of work. We were doing patrols over the Army and over Messina, but otherwise we were not pushed too much at all. When we were going up to Falcone we stopped on Mount Etna overnight. It wasn't erupting at that time and we eventually got to Falcone on the north coast, where we set up our camp again. At Falcone we started being very busy again, and now we were preparing for the invasion at Salerno. We were fitting ninety-gallon drop-tanks on the aircraft for every trip, and this was quite a hectic time.

On the 8th the squadron began to think it would never settle in one place when it was informed that its role in the invasion would take it further north to support further landings south of Naples. Once again preparations were made to move.

Operation Avalanche commenced on the 9th, with the US Fifth Army landing at Salerno, south-east of Naples. Meanwhile British forces had captured Taranto unopposed. On the 9th everyone was heartened to hear that Italy had surrendered unconditionally, and the squadron began patrolling the invasion beaches south of Naples. To enable this the Spitfires were fitted with ninety-gallon overload fuel tanks which gave them an endurance of approximately 2 hrs 40 min, though two aircraft managed to remain airborne for 3 hrs 40 min with these tanks. Rodney Scrase wrote of these long-range operations:

We used Falcone on the north coast of Sicily as our base from which to fly for the invasion of Italy – Peaches Beaches was the name given to the strip of coast south of Salerno which we were to patrol. That was 180 miles away and about as far as we could go using slipper tanks and still carry out an effective patrol. My logbook records flying times of 2 hrs 30 min to 2 hrs 45 min for these missions. About one-third of the way to our patrol point was the Aeolian island of Stromboli – a live volcano. Our heading point, showing puffs of smoke and occasional bursts of red flame, served as marker. From there all one had to do was to head north.

On the 10th the advance party set off for marshalling yards near Milazzo where the vehicles and equipment were to be waterproofed prior to embarkation on invasion shipping for Italy. The squadron's new role would be in support of the Fifth Army in the Salerno sector. The pilots busied themselves with patrols over a beachhead codenamed Peaches, and during one such patrol on the 10th Flt Lt Johnson was badly shaken when his Spitfire overturned on take-off. German troops occupied Rome on the 10th and disarmed all the Italian troops in Italy.

DFC Citation

LONDON GAZETTE, 10TH SEPTEMBER 1943

Keith, F/O George Noel

Flying Officer Keith is a fine section leader whose skill and determination have been outstanding. He has destroyed seven aircraft in recent operations.

On the 11th, as British troops occupied Brindisi, Flt Sgt Leech became the squadron's first member to set foot on Italy when he landed at Paestua with engine trouble. He returned to base later in the day. Plt Off Newman arrived to replace the injured Greggs Farish as engineering officer.

On the 12th the squadron was back in the thick of it and increasing its victory score. On the day's first patrol the Spitfires encountered seven Bf 109s in the Naples area. Plt Off Ingalls and Flt Sgt John Connolly both shot one down, while Connolly damaged another. A fourth was damaged by Flg Off Smith, whose Spitfire was hit by flak. Plt Off Bruce Ingalls had to crash-land at Milazzo on the return when he ran out of fuel.

CHAPTER FOUR

Italy

The squadron began operations from Italy on the 13th from Tusciano, and once again damaged a Spitfire on arrival. This time Sgt Clarkson escaped unhurt. The first sortie was a Dakota escort to Stromboli, and later they returned to patrols over Peaches beach. Rodney Scrase recalled the move:

On the 13th it was time to fly over to our newly constructed landing-strip at Tusciano, close to the river of that name and with British artillery units almost in the field next door. Not only were we close to our own artillery, but also to warships of the combined Anglo-American fleet, whose heavy guns were pounding the Germans. It was very much a question of escalation. That had led to the use of Dornier 217Ks of KG100, which, using guided bombs, hit and seriously damaged a number of our warships, including HMS Warspite.

The ground crew advance party came off the beach during the day and the pilots were treated to some night-bombing by the enemy, who dropped bombs in the vicinity of the squadron's campsite in the darkness. One enemy aircraft was brought down north-east of the camp by the anti-aircraft guns, which caused little sleep to be had while they pounded away. While the advance party was landing, heavy German counter-attacks were being made by six divisions around Salerno, pushing the Fifth Army back to within five miles of the beaches. This setback forced the Allies to consider evacuation of the invasion force. The next day the fighting was still heavy, with the Germans launching a further counter-attack. The rear party began the same trek as the others on the 14th but ended up with a long and tedious wait at Milazzo until 21 September, as no shipping space was available for it. Irvine Wright landed at Salerno with the 'A' Party:

I was with the 'A' Party going into Salerno on a 5-ton Thorneycroft lorry rather overloaded with ammunition, etc., and almost as soon as we got onto the beach the track-rod went and the two front wheels were trying to go in opposing directions. Fortunately the Army had a big Scammell recovery vehicle standing by and it picked us up as though we were a toy. The beach was no place for loitering at that stage.

Jack Lancaster remembered waiting in the bay to land under shellfire:

We had a bit of shelling when we were sitting out in the bay, and the captain of our ship decided that it wasn't a very healthy place and he'd like to get rid of us and put us ashore. We went ashore and the old Army chappy on the beach, the Beach Master, said, 'What the heck have you come for? The Germans are not far away and there's still hell on round here. The best thing you can do is dig a trench and get stuck in there because there'll most likely be a lot of shelling going on tonight, and keep yourself well prepared, you might be used as infantry eventually.' We thought this was brilliant. We settled down, had a bit of food, and during the night we heard a Tiger tank come up about 200 yards away, but it turned round eventually and went back, thank goodness. The night was spent rather in trepidation, but we managed to live through it.

Patrols and escort continued at a steady rate, and the score was increased again on the 15th when Sqn Ldr Daniel shot down a Bf 109 over Peaches. Later in the day Flg Off Smith probably destroyed an Fw 190 and Flt Lt Johnston damaged another.

The focus of patrolling on the 16th was Peaches again. Flt Sgt Piper shot down a Bf 109 on the second patrol but encountered engine trouble and crash-landed within enemy lines and was reported missing. Piper's victory was the 200th enemy aircraft destroyed by the squadron. On the same patrol Flg Off Barnfather damaged a Bf 109, and on the last patrol of the day Flt Lt Pearson and Flg Off Smith each shot down an Fw 190. Rodney Scrase flew a patrol with Roy Hussey:

September 16th was a day I shall always remember. Flying as No. 2 to Roy we were vectored onto enemy plots over the Bay of Salerno, where British and American warships were providing maximum possible support to our ground troops, who only two days after the landings were having a tough time. We were at 20,000 ft and heading towards two Do 217s. At that moment I had trouble with my second-stage supercharger, which kept cutting in and out. Roy flew on ahead and shot down the first Dornier. By the time I had sorted out my problems, he had caught up with the second aircraft and got that one too. As I came up alongside the crew were baling out, but the last, who was in too much of a hurry to pull his rip-cord, went down with his plane, the parachute see-sawing up and down the tailplane. These aircraft were using a new form of bomb – a 3,000 lb Henschel 293 released by one aircraft and then guided by the second plane onto the target by the 'bomb aimer', who used radio control to make adjustments to its flight. Over the two days the Dorniers were able to inflict considerable damage to our ships – sinking a US cruiser and damaging several of the ships as well as damaging our own battleship – HMS Warspite.

On the 16th the US forces halted the German counter-attack against the bridgehead, and by the 17th the Germans began to withdraw from around Salerno as the Eighth Army linked up with the Allied forces in the bridgehead. On the 17th Sqn Ldr Daniel and Flt Lt Jupp set off to escort P-38s tasked with ground attack. The P-38s did not turn up, so Daniel led Jupp in a little ground attack of their own, shooting up aircraft on an enemy airfield. By the 18th the Eighth Army was advancing steadily and closing the gap between it and the Fifth Army's Salerno salient. The squadron kept up the patrolling, and Alan Gear turned up again, having been released from hospital.

On the 20th the squadron was on the receiving end when two Fw 190s made low-level bombing and machine-gun attacks on the airfield. Though casualties were suffered, none were from 72. The *Luftwaffe* was determined to get at the Allied shipping off Salerno, and the squadron was kept busy patrolling the beachhead in efforts to stop them getting through. The patrolling brought more successes, and Plt Off Hussey shot down two Dornier Do 217 bombers over the

Plt Off R.H. 'Roy' Hussey among *Luftwaffe* wreckage on Sicily. Hussey had shot up this Ju 52 as it was unloading troops the previous day, and was able to observe the results when the airfield was captured. (72 Sqn)

beachhead. The Eighth Army captured Bari on the 20th, and two days later began to be reinforced by the British 78th Division, which began landing there.

Sgt Piper, posted missing on the 16th, turned up on the 21st with a tale to tell. Having extricated himself from his Spitfire he first befriended an Italian soldier accompanying several other Allied troops seeking to escape through enemy lines. The Germans were extremely keen to capture Piper, and patrolled the area of the downed Spitfire aggressively, searching houses and buildings. Meanwhile, Piper and his companions had evaded them and reached Campagnia on the 21st. They were apprehensive about entering the town in case it was still in enemy hands, but in the event the Americans held it. Piper was being returned by road by the Americans when he spotted some Piper Cub liaison aircraft in a field, and one of the pilots offered to fly him back. The offer was accepted and Piper returned to the squadron in style!

The squadron rear party landed on the beach on the 22nd and the airfield was visited by a hit-and-run raider who dropped bombs close to the runway. The rear party had its first taste of enemy fire, too, as it landed under enemy shell fire, eventually reaching the airfield in darkness.

On the 24th the wing leader, Wg Cdr Dundas, led the squadron on a patrol of Salerno and shared in the destruction of a Ju 88 with Canadian Flt Sgt Tom

Larlee. Patrols continued for the next few days, but the weather then took a hand, and by the 27th the heavy rain had made the airfield unserviceable. Flying resumed on the 28th, but that night a violent thunderstorm and torrential rain brought a dismal night to many of the squadron, whose tents were blown away. The airfield was u/s again the next day. Fortunately the weather improved and greatly assisted in drying-out the sodden equipment and tents. The airfield was still unfit for flying by the end of the month.

Bar to DFC Citation

LONDON GAZETTE, 28TH SEPTEMBER 1943

Daniel, Stephen Walter, Acting Squadron Leader

This officer has led his squadron on operations resulting in a succession of victories in which his fine fighting spirit and exceptional ability have been a material factor. He has personally destroyed at least ten enemy aircraft and damaged many others.

During the operations at Salerno Jack Lancaster and a party of engineers were sent out to an American airstrip to repair a damaged Spitfire:

I took some lads out to one of our aircraft which had force-landed at one of the other strips that was occupied by the Americans. Talking to one of their American fitters I noticed that he had a wonderful toolkit, and they were so generous that I came away with about half of it. Things that were absolutely wonderful, that would be very useful to us, but which we didn't have any idea of their existence.

Conditions on the ground at Tusciano were Spartan in September, and Rodney Scrase recalls one attempt to improve the rations for the squadron:

On the ground it was hard going. Mosquitoes and hard temperatures, poor tented accommodation and basic rations. We thought this would be somewhat livened up when our cooks slaughtered one of the cows in the nearby field. The squadron's Coles crane was used from which to hang the beast, but no one was prepared to wait and let it hang properly, so it was a tough old animal to eat.

Other events during the month included the landing on Corsica of French Commandos to assist the resistance in the fight against the Germans there, and by 4 October they were in complete control of the island. The Italian resistance forced the Germans out of Sardinia.

An unidentified pilot with a captured Fw 190 at Capodochino airfield, Naples. (72 Sqn)

While Naples fell to the Allies, the squadron managed one operation on 1 October before more torrential rain on the 2nd shortly after a second sortie closed the airfield again. Hitler ordered a German defence of Italy based on a line south of Rome, and the British 2nd Special Service Brigade was landed at Termoli on the Italian east coast, quickly linking up with troops moving north through the Foggia area. There was some good news, though, as Sqn Ldr Daniel was awarded a DFC. Flying restarted on the 5th, but by the 7th the rain had the upper hand again and the airfield was swamped. On the 6th the US Fifth Army captured Capua and Caserta, but was halted the following day on the River Volturno, twenty miles north of Naples, by a stiff German defence. By the 10th the squadron had been notified that along with the rest of 324 Wing it was to prepare for a move to an airfield in the Naples area. An advance party set off by road for Naples on the 11th and scoured the city for billets for the squadron. It located a large suite of well-equipped offices and took them over. Jack Lancaster was with one party moving up to Naples:

On the way we went through one or two small villages which had been completely wiped out, and there were a few old women there still trying to sort out a bit of what the Germans had left them – and what we had left them. It was quite heart-rending to watch these people who had lost absolutely everything. The fortunes of war.

Having found suitable indoor accommodation, the scroungers on the squadron began finding ways to furnish it and make life a little more comfortable, as Jack Lancaster recalls:

It was fairly obvious that we were going to be in Naples quite some time, as the Army was held up and all around Monte Cassino there was tremendous fighting going on. The CO decided that he ought to get some better accommodation for us, and he arranged the requisition of a block of flats on Via Firenzi in Naples, and the whole squadron moved in there. I think the officers were in the top and then the sergeants and by rank coming down to the ground floor. It was very, very cold when we were in Naples that winter. People were lying in the street due to hypothermia. A lot of Napolese had a lot of problems with feeding. However, we didn't do too badly and we generally enjoyed our stay in Naples. One of my lads came to me one day and said, 'Hey, Sarge. Have you got a bed to sleep on?' I said, 'No, I haven't had a bed since I was in England.' He said, 'Would you like a bed?' I said, 'A camp bed? Yes.' He said, 'Can you spare a bottle of whisky?' I said, 'I'll give two bottles of whisky to get a camp bed.' And he said, 'Right, I just want one bottle and I'll get you a camp bed.' How these lads got these camp beds is something that is beyond belief. The following day he came to me and he said, 'How about this?' and provided me with a brand-new American camp bed which I kept right to the end of the war.

A wrecked Messerschmitt Bf 109 at Capodochino. (72 Sqn)

Sqn Ldr S.W.F. Daniel and a ground-crew corporal in Italy in 1943. (72 Sqn)

Meanwhile the Spitfires left Tusciano for Naples in the afternoon. Once the remainder of the squadron arrived they were all accommodated under one roof in the five-storey building.

On the 12th the US Fifth Army resumed its assault along the Volturno river, and by the next day elements of the Army were on the far bank. However, by the 19th the offensive had stalled due to bad weather and the skilful defence of the river line by the Germans. The Americans halted to gather strength before resuming the assault on the 31st. Montgomery meanwhile had begun his new offensive on the 27th.

Operations resumed on the 13th with four patrols in the Volturno area. While the pilots patrolled around Volturno over the following days, the ground crew busied themselves exploring the wrecked airfield trying to locate suitable working quarters. Rodney Scrase recalls Naples in some detail:

In Naples we were billeted in very splendid flats in the streets adjoining the main railway station. They had probably been reserved for use by wealthy Fascisti. The contrast between our life in the field in Tunisia or in Sicily was beyond belief. Now restaurants and bars offered a very real social life where you met people of all kinds. You were juggling the demands of military service with the reality of the world around you. Our quarters were cleaned and tidied by local folk – very likely the servants employed by the previous residents. The price of goods and services increased day by day as the locals realized we were totally unaware of the cost of life in Naples. They had lived through the years when Mussolini got the trains to run on time, but even he had not been able to get Neapolitans to behave in an honest manner.

As squadron pilots, our favourite dining spot was the Giardini degli Arnaci (Orange Gardens) high up on the hillside and with lovely views across the Bay of Naples. Cars 'commandeered' by some of our pilots meant there were drives along the road network to this or some other restaurant. At a visit to the Opera House – the San Carlo – I made a foolhardy leap from a balcony onto the table some distance below. By great good fortune I landed safely and did myself no physical injury. We made a friendly swap with soldiers on an American Army truck. As we drove up a hill to Capodochino they gesticulated and asked us to stop. We did so. They wanted to know whether we had any victuals to exchange. We swapped our surplus tea for their coffee.

A quite different contact was one we had with two Italian Air Force officers. They wanted us to attend a meeting where they – Royalists – were hoping we would speak in support of their King and play down the Republican cause supported by many of the locals. Needless to say, we steered well clear of such activity.

The Army was advancing beyond Naples to a line along the Volturno and the town of Capua. Much of our flying time was given to providing cover for destroyers engaged in shelling the coast towns such as Minturno.

The pilots had a field day on the 16th while on a recce of the Gulf of Gaeta. The Spitfire pilots spotted over twenty Fw 190s and a dozen Bf 109s giving escort to another group of Fw 190s, and wasted no time in attacking. In all, the squadron destroyed six and damaged two. Sqn Ldr Daniel (JF513) destroyed two Bf 109s, Flt Sgt Clarkson (EF656) shot down two Fw 190s, Plt Off King (JK599) and Flg Off Barnfather (MA444) both destroyed Bf 109s. Flt Sgt K.C. 'Red' Weller (JK132:RN-B) and Australian Flt Sgt Connolly (MA462) completed the tally with a Bf 109 damaged each. The only loss to the squadron was Canadian Flt Sgt J.W. Larlee's Spitfire (EN258), which was hit by cannon fire and which he crashed on landing, escaping unhurt. The *Luftwaffe* took its revenge on the squadron on the 21st with an evening air raid which lasted half an hour. Flt Sgt Scott and Flt Sgt Ron Gridley, both pilots, were caught in the open and were injured by shrapnel.

On the 28th, 324 Wing instituted a rota which allowed each of the wing's five squadrons one day in five completely free of operations. Liberty runs were arranged, and most of the squadron took the opportunity to visit Pompeii and Sorrento. The idea was well received.

On the 29th, the CO, Sqn Ldr Daniel (JF513), increased the tally again when ten Fw 190s were sighted. He shot down one south of Rome while on a recce of the area with six Spitfires.

Ron Gridley modelling RAF desert kit. (Betty Gridley)

November 1943 saw the squadron settled at Naples in a routine of bomber escorts and fighter sweeps. On the 4th the squadron flew a single operation which proved to be an unlucky one for the Germans, with Flt Lt Arthur Jupp (JG722) knocking down an Fw 190 and Flg Off Smith (JL368) destroying a Bf 109 over Cassino. By the 4th the US Fifth Army had captured Isernia, fifty miles north of Naples, and had linked up with the Eighth Army advancing north-west from Foggia. The following day squadron personnel had a grandstand view as enemy bombers attacked Naples docks for over an hour. One bomb fell on a road junction 300 yards from the 72 Sqn billets. The US Fifth Army in the meantime had reached the River Sangro.

On 10 November 324 Wing bade farewell to 243 Sqn, which was moving east to 322 Wing. This left 324 Wing with 72, 93, 111 and 43 Squadrons. Awards for service in the North African campaign finally caught up with the squadron, and WO Norton received the MBE, Flt Sgt Landon the BEM and Flt Lt W.F. Le Petit, Flg Off Greggs Farish, Flt Sgt H.F. Dow, Flt Sgt W. Mann, Sgt F.W. Arthur, LAC Mike McCaul, AC1 J. Foot and AC1 G.C. Peterson all received Mentions in Dispatches.

The *Luftwaffe* had an unlucky day on 13 November. On the first patrol of the day Flt Sgt Morris (LN259) shot down one Fw 190 and damaged another, and on a bomb line patrol later the squadron met a formation of Fw 190s and Bf 109s north of Gaeta and set about them. Sqn Ldr Daniel (LZ949) destroyed a Bf 109 and Flg Off McLeod (JL384) also shot one down, but the most unusual kills went to Flt Sgt Tom Larlee. He took on two Bf 109s and dived after them at high speed from 22,000 ft. He pulled out at about 10,000 ft, having reached a speed in excess of 500 mph, but the Messerschmitts continued to dive and failed to pull out, crashing within 200 yards of each other. Larlee had not fired a shot! In what was becoming something of a habit with the squadron, Larlee returned to base with a damaged aircraft, overstressed in the pull-out; the starboard undercarriage would not lower, forcing him to crash-land the Spitfire (LN259). Once again the pilot walked away from it. Rodney Scrase remembered the battle:

We did have one major engagement with Me 109s described in my logbook as a freelance delousing sweep. The lice were shot down – five of them.

On the 15th Gen Mark Clark called a halt to the Fifth Army offensive, and in the north civil unrest in Milan forced a state of emergency to be called as the Germans took 1,750 hostages and sited machine-guns on street corners, enforcing an 8 p.m. curfew.

On 17 Nov Flt Lt Tom Hughes returned to the squadron after a brief period with 43 Sqn, and took over as 'B' Flight commander from Flt Lt Johnston,who was tour expired. On the 24th the squadron was honoured by a visit from AM Sir Arthur Coningham KCB, DSC, MC, DFC, AFC when he 'dropped in' at dispersal and chatted to the pilots.

Ron Gridley collecting grapes wearing a pith helmet. (Betty Gridley)

The squadron had slipped into a routine of bomb line patrols, shipping escorts and recces that brought little air action from the *Luftwaffe*, which was by now badly outnumbered and overstretched. By the 20th the Eighth Army was across the River Sangro, and Hitler withdrew Rommel to oversee the construction of the 'Atlantic Wall'. *Feldmarschall* Albert Kesselring was brought in to command German forces in Italy and hopefully stem the Allied advance. By the 23rd the Allies were across the River Sangro in strength, and four days later the Eighth Army joined the assault, establishing a second bridgehead across the river by the 28th. On 26 November the squadron suffered its first ground crew casualty in some time when an accident occurred near the 'A' Flight Armoury tent. One of the airmen picked up a small unexploded bomb and then decided to throw it away, whereupon it exploded, seriously injuring AC2 Walker and injuring LAC Stewart. Walker died a few hours later in hospital of abdominal wounds from the shrapnel.

On the 28th the squadron turned to ground attack when enemy transport was sighted on the road between Capistrello and Vincenzo. Flt Lt Hussey (JL368) claimed two trucks and a staff car left on fire, and a tank carrier and tank damaged, while Plt Off Ingalls (EF648) damaged two staff cars and Flt Sgt 'Red' Weller (ER635:RN-M) scored hits on two tank carriers and tanks, and damaged two trucks and a staff car.

BRADFORD TELEGRAPH & ARGUS 17 NOVEMBER 1943

R.A.F.'s GRATITUDE

When the Bradford Local savings Committee were making arrangements for the commemoration ceremony connected with the City's Wings for Victory Campaign an invitation to attend the function in the New Victoria Cinema on 29 August was extended to No. 72 Squadron of the R.A.F., which was attached to Bradford in June 1939. Actually the location of the squadron is not known, and it was not surprising that the unit was not represented at the ceremony. The invitation, however, was passed on by the Air Ministry, and to-day a reply had been received from the Squadron Leader intimating that the squadron left England nearly a year ago.

He expresses his gratitude to the committee for wishing to give the squadron a prominent place in the ceremony, and regrets that it was not possible for him and his men to co-operate, and adds: 'I take the belated opportunity of congratulating your city on the magnificent financial result achieved. Such support is greatly encouraging to the Forces.'

It will be remembered that Bradford's Wings for Victory Week last April produced £2,989,679 against a 'target' of £2,500,000.

December opened with the British 10th Corps, under the US Fifth Army, striking at Garigliano, and by the 6th the US Fifth Army had taken Monte Carnino. Before leaving North Africa for Malta the squadron had deposited a large amount of kit and equipment in storage at Souk el Khemis, and received some bad news about it on 5 December, when it was reported that the ship transporting the equipment to Italy had been sunk during a heavy air raid on Bari on the night of 2/3 December. The first of many South Africans to be associated with the squadron during its sojourn in Italy arrived on 8 December in the form of Maj A.C. Bosman DFC. Maj Bosman was made supernumerary, and was earmarked to eventually replace Sqn Ldr Daniel as CO. The squadron also received its first French Canadian, when WO Turgeon arrived the same day. The following day the squadron was hit badly when both Flt Lt Pearson and WO Larlee were posted missing. Pearson (EF648) was last seen as he descended in the Rome area to strafe enemy transport, and Larlee (EF656) called on the radio about fifteen miles south of Rome to report that he had engine trouble and would have to bale out. None of the pilots saw him jump. The squadron lost another Spitfire the following day, when the newly arrived WO Turgeon (EE811) had to crash-land near Gingliano. He made an exceptional landing in a small clearing in an apple orchard, which so impressed the very shaken apple sorters nearby that they gave Sqn Ldr Daniel and the intelligence officer, Flg Off Brill, a large quantity of their best apples, having already bestowed food, fruit and drink on WO Turgeon. The Eighth Army crossed the River Moro on the 10th, and on the 12th Flg Off Rodney Scrase scored another victory, knocking down a Bf 109 near Frosinone. On the 15th Scrase had a very close call:

While escorting A-20 bombers to Frosinone we came across formations of 109s and 190s. They attacked the bombers, we attacked them. I claimed an Me 109G destroyed. Other pilots claimed a number of enemy aircraft damaged. Then I had a shaky set-to with another Messerschmitt – the perspiration was pouring off me as I turned and turned, but without any success against him. Eventually we both flew off home, the fight leaving me and my pals very short of fuel. After refuelling I was told I had just about one gallon left in my tanks.

Heavy fighting had been going on around the village of San Pietro, which finally fell to the Americans on the 17th, and by the 21st the 1st Canadian Division of the Eighth Army was battling fiercely to capture Ortona. Fighting for Ortona went on until it was finally cleared of German opposition on the 28th. The 18th saw the loss of Flt Lt Tom Hughes (EN258) on a bomber escort near Capua. He had turned back early and was not seen again. Tom Hughes survived, badly injured, and was made a POW. The squadron's fortunes changed on the 19th with a very successful day's shooting. On a morning bomber escort to Acre, Flg Off McLeod (MA444) destroyed an Fw 190, and both Flt Sgt Coles (MA637) and WO John Connolly (EN491) shot down Bf 109Gs. Later in the afternoon the squadron flew a bomb line patrol and Flt Lt Hussey (JL384) shot down an Fw 190 and damaged another, while Sgt Pullan (MA444) damaged a Bf 109. These victories were countered by the loss of Flt Sgt Bouchier (MA511), who was hit by flak while chasing another Bf 109. His Spitfire crashed four miles south of Ceccano, well behind enemy lines. There was also a change of command on the 19th, when Maj Bosman finally replaced Sqn Ldr Daniel, who departed on Christmas Eve.

The war did not stop for Christmas, and there was one bomb line patrol flown during which Flt Sgt 'Red' Weller (JG722:RN-D) was hit by flak and had to bale out. Weller was fortunate that the winds carried him just inside Allied lines. On landing he was sheltered by some Italians until American troops arrived and returned him to the squadron in good time for Christmas dinner! Irvine 'Rio' Wright was a ground crew member of the squadron and recalls Weller being shot down:

Red Weller was unfortunate to be shot down on the morning of Christmas Day 1943 while we were at Naples, and as a result of wearing a borrowed 'chute, which was not properly adjusted, he ended up damaging a rather delicate pair of vital organs!

The squadron's next operation was on the 27th, when Flg Off McLeod (JL127) damaged a Bf 109 on a bomb line patrol in the Ceccano area. Six Bf 109s, five Fw 190s and a single Macchi MC202 were encountered. The Focke-Wulfs were giving top cover to the Messerschmitts, which apparently had not sighted the Spitfires of 93 Sqn below them. The enemy fighters pulled up into the sun and 72 Sqn engaged them, resulting in McLeod's claim. Three days later on the 30th the bomb line patrol bounced eight Fw 190s bombing the railway near the Gulf of Gaeta, and Flt Lt Hussey (ER635) was the only pilot of the squadron able to catch the Germans up. He damaged one of them, and it flew off along the coast at low level after jettisoning its bombs.

January 1944 opened with Gen Mark Clark taking command of the US Seventhth Army in addition to his command of the US Fifth Army. The Fifth Army opened the offensive against German forces entrenched along the Gustav Line on the Rapido river on the 3rd. The centre of the line was at Cassino, which was a tough nut to crack and caused much trouble for the Allies over the coming weeks. Maj Bosman had only been with the squadron for a few weeks when he was posted to take over No. 7 SAAF Wing on 3 January 1944. His replacement as CO was Sqn Ldr J.M.V. Carpenter DFC, posted in from No. 145 Sqn. 'Chips' Carpenter was pleased to be promoted, but reflected the feelings of many in a letter home on 1 January:

> *Just a line to let you know I am now a squadron leader and have been given 72 Squadron. Great news, very excited but at the same time anxious and terribly <u>afraid</u>. However, I hope, and will do my best to make it a go. No more now as I'm on my way in a moment. Say a little prayer for me.*
> *Lots of love John*

By 8 January the squadron's well-worn Spitfire Mk Vs were all gone, replaced by newer Mk IXs. On the 13th more awards reached the squadron; DFCs for Flt Lt R.J.H. Hussey DFM and Flg Off K. Smith, and a DFM for Flt Sgt K.E. Clarkson, who had been posted, tour expired, the week before. The following day the squadron was informed that it was to move again, this time to Lago. The advance party left on the 15th. As the advance party moved out, the Germans were withdrawing across the Rapido river in the area of Monte Trocchio, which was captured by the Fifth Army. French troops under Gen Juin captured Monte Santa Croce. The rear party moved on the 16th and the first operations were flown from Lago on the 17th. There was an influx of SAF pilots to the squadron on 20 January, when Lt Jack Franks, Lt P.J. van Schalkywyk, Lt J.M. Jackson and Lt I.M. Richardson arrived from the 324 Wing Training Flight. Rodney Scrase describes the new campsite:

> *On the 16th of the month we said goodbye to Naples and went off to Lago, an airfield by the sea and just north of Castel Volturno. Although this was a canvas*

72 Sqn Spitfire Mk IX in Italy.
(K.C. Weller)

Christmas Dinner
menu at Naples 1943.

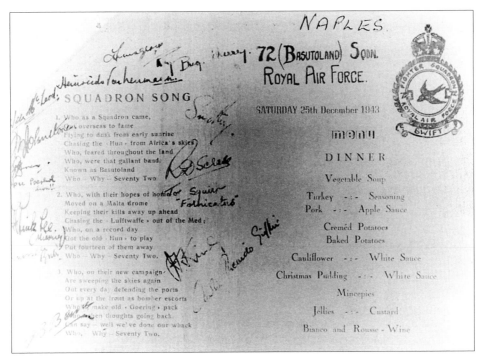

Centre pages of Christmas Dinner menu with signatures of squadron members.

encampment, at least we had the pleasure of sea bathing. In the small village, twenty miles from Capua, there was an atmosphere more closely resembling that of the Medjerda valley [in Tunisia]. Just a few days later came the landings at Anzio and Nettuno. We had some activity – but limited in scale, and encounters with the enemy were by chance.

On the 20th, US troops assaulting the line on the River Rapido were halted and thrown back across the river by the defending Germans. On the 21st four of the squadron Mk IXs were providing escort to a convoy when Flt Sgt C.M. Scott's aircraft (MA443:RN-T) developed engine trouble. Scott baled out and was successfully picked up. Life at Lago for the ground crew became a little more settled, and the adjacent beaches gave the men the opportunity for some relaxation from time to time, as Jack Lancaster recalls:

Lago was just north of Capua, just by the village of Montrigoni, and we had a very nice little airstrip here. The whole wing was on this airstrip, and we more or less had a regular sort of existence there, no great panics at all. However, Monte Cassino was only about ten miles away and the noise of the guns from there was deafening throughout the night. We were very fortunate that we weren't on the receiving end. When the weather got better, as our strip was only a few hundred yards away from the sea, we did manage to get a dip in the sea now and again.

DFC Citation

BRADFORD GAZETTE, 7 JANUARY 1944

Hussey, Roy Jack, Acting Flight Lieutenant

An outstanding pilot, this officer combines courage and accurate shooting with cool judgement and fine leadership. Since being awarded the Distinguished Flying Medal he has taken part in the Sicilian and Italian operations with conspicuous success, destroying a further five enemy aircraft, bringing his total victories to at least ten hostile aircraft destroyed and others damaged. On one occasion in September 1943, Flight Lieutenant Hussey shot down two Dornier 217s within the space of two minutes. At all times his fine fighting spirit, courage and devotion to duty have been worthy of the highest praise.

The Anzio landings commenced on 22 January. The US Fifth Army landed two divisions, over 36,000 troops and 3,000 vehicles, under Maj Gen John P. Lucas, thirty miles south of Rome. As the landings progressed, albeit slowly and cautiously, an enraged Hitler ordered the Gustav Line to be held at all costs. 72 Sqn flew its first sorties in support of the landings the same day, escorting Bostons on a mission. Over the following days the squadron was busy providing cover to the landing-beaches codenamed Shingles. On the 24th Spitfires of the squadron were over Shingles when they sighted four Fw 190s attempting to bomb the convoys. The Fw 190s were unsuccessful and lost one of their number when Flt Lt Hussey (MH611) and Flg Off

Roy Hussey. (J. Corbin)

King (JL384) shared in its destruction. As 72 Sqn fought over the beaches, French troops were fighting their way through north of Cassino, and the Germans had halted the advance of the Allies on the beachhead. By the 27th the French were being strongly counter-attacked by the Germans around Cassino.

The first sorties on the 27th brought success to Flg Off Rodney Scrase (MH699) when twenty to thirty Bf 109s and Fw 190s were sighted over the beachhead. The Spitfires waded in, and in the dogfight Rodney Scrase destroyed an Fw 190. He describes the encounter:

Flying as Black 1, I found and destroyed an Fw 190. This was ten miles south-west of Rome. Following the early days after the Shingles beach landing, we did get

---

DFC Citation

LONDON GAZETTE, 7 JANUARY 1944

Smith, F/O Kenneth RAFVR

An inspiring leader, Flying Officer Smith has taken part in the North African, Sicilian and Italian campaigns. He has throughout displayed courage and determination and on three occasions has brought his aircraft back to base considerably damaged by anti-aircraft fire. This officer has destroyed at least three enemy aircraft and damaged others.

---

some enemy reaction, but it was very much in-and-out flights by enemy aircraft bombing or striking at our ships off the beach. I was now serving aa deputy flight commander.

The third patrol over the beaches on the 27th brought more successes. Flg Off McLeod (MA444) and Flt Sgt Leach (MH658) both destroyed Bf 109s, Plt Off Bruce Ingalls (MA637) shot down an Fw 190 and WO Turgeon (LZ861) damaged a second. The wing leader, Gp Capt Duncan Smith, led the squadron on a sortie on the 28th which resulted in his Spitfire (coded DS) being seriously damaged by flak. He returned safely, however. Rodney Scrase recorded other events during the month:

In January we became an all Mk IX squadron again. My plane MH669:RN-N was to be my pride and joy. Most of the sorties we made during January were at four- or six-aircraft strength. For a number of these I was leader. On the non-flying side, January was a month when, in company with Roy Hussey, and ably conducted by an Italian guide, we climbed Mount Vesuvius. At 4,200 ft it was not a great height, but one needed a guide to be able to get there and back safely. This at a time when the volcano was not quiescent. The trick for the guide was to get us to give him a coin, which he then pressed into the next flow of molten lava to land nearby. I still have my souvenir, a 1942 Italian coin with its black lava surround. Vesuvius was showing danger signs, and some months later there was a major eruption, which altered the shape of the crater.

The Germans were not intending to give up the Anzio area, and they fully intended to throw the Allies back into the sea. On the 30th they wiped out a complete US Ranger battalion in the area. Fighting at the Rapido was still fierce, and against strong opposition the US 34th Division crossed the river on the last day of the month.

February 1944 commenced with the usual round of patrols and escorts, and on the 3rd ten Spitfires were equipped with ninety-gallon tanks to escort thirty-six Marauders, in company with 43 Sqn, to Civitavecchia. The rendezvous with the Marauders did not happen, due to cloudy weather, and the fighters returned to base. One Marauder was seen to ditch, and a 72 Sqn pilot landed at Nettuno to pass on the details of the ditching, the first of the squadron to land inside the beachhead at Anzio. On the ground an attempt to break out from the beachhead ended on the 3rd, with the Allies only advancing three miles in three days, and being halted by a strong German counter-attack. Nettuno was to become a regular diversion for aircraft damaged or short of fuel, and on the 5th Sgt Pullan (MA521) force-landed there with

Roy Hussey in the rear seat of the captured Caproni Saiman 200. (T.B. Hughes)

engine trouble. After repairs he returned to Lago. On the 5th US troops had reached to outskirts of Cassino, but were thrown back by the Germans. Two days later, having stopped the Allied advance out of the beachhead on the 3rd, the German commenced a full-scale attack on the beachhead with the intention of throwing the Allies back into the sea. By the 9th they had forced their way into the beachhead as far as Aprilia.

On the 7th eighteen Spitfires of 72, 43 and 111 Squadrons escorted Mitchells to Viterbo. Large numbers of long-nosed Fw 190Ds were sighted north of Rome, and one was shot down by Flg Off Bruce Ingalls (MH562) and Sgt Pullan (MA637). On the 10th the pilots found themselves the subject of some unwanted attention when two American Liberators, who had been flying in company with the Spitfires for over five minutes, opened fire on them. Fortunately, no hits were scored.

On the Cassino front American troops were relieved by New Zealand and Indian forces on the 11th, and on the same day the Allies at Anzio had been pushed back to what would be their final defence line. The situation in the beachhead was becoming desperate. On the 13th the German attacks at Cassino were halted and the Allies warned the Italian occupants of the hilltop monastery that it would be bombed

Australian WO Morris totted up an admirable score on the first beach patrol of the 13th when more than ten Fw 190s were encountered. Morris (MH611) destroyed one Fw 190, damaged two more and in all attacked five enemy aircraft. Flg Off McLeod (LZ915) added to the score, damaging another Fw 190.

The tally on the scoreboard was further increased on the 14th, on the last beach patrol of the day. A large group of Fw 190s escorting eight Bf 109s was attacked, and Flg Off Rodney Scrase (MH699) destroyed one Bf 109, while Flt Sgt Leach (MA638) and Sgt Coles (MH604) both damaged Bf 109s

The stronghold at Monte Cassino had been holding up the Armies' advance for some time, and the decision was taken to reduce it by bombing. The monastery and town were devastated by bombers dropping 422 tons of bombs. At the same time the New Zealand and Indian troops began their offensive to take the position, which was defended by the élite paratroopers of the German 1st *Fallschirmjaeger* Division.

On 15 February Rodney Scrase was airborne on escort to the bombers, and witnessed the attack:

In 1944 the bombing of Monte Cassino on 15 February will always be a memory I hold with sadness. Flying at 15,000 ft as Red 1 in my 'own' Mk IX MH699:RN-N, I was leader of the escort to the Marauders flying in two groups of six. We saw all too clearly what was happening, and my comments that it was a wonderful show were widely reported in the press back home. Little did we realize it would be another three months before the Allies could finally break through on the road to Rome.

The Germans were determined to push the Allied invasion back into the sea, and were employing bombers and fighter-bombers, escorted by more fighters, to achieve this in the air. On the ground Kesselring launched seven divisions into the attack. 72 Sqn did not have long to wait to increase its score with this high level of enemy air activity, and on the 16th it encountered more than twenty Fw 190s approaching Anzio in a dive. The Spitfire pilots quickly engaged the Germans, and Flg Off Bruce Ingalls (MH562) shot down an Fw 190. The third patrol of the day bounced some fifteen Bf 109s over Anzio, and South African Lt SV Richardson (MA444) damaged one of them. On the fourth patrol Flg Off McLeod (MA444) chased one of fifteen or so Fw 190s seen over the beaches until he was just south of Rome, when it escaped damaged. To add to the day's successes the squadron was informed that Flt Lt R.J.H. Hussey DFC DFM and Flt Lt R.C. Prytherch DFM (who had gone missing over Sicily) had been awarded Mentions in Dispatches. Over the days that followed Flg Off Barnfather left the squadron tour expired and Flt Lt Cox DFC left to take command of 92 Sqn on promotion.

By the 18th the Allies had been forced to break off their attacks, bloodied and battered, at Cassino, while on the Anzio front the Germans made further gains initially before being forced back by the combined efforts of Allied artillery and warship bombardment. The 19th brought more action. Ten Spitfires on the day's second patrol spotted eleven Fw 190s over the beaches and gave chase. Plt Off J.F. King (LZ915) caught up with one of them and opened fire, and destroyed it over Tivoli. The German pilot baled out. During the fight Sgt Coles's Spitfire (MA637:RN-Y) was hit and he crash-landed safely near Nettuno.

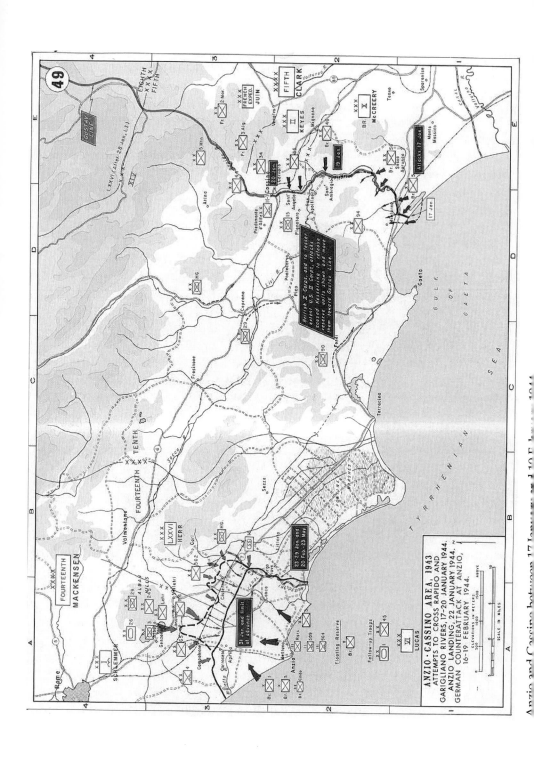

ANZIO - CASSINO AREA, 1943
ATTEMPTS TO CROSS RAPIDO AND
GARIGLIANO RIVERS, 17-20 JANUARY 1944.
ANZIO LANDING, 22 JANUARY 1944. ~
GERMAN COUNTERATTACK AT ANZIO,
16-19 FEBRUARY 1944.

The fighting over the beaches was hotting up, and on the 20th the squadron bounced two sections of more than twenty Bf 109s and Fw 190s. The score rose rapidly as the ten pilots of the squadron fought a fierce battle. WO Norris (MH611) and Flg Off Bruce Ingalls (MH699) both destroyed Fw 190s, WO Turgeon (EN242) damaged a Bf 109, South African Lt Van Schalkywyk (EN534) damaged an Fw 190 and Sgt Street (EN491) damaged two more Bf 109s. 'B' Flight received a new commander when Flt Lt G.H. Mayes arrived on the 20th, to replace Flt Lt Cox.

By the 23rd the Germans had driven the Allies even further back toward the Anzio beaches, and Gen Lucas was sacked and replaced by Maj Gen Truscott. For the next week the air over the beachhead was relatively quiet, with no enemy aircraft inviting the squadron to attack. On the 28th WO Connolly was posted tour expired, and Flt Sgt Red Weller left for the UK. The squadron's last successful sortie for the month was on the 29th, when the wing leader, Gp Capt W.G. Duncan Smith DSO DFC (code DS), led eight 72 Sqn Spitfires on the Anzio beach patrol. The Group Captain attacked one of two Bf 109s on a recce sortie and damaged it. On the ground the Germans launched their third major offensive at Anzio.

At Anzio the German attacks ceased on the 3rd after the loss of some 3,500 men and thirty tanks in four days of bitter fighting attempting to push the Allies into the sea. March 1944 began quietly for the squadron, with the only items of note being Flt Lt Rodney Scrase being posted tour expired on the 7th and the awards of Mentioned in Dispatches to one of the ground crew, Cpl W.A. McMillan, and to Pilot Sgt A.M. Griffiths, who had been killed in action over Sicily. On the 10th the squadron also saw Flt Lt Ingalls leave to take up a flight commander post with 417 Sqn. In replacement two Australians arrived, Flt Lt Terry and Flg Off Fisher. By the 12th the weather had turned particularly nasty and many parts of the 72 Sqn camp were flooded. On the Cassino front the Allies renewed their attempts to capture the mountain from the Germans on the 15th. Cassino was pounded to rubble in the attempt, with the air forces dropping 1,250 tons of bombs and the artillery firing 195,969 rounds over a seven-and-a-half-hour period. Even so, the troops made slow headway against the determined defending paratroopers.

The squadron lost another pilot on the 16th on a twelve-aircraft patrol over Arca and Ceprano. A single, very lucky, burst of flak at 12,000 ft took the starboard wing off Flg Off McLeod's Spitfire (MA444), and he baled out three miles south-west of Ceprano, where he was seen to touch down. Better news was received about Canadian Flg Off W.J. Cameron, who had been reported missing; he was now a POW.

The long lull in combat was broken on the 17th during a patrol over Anzio. At least fifteen Fw 190s were spotted approaching the beachhead from the mouth of the River Tiber, intent on bombing the troops below. On sighting 72 Sqn they jettisoned their bombs before reaching the target, and in the dogfight which

Flt Lt D.G.S.R. Cox discusses with ground crew the work to be done to his Spitfire following a sortie over the Nettuno area near Anzio. (72 Sqn)

ensued Flt Sgt Leach (MB807) probably destroyed one Fw 190, while Flt Sgt Ware (MH560) damaged two Fw 190s. It was not a one-sided fight, though, and Canadian WO Turgeon (MA521:RN-S) was missing, last seen mixing it with the enemy. Balancing the loss of Turgeon was the news that Flt Lt Tom Hughes, who had been shot down in December 1943, was a POW. At Cassino the new

Zealanders captured Cassino railway station. The following day Australian Plt Off Alf Taylor was posted in. The 18th also saw the squadron begin patrols over the Cassino front, an area which would bring them more action in the following weeks. As they patrolled over the front the New Zealanders launched a

Flt Lt Cox departs as the ground crew set to rearming the Spitfire and rectifying faults. (72 Sqn)

72 Sqn Spitfire Mk IX beating up the airfield as others taxi out for take-off. (J. Lancaster)

tank assault on Monte Cassino which was repulsed with the loss of all seventeen tanks. On the 19th the squadron was given the responsibility of escorting a Fairchild carrying General Hawkins to and from Nettuno, which was carried out without incident. Flt Lt Terry, who had been with the squadron for less than two weeks, left on the 24th to take command of a flight of 43 Sqn. Also on the 19th the RAF launched Operation Strangle, designed to disrupt German lines of communication throughout the whole of Italy. By the 22nd the Allied troops had battered themselves senseless in frontal attacks at Cassino, and Alexander called a halt to further frontal attacks. On the 24th the Germans began bombarding the Anzio beachhead using long-range guns backed up by *Luftwaffe* aircraft dropping guided bombs. The result was a large number of casualties in men, equipment and ships.

Action awaited the ten pilots on beach patrol on the 26th. The Germans tried to creep in with at least ten Bf 109s, but they were spotted by 72 Sqn. Lt Van Schalkywyk (MH562) shared in the destruction of a Bf 109 with Flt Sgt Scott (MH635) fifteen miles north-west of Anzio. The dogfight took place at high speed and very low level, with Spitfires and Messerschmitts racing between the trees. Flt Lt Musgrove pulled up to 800 ft chasing one Messerschmitt, and was hit by intense light flak which brought his Spitfire (MA561) crashing to the ground.

On the 27th the squadron was patrolling over the beaches when fifteen or more bomb-carrying Fw 190 fighter-bombers, escorted by the same number of Bf 109s, were sighted trying to reach and bomb shipping in the beachhead at Anzio. Sighting the Spitfires, the Fw 190s jettisoned their bombs before reaching the

Engineering officer Greggs Farish photographed following his departure from the squadron. Farish was subsequently court-martialled for flying the Spitfire in this photo into the Anzio beachhead to repair another aircraft. His flying experience was limited to a few flights in the Caproni Saiman 200 captured by the squadron. (J. Lancaster)

shipping, and fled, but not before American Flt Lt J.A. Gray (MH623) damaged one of them. The escorting Messerschmitts also turned tail, but a determined Lt Van Schalkywyk (MH562) chased one and probably destroyed it over the western outskirts of Rome. South African Lt S.V. Richardson (MH560) did not return from the sortie. The squadron had been ordered to land at Nettuno on completion of the patrol, and once on the ground the pilots were informed by observers on the airstrip that a Spitfire had been observed to dive into the sea with a pilot hanging from his parachute which was draped over the tailplane of the aircraft. It is believed that this was Richardson.

The number of tour-expired pilots leaving the squadron continued on the 28th, with the departure of Flt Lt Gray, Flg Off Ingalls, WO Morris and Flt Sgt Scott. They were replaced by three new pilots at the end of the month: Flt Lt Mitchell, Flg Off Hendry and WO Jacobs. Jacobs had previously been with the squadron in North Africa, and had been injured in the eye by a Perspex splinter.

April 1944 brought numerous changes to personnel on the squadron. Among those posted in were Flt Lt B.J. Blackburn from No. 145 Sqn, to replace Flt Lt J.D. Gray, who was tour expired, as 'A' Flight commander. Flg Off J.F. King and WO L.C.R. Morris also departed tour expired, and were replaced by Lt K.D. Davidson SAAF and Sgt Jeffrey 'Dickie' Bird, both posted in from No. 324 Wing Training Flight. There was some movement among the ground crew also, as 324 Wing had decided to set up a servicing echelon at Nettuno to work on aircraft operating in the beachhead. To that end the squadron provided one NCO and two airmen. By the 12th, Sqn Ldr J.M.V. Carpenter DFC was also tour expired, and he was replaced by Sqn Ldr C.I.R. Arthur from Rear HQ Desert Air Force. On 13 April the squadron personnel began to receive some much-needed rest from the constant frenzy of operations and servicing, when fifteen airmen left on six days' leave at a rest camp in Bari, the first organized leave since the squadron had gone overseas in November 1942. Further postings occurred on the 14th with the arrival of Lt D. Kemlo SAAF and Sgt W.A.R. Morris. Dickie Bird in his first week with the squadron had a rude introduction to the hazards of operational flying, which did not always involve the enemy, on the 14th, when, having flown into a strip at Anzio, his Spitfire MJ992:RN-M was struck by a Mustang which was taking off, smashing the Spitfire's propeller with its wing.

News reached the squadron on the 16th of the award of DFCs to Flg Off Rodney Scrase and Australian pilot WO J.T. Connolly, both recently tour expired. The beachhead at Anzio was not a very safe place to operate from, and the airstrip was often shelled.

The squadron's pilots often stayed overnight there, having landed from an operation, and they would try to find a safe place to hide, as Dickie Bird recorded: 'Anzio patrol. Landed at Anzio, stayed the night – in the hole.' Further arrivals were Flt Lt R.F. Starnes and Flg Off D.P. Sampson on the 26th. April was remarkable only in that numerous patrols and escorts to bombers and fighter-bombers were flown with a complete absence of enemy air activity, and no gains or losses to the squadron other than Spitfire MH329 flown by Australian WO Jacobs, which lost power on take-off, crash-landed and overturned at Lago on 4 Apr. Throughout April the squadron's war-weary Spitfire Mk IXs began to be replaced by new Spitfire LF Mk IXs, and it was completely re-equipped by the end of the month.

Australian Plt Off Alf Taylor. (72 Sqn)

Refuelling a Spitfire Mk IX. (J. Lancaster)

May 1944 began with a series of sweeps and bomber escorts interspersed with non-operational days due to poor weather. Flt Lt K.W.D. Creed was posted in, Sgt A.W.R. Norris left to 93 Sqn and the NCO i/c the Equipment Section, Sgt H.J. Horner, was commissioned. The lull in enemy air activity ended on the 7th, and the squadron had one of its best days yet. Twelve Spitfires took off for a sweep to the north of Rome and encountered eighteen Bf 109s over Lake Bracciano. The pilots wasted no time in getting in among the Messerschmitts, and Sqn Ldr Arthur (MJ407) and Flt Lt Blackburn (MJ718) both destroyed one, South African Lt Van Schalkywyk (MJ171) shot down two and New Zealander Flt Sgt J.T. Aspinall ((MJ992) destroyed a fifth. Two more Bf 109s were destroyed and a further damaged by Flg Off R.B. Hendry (MH784), and Sgt Dickie Bird (EN250) completed the tally with two more, to bring the score to nine destroyed and one damaged. The victims were all from *I/JG4*. On return to Lago the victorious pilots were immediately surrounded by public-relations photographers, and the photos and story were radioed to London and published in the following day's papers. General Barcus of the US 6th Fighter Wing sent a signal:

Congratulations on a superior show this morning. You may well be proud of Seventy-two Squadron. Please relay our best wishes.

Dickie Bird noted in his logbook:

Met twenty 109s. Nine destroyed. Two myself, both flamers.

DFC Citation

LONDON GAZETTE, 7TH APRIL 1944

Scrase, Rodney Diran, F/O

This officer has served in the North African, Sicilian and Italian campaigns. His fine fighting spirit and outstanding leadership have resulted in many successful combats for the squadron. He has himself destroyed at least four enemy aircraft and damaged others.

The following day the squadron was caught on the hop by the Germans. Two Spitfires were providing escort to an ASR launch when two Bf 109s dived out of the sun and strafed the launch, escaping at well over 400 mph before the startled Spitfire pilots could react and give chase. On the 9th two more pilots arrived, Lt A.A.N. Batchelder SAAF and Sgt G.W. Thompson. They were just in time to be kept awake along with the rest of the squadron by a terrific artillery barrage laid on to soften-up enemy defences on the 11th in preparation for the advance on Rome. The barrage was provided by some 2,200 guns preparing the ground for the advance of the US Fifth and British Eighth Armies. The following day the Germans responded to the advance with fierce counter-attacks, but by the 13th the Allies had captured Sant' Angelo and Castelforte, opening up the way to Rome.

Patrols of the Cassino front recommenced on the 14th, but did not entice the enemy to action. Further postings occurred with the arrival of Flt Lt R.W. Turkington DFC and Flt Lt J.A. Ormerod, who would take over 'A' Flight from Flt Lt 'Blackie' Blackburn, who was now tour expired. Flt Lt P.R. Street also left, tour expired, and the squadron also took advantage of the leave scheme and sent a further batch of airmen to Bari on the 15th. The Germans began to withdraw from the Gustav Line on the 15th to new positions at the Dora Line (also known as the Adolf Hitler Line), thirty miles to the south of Rome.

Flt Sgt Johnny Aspinall. (72 Sqn)

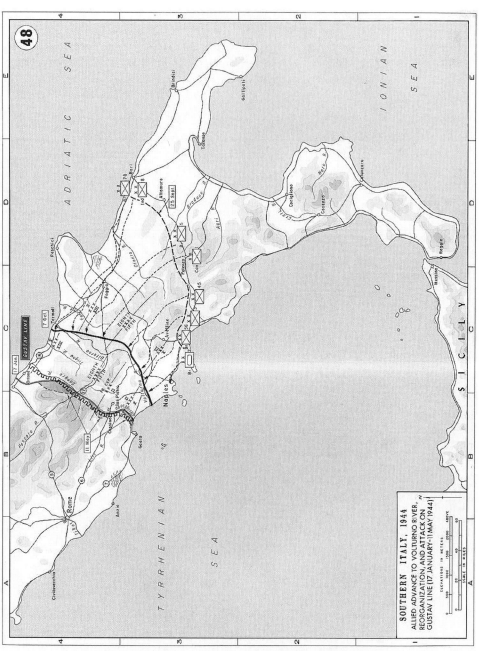

Allied advance to the Volturno river, and the attack on the Gustav Line, 17 January to 11 May 1944.

The reluctant *Luftwaffe* put in an appearance on the 16th during a last-light patrol by eight Spitfires over Lake Bracciano. Two Bf 109s were spotted, and Sqn Ldr Arthur (MJ401) and Canadian Flg Off Johnny Howarth (MK111) shared in the destruction of one of them. Dickie Bird, flying MJ190:RN-D, was also involved, and noted:

> BLP Cassino. Met two 109s, one destroyed – shared CO and Johnny – not even a look.

The following day the squadron received the news that WO Turgeon, missing since 17 March, was a POW. Most sadly, though, they also discovered that his mother had collapsed and died on the doorstep of her home on receiving the news that he was missing.

By the 17th, Kesselring had ordered the evacuation of Cassino, and French troops had broken through in the area to a depth of twenty-five miles. The following day Polish troops finally captured the town of Cassino, and on the 19th British troops overran the airfield at Aquino in the Liri Valley, south-east of Rome. By the 20th the US Fifth Army had captured Gaeta.

By the 22nd the squadron had been warned to stand by for another move of base, and news arrived of the award of the DFC to Flt Lt Ingalls, who had recently left the squadron. The following day the planned move of base was cancelled. By the 26th the move was on again and planned for 3–5 June. The new airfield was at Tre-Cancelli, close to the airstrip at Nettuno. With the capture of Cassino and the breakthrough at the Gustav Line, a renewed offensive began by the Fifth Army from the Anzio bridgehead towards Rome on the 23rd. South-west of Monte Cassino Canadian troops broke through the hastily prepared Dora Line, and on the 24th US troops took Terracina and subjected the retreating Germans to heavy air attacks. The Fifth Army made first contact with troops in the beachhead at Anzio on the 25th, and the following day troops from Anzio captured Cori, which was twenty-two miles inland. The advances had been a long time coming. Gen Clark directed four divisions towards Rome and another to Valmontone on Highway 6 to cut off the retreating Germans.

Canadian WO Larlee turned up on the 26th. He had been posted missing on 9 December 1943, and had been hiding and evading capture behind enemy lines for five months. On the 28th, ground crew numbers at Lago were further depleted, with a second batch of twelve airmen led by a SNCO being dispatched to bolster the Wing Servicing Party at Nettuno. On the 29th, British troops had reached 'The Factory', ten miles north of Anzio.

It was the penultimate day of May before the squadron encountered the *Luftwaffe* again. Early in the morning the second patrol of the day, consisting of six Spitfires, came across some twenty Fw 190s and Bf 109s near Viterbo. The Spitfires chased the enemy fighters as far as Lake Bolsena, but only one pilot had success: Flt Lt R.F. Starnes DFC (MJ778) managed to damage one Bf 109 three miles south of the town. Dickie Bird recorded:

Bomb Line Patrol Rome. Met 12+ 109s and 190 – Gen types stayed together no one could get a smell.

More success followed on the fourth morning patrol. Six Spitfires scoured the Rome area, sighting twelve Bf 109s at 24,000 ft over Lake Bracciano. The Spitfires latched onto two of the Messerschmitts and chased them ten miles north-west of Terni, where Lt Van Schalkywyk (JL364) and Sgt Dickie Bird (MJ128) shared in shooting one of them down. Dickie Bird noted: 'Met fifteen 109s. Engaged one and destroyed it – Hun bailed.' In the afternoon three more patrols were flown, and on the final patrol WO W.J. Johnston (MJ190) radioed that his oil pressure was dropping and he would return to Nettuno. Shortly afterwards he called again, this time to say he would have to bale out. Nothing further was heard from Johnston. This was not the only casualty of the day, though, as the ground crew also suffered while on the way back from a liberty run to Naples. The lorry they were travelling in overturned, and eight ground crew were taken to hospital, four later being released after treatment, and the remainder being retained. Dickie Bird almost became a casualty, too, on his last patrol of the day in MJ552:RN-F. His flight lasted all of ten minutes and ended in a crash-landing recorded in his logbook thus:

Glycol leak – all in cockpit – could not see a thing – managed to get on runway but tyre burst – went on my back.

The 30th found the Eighth Army well on its way to Rome from Cassino, having captured Arce, fifteen miles north-west of Cassino.

As the final decisions were being made in early June 1944 for the invasion of France by Allied forces from Britain, the Allies fighting their way up the length of Italy were more concerned with breaking out of the Anzio beachhead to

---

DFC Citation

LONDON GAZETTE, 23RD MAY 1944

Ingalls, F/L Bruce Johnston

Flight Lieutenant Ingalls joined this Squadron in Malta and flew many sorties during the invasion of Sicily, subsequently he took part in the Salerno operations and has been flying with the squadron on all occasions during the Italian campaign. On many occasions it has been due to this officer's accurate reporting of the presence of enemy aircraft that this squadron has been able to engage them. He has destroyed at least five enemy aircraft and damaged others.

Spitfire Mk IX ?K171:RN-O on 19 April 1944. (72 Sqn)

Sgt Irvine 'Rio' Wright and Flt Sgt Daw at Sorrento in April 1944. (I.A. Wright)

Another photo of Sgt Irvine 'Rio' Wright and Flt Sgt Daw at Sorrento in April 1944. (I.A. Wright)

Nine down in four minutes. The successful pilots. L to R: Front – Lt Van Schalkywyk, Flt Lt Blackburn, Sqn Ldr C.I.R. Arthur. Rear – Flt Sgt Aspinall, Flg Off Hendry, Sgt Bird. (72 Sqn)

capture Rome and to crack the extremely tough nut of Cassino. By 1 June British troops had captured Frosinone, and the 2nd found US troops only twenty miles from Rome. The operational tempo for the flying squadrons increased, and the early days of the month saw a very large number of patrols. By the 3rd the squadron, which had previously been concerned with providing air patrols and bomber escorts, found itself once more supporting the ground forces in strafing and bombing. On a patrol covering a large area including Guidonia, Rome and Terni, the CO, Sqn Ldr Arthur, shot up a large diesel bus, putting it into a ditch, and also strafed a petrol dump, blowing it sky high. A further large enemy vehicle was damaged, but despite the size of the area scoured no other enemy transport was seen. Rome was declared an open city on the 3rd, and Hitler finally allowed Kesselring to withdraw from the city. The following day the US Fifth Army entered the city.

While the Spitfires were busy dealing with the enemy, the ground crew advance party had struck tents, packed equipment and was ready to move to

A posed photo of the successful pilots, with Flg Off R.B. Hendry on left describing his combat to L to R: Flt Sgt J.T. Aspinall, Sgt J. Bird, Flt Lt B.J. Blackburn, Lt P.J. Van Schalkywyk and Sqn Ldr C.I.R. Arthur. (72 Sqn)

Tre-Cancelli. The party set off that night and after driving through the night arrived tired but safe at Tre-Cancelli in the early hours of the morning. By lunchtime a suitable campsite was found, and the tents and cookhouse erected. At first light on the 5th a patrol led by Wg Cdr Le Roy Du Vivier DARG DFC*, swept the Rome area, landing at Nettuno to refuel before flying into Tre-Cancelli. The remainder of the Spitfires flew directly from Lago to the new airfield.

As Allied troops began landing on the Normandy beaches on the morning of 6 June, and French troops took Tivoli in Italy, 72 Sqn continued its own war against the enemy with three patrols escorting minesweepers working in the mouth of the River Tiber. The rear party had left Lago and arrived unharmed at Tre-Cancelli despite an ammunition truck exploding on the road a few miles from Anzio. WO W. Johnston, who had gone missing on 30 May, also made a return to the squadron with a tale to tell. He had force-landed in the Tiber area and was forced to hide in nearby cornfields while German troops searched for him. Unable to locate him, the Germans sprayed the fields with automatic fire, but Johnston hugged the earth and was not hit. Later he was assisted by some Italian country folk, who hid him until the arrival of British troops.

On the 7th the squadron suffered another casualty among the ground crew when LAC W.S. Mackie was injured while standing next to a burning rubbish

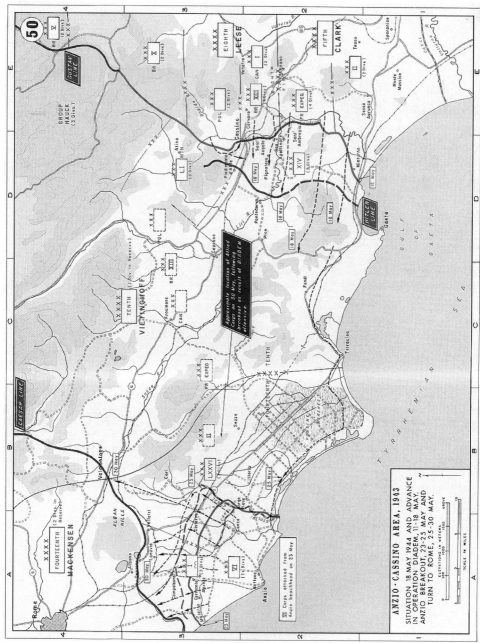

Anzio and Cassino between 11 and 30 May 1944.

L to R: WO Weedon, Sgt Irvine Wright, Sgt Pointer, Sgt Waite, Flt Sgt Daw. (I.A. Wright)

72 and 111 Sqn Spitfires in Italy 1944. (72 Sqn)

fire. Something in the fire exploded, and Mackie received injuries to his ears, and was treated and taken to hospital. The 7th also saw the capture of Civitavecchia by US forces. The next day Sqn Ldr Arthur was awarded the DFC. On the 9th the squadron received news in a letter from his father that Flg Off McLeod, who had been shot down on 16 March, was a POW, and Flg Off John King was gazetted for the award of the DFC. By the 9th Civita Castellana had been captured and US forces were fifty miles north-west of Rome.

DFC Citation

LONDON GAZETTE, 9TH JUNE 1944

Arthur, S/L Charles Ian Rose

In May 1944 this officer flew the leading aircraft of a formation which engaged a force of eighteen enemy aircraft, nine of which were shot down without loss. By his skilful and determined leadership, Squadron Leader Arthur played a worthy part in this brilliant success. This officer has taken part in a very large number of sorties and has displayed outstanding devotion to duty. He has destroyed two enemy aircraft.

The squadron had hardly settled in at Tre-Cancelli when it was told it was to move again, and on the 11th liberty runs began to the newly liberated city of Rome. During this relatively quiet period Flt Lt D. le S. Fisher, Plt Off J. Coles and the recently returned WO W.J. Johnston all left the squadron tour expired, and the squadron advance party left for the new airfield at Tarquinia. The party drove through the night on a journey of seventy miles, and had breakfast prepared when Sqn Ldr Arthur and Gp Capt Duncan Smith arrived in their Spitfires with news that the remainder of the squadron's aircraft would arrive that afternoon. Once the aircraft left Tre-Cancelli, the rear party set off, arriving the following day, once again driving through the night. The Spitfires meanwhile flew a sortie led by Gp Capt Duncan Smith, and found some difficulty in landing back at the airfield due to dust and low cloud hanging over the runway as the evening temperature dropped. By the 14th the advance was now sixty-five miles north-west of Rome and Orvieto had been captured. Two days later the Eighth Army took Foligno and Spoleto east of Orvieto, and was approaching Perugia. On the 17th the small German garrison on the island of Elba off Italy's west coast was evacuated, and the Eighth Army captured Assisi on the 18th.

On the 18th Flt Lt Starnes left to become a flight commander with 145 Sqn. The squadron was settling in reasonably well at its new base, and a lifting of the restriction on mentioning place names in letters home for locations south of a line stretching from Naples to Bari meant that many spent the 19th writing home of their adventures, causing a flood of mail for the squadron's censors! The Eighth Army captured Perugia on the 20th.

Operationally the squadron was finding the new airfield slightly more problematic. In addition to the landing difficulties a few days previously, taxiing also brought problems, with two aircraft bogged down while heading for the runway on the 20th and a third put on its nose taxiing back from the runway on the 21st.

72 Sqn ground crew in Italy in 1944. Cpl Alex McMillan rear 2nd right. (J. Lancaster)

By now the squadron was becoming used to packing every few days, so it came as no surprise when orders arrived for yet another move, this time to Grossetto. The advance party set off on the 24th in what was now a well-practised operation, and arrived at Grossetto at 0600 hrs, setting up the tentage in record time. The Spitfires flew in the following day, followed by the rear party, which arrived late that night.

The squadron flew its first operation from Grosetto on the 26th. Twelve Spitfires flew an armed sweep over Bologna, during which the 'B' Flight commander, Flt Lt G.H. Mayes (MK353:RN-Z), was hit by the first accurate burst of flak. He continued on course, descending, for a while before finally baling out over Firenzuola. His parachute was seen to open and he appeared to be unhurt. The pilots flying with him returned hopeful that he would evade capture. Events such as this were taken in a matter-of-fact fashion by the pilots, and Dickie Bird noted the loss of Mayes in his logbook: 'Sweep. Flak 10/10. Flt Lt Mayes stepped out N. Florence.' Jack Franks witnessed the shooting down:

I was flying as No. 2 to Gordon Mayes on a fighter sweep over northern Italy on 26 June 1944 when a salvo of four 88 mm shells came up and burst below and between us, throwing all the shrapnel up and into Gordon's spitfire. This was followed immediately by the heaviest AA fire that I had ever experienced. The rest of the squadron immediately withdrew to a safe height above and to the one side of the AA fire. The fire was so heavy that I felt that I could get out and walk on it.

During all this time I had remained circling around Gordon's Spitfire. I pulled in close and below him, and I could see that his plane looked like a sieve underneath and the glycol was pouring out. I remained close by until he had glided down from 14,000 feet to about 9,000 feet; he then called up on the radio and said that he was baling out. I saw him jettison the canopy, turn the Spitfire over and drop out. When I saw him safe in the parachute I climbed up and joined the rest of the squadron.

On the 29th the flak scored hits again, damaging one Spitfire during a last-light patrol by five Spitfires over Pontedera.

DFC Citation

LONDON GAZETTE, 9TH JUNE 1944

King, John Fergus, F/O

Flying Officer King has served with the squadron in North Africa, Sicily, Malta and Italy and has completed many operational sorties during which he has destroyed three enemy aircraft and damaged another. At all times he has shown exceptional eagerness to engage the enemy together with sound judgement and leadership and had led his flight on many successful operations. As a Deputy Flight Commander, he has displayed outstanding enthusiasm and ability in his duties.

DFC Citation

LONDON GAZETTE, 9TH JUNE 1944

Morris, Lionel Charles Robert, Warrant Officer

Warrant Officer Morris joined this squadron in North Africa and served in the conclusion of that campaign, later taking part in the invasion of Sicily and Italy and the landing at Salerno. He has proved himself an extremely efficient pilot. He has destroyed three enemy aircraft and, on one occasion, attacking a force of five enemy fighters, pursuing them far into enemy territory and destroying one. He has always shown outstanding keenness to engage the enemy.

Jack Lancaster on a 'day off' at Tarquinia. (J. Lancaster)

72 Sqn ground crew. Front left, Sgt Jack Lancaster. (J. Lancaster)

During the month several pilots were posted tour expired: Flt Lt R.W. Turkington, Flg Off J. Howarth, WO P.H. Ware, Flt Sgt G. Pullan all left. Their replacements included two Canadians, Flg Off J.F. Davies and Flg Off W.R.C. Bunting, as well as Sgts Milner and Kester. In addition to these arrivals, a further pilot arrived to replace the missing Flt Lt Mayes as 'B' Flight commander – Flt Lt Prince Emanuel Galitzine from 95 Sqn. Jack Franks remembers the 'Flying Prince':

Emanuel Galitzine was my flight commander on 72 Squadron 324 Wing Italy. Flight Lieutenant Galitzine replaced Gordon Mayes as flight commander of 'B' Flight when he was shot down. Our new flight lieutenant was a man with a terrific personality and was well liked on the squadron. He and I formed quite an association and we flew many missions together, including the shooting-down of the first German flying-boat in the south of France area. We were known as the 'strafing foursome' on the squadron. I left the squadron in Lyon after completing my tour of operations and an extension. As I was leaving, Emanuel asked me to lend him thirty pounds. Three months later I received a letter from my Barclays Bank of SA, informing me that thirty pounds had been paid into my account by Flt Lt Galitzine in London.

Flt Lt Prince Emanuel Galitzine.

On the last day of the month everyone on the squadron had cause for rejoicing when the NCO I/C the NAAFI supplies, Cpl H.J. Pollard, returned from a long and arduous journey with enough beer to provide three-and-a-half bottles for every man on the squadron. As far as the squadron was concerned, Pollard was the most popular man in the RAF that night.

The town of Siena was evacuated by the Germans on 2 June, and the next day French troops occupied it and were now only thirty miles south of Florence. The pilots were still finding the conditions at Grossetto difficult in July, and on the 3rd South African Lt D. Kemlo crashed his Spitfire (MJ552:RN-F) on take-off. The aircraft turned on its back, but luckily Kemlo was only slightly injured. Dickie Bird had flown 'F' on many occasions and was feeling its loss, having been the last to fly it before Kemlo recorded in his logbook:

Next trip F does Kemlo rights [sic] it off; taking off.

The 72 Sqn 'travelling circus' was on the move again on the 4th, with the advance party leaving for Piombino, a short journey of only two hours. The

Sgt Pilot Charles Kester of 72 Sqn with Spitfire Mk IX, Italy 1944. (72 Sqn)

Spitfires flew over on the 5th, and the rear party arrived that evening. Few sorties were flown in the days after the arrival at Piombino as the weather had taken a hand, swamping the airfield and campsite and forcing the squadron personnel to dig irrigation ditches to drain tents and messes. Hardly had the squadron settled in when it was told it was on the move again. As the squadron prepared to move, the Eighth Army captured Osimo, twenty miles south of Ancona, on the 6th.

Citation for Bar to DFC 7th July 1944

SQUADRON LEADER J.V.C. (CHIPS) CARPENTER DFC

Citation submitted by Group Captain Duncan Smith – OC 324 Wing

This Officer has an exceptional record having been engaged on operational flying almost continuously since the outbreak of war. He has been in command of this Squadron since January 1944. The many successes achieved by the Squadron during that period are in no small measure due to the fine leadership of S/Ldr Carpenter and the inspiring example he has set of steadfastness and devotion to duty. Since being awarded the DFC this officer has destroyed a further 3 enemy aircraft, bringing his total victories to 8 enemy aircraft destroyed.

DFC Citation

LONDON GAZETTE, 7TH JULY 1944

Blackburn, Basil John, F/L

Flight Lieutenant Blackburn has displayed the utmost zeal and determination as a pilot and flight commander. In May 1944 he led his flight into combat with a force of 18 enemy aircraft. Seven of the enemy were destroyed, one by Flight Lieutenant Blackburn personally. By his example of coolness and courage in the face of enemy opposition, this officer has produced a marked effect on the efficiency of his flight. He has destroyed at least three enemy aircraft.

CHAPTER FIVE

Corsica and Southern France

This time they were going to Corsica. For the move the advance party would be made up of ground crew from both 72 and 43 Squadrons, followed by another party from 93 and 111. The first party left Piombino on the 15th, led by Flt Lt Brill and Lt Van Schalkywyk, moving to a staging area at Civitavecchia. At Piombino, meanwhile, the squadron continued to fly bomber escort and bomb line patrols, as it had since the beginning of the month despite all the moves of base. The advance party embarked on an LST on the 16th and then anchored for the night before proceeding to Corsica on the 18th, arriving at Porto Vecchia in the south-east of the French island. The convoy set off on a long journey, eventually arriving at Calvi airfield on the morning of the 19th. Jack Lancaster recalled the long journey to the new airfield:

We had quite a long journey across the island. It was right through the mountains and that was a bit of a hairy drive with a 1,000-gallon petrol tanker. We arrived at Calvi, which was a very small strip.

As the ground party made its way to Corsica, the Eighth Army captured Arezzo and reached the River Arno on the 16th, and the Polish II Corps took Antona on the 18th. The pilots back at Piombino were kept busy patrolling, and on the 19th, as the US 34th Division captured Livorno, they were tasked with the interception of a recce Me 410. That evening it was sighted, and Flt Lt Ormerod (MJ718) chased it for over 100 miles before he closed enough to open fire, damaging it before it escaped north-north-west of Corsica.

The Spitfires left for Calvi on the 20th with the rear parties following on. The squadron was not the only unit preparing for the invasion of southern France, and the French units fighting on the Italian front were withdrawn on the 20th to prepare themselves for their return to their homeland. On the 23rd the US 34th Division captured Pisa. Patrols commenced immediately, and on the 25th the squadron flew its first operation over France since leaving England in 1942, escorting A-20s. On the 28th the Spitfires flew as escort to twenty-four A-20s bombing Lavagna. On the return sea crossing Sgt Dickie Bird (MJ626:RN-D) developed engine trouble and had to bale out forty miles north-west of Cap

Corse. Air-Sea Rescue was alerted, and after only thirty minutes in the water he was picked up none the worse for his experience. Dickie recorded the incident:

Returning to base 12,000 ft engine packed up – glided down to 2,000 ft and baled out 50–60 miles N. Corsica picked up by ASR Launch 175.

In the afternoon a fire broke out in the living area of the newly arrived 'B' party at Calvi. Every available airman grabbed fire extinguishers and anything else they could find to fight the serious fire and stop it spreading. After an arduous hour of fire-fighting the blaze was extinguished, with the loss of only the tent and equipment of four airmen.

On 2 August the squadron flew a sweep over the Marseille area, and later sighted seaplanes on Lake Berre. Following up on the sighting, the squadron flew a further sweep on the 3rd, paying particular attention to the lake. Flt Lt Emanuel Galitzine (MH763) and Lt Davidson (MK171) bounced one Dornier Do 24 as it was taking off, and shot it down.

During this period leading up to the invasion of southern France, the squadron became somewhat fragmented, with the pilots initially continuing to fly operations from Calvi, while the ground crew were split into 'A' and 'B' parties. The 'B' party moved to Santa Maria in Italy, and then on the 5th to Naples, for embarkation as part of the invasion forces. It was taken to a transport ship, the *George C. Meade*, in Naples Bay. The 'B' party had a long wait aboard ship before finally sailing for France on the 13th under a strong naval escort. By the 17th those on board were sitting off the coast of southern France and they could hear the gunfire in the distance and observe blasting and mine demolition on the beaches. Nerves were kept on edge throughout the voyage by constant alerts both day and night; however all the sightings were of friendly aircraft. The 'B' party landed on Green Beach at 0900 hrs on the 18th, and proceeded by road to Ramatuelle airfield, where it began to prepare for the arrival of the squadron Spitfires. Dispatch rider Darryl Briggs was one of those who boarded the *George C. Meade*:

We landed at St Tropez from the US liberty ship George C. Meade before taking the 'Route Napoleon', on which some of our lads were killed when a vehicle crashed over a drop in the mountains. Eventually I arrived at Bon aerodrome at Lyon, with a couple of mates, in the evening.

We had a look around, and on seeing a great pile of coffins against a wall it was suggested that an enthusiastic funeral bod was hoping for business, and what about swiping one and fixing on my bike as a chair?

We had for some time been aware of that horribly familiar smell of death, but carried on around the side of the hangar and then — — ! A small crowd of people, mostly women in black, were on their knees scraping away with their hands in the mud, uncovering lengths of corrugated sheets, probably roof fitments. A priest stood waiting. Carefully they uncovered a great row of bodies. The victims had been lined up on this trench and shot. Those that lay on the sheeting included men, women and children, hands tied behind their backs.

All thoughts of the 'chop' had gone, and we went back to the unit quite depressed. That evening I met a French captain, Dr Rolande Andrieu, and his wife, a Polish lady. In the house three men had machine-guns and rifles, which they were servicing. I was made very welcome and had many meals with them until we pulled out.

The 'A' party, meanwhile, set off on the 20th, routeing via Capri for a staging area at Ile Rousse. Boarding LST 482 during the afternoon of the 21st, it sailed north and in the early hours of the 22nd was in sight of France. The men disembarked that evening and set off for Ramatuelle, arriving in groups on the 23rd. No sooner had they arrived than it was announced that another 'A' party was to be formed and moved out immediately for Sisteron airfield. The party set off on the 140-mile journey, stopping overnight at Draguignan. Setting off again on the morning of the 24th, it had been on the road for just over an hour when a serious accident occurred just north of Comps. One of the 3-tonner trucks struck the rear of a 43 Sqn truck, overturning it. The 72 Sqn truck ran off the road and rolled over several times down a steep bank. Two airmen from 43 Sqn, Cpl George and LAC Wilkinson, were killed, and four other airmen were injured – Cpl Perry, LAC Scott and AC1 Walker of 72 Sqn, and LAC Taylor of 43 Sqn. All four were taken to hospital while the convoy continued on to Sisteron, arriving at 1600 hrs. Cpl George and LAC Wilkinson were buried at Sisteron airfield on the 25th. Jack Lancaster remembers the tortuous journey through southern France:

I was driving the old 1,000-gallon tanker and Cpl Spencer was with me. We went along to St Tropez and then along to Cannes and eventually turned up through Grasse toward Sisteron. On the way we, as per usual, went on the wrong road, and Cpl Spencer said, 'Hey, hey Jack, look out! What's that up there?' It was a Tiger tank. Fortunately, the Germans had gone, long gone, but we weren't going to take any chances, we just turned around and got back on the right road.

On our way up to Sisteron we passed a number of French houses and we didn't get any sort of greeting whatsoever. When we got to Sisteron the Maquis had taken charge of the local pub and they were completely bonkers. They'd fire their guns in the pub and anywhere they could. They were a completely wild lot and we weren't too happy about them at all. We left Sisteron eventually and went up to Lyon.

At Sisteron we did not have any fuel for the aircraft, and this was flown in by some American Liberators, who emptied from the aircraft. They took out fifty-gallon drums and they had small petrol-engine pumps, and they took petrol out of their own aircraft tanks to fill up the drums for us.

The 'B' party left Ramatuelle on the 25th, arriving at the new airfield on the evening of the 26th. By the following day all the stragglers had arrived and the squadron was able to operate as a complete unit for the first time since 15 July.

While the ground crew were invading southern France the pilots had been kept busy too. Fighter sweeps continued, and the squadron received its first Mk VIII aircraft as a replacement on the 6th. The Mk VIII would have a short life. Everyone wanted to fly it, but on the 8th Flg Off Hendry experienced some trouble on landing it, and the Spitfire was written off. Hendry was unhurt in the crash. News reached the squadron that Flt Lt Mayes, missing since 26 June, had survived and was now a POW, the information coming in a letter from his aunt. Not satisfied with breaking the Mk VIII, the squadron damaged another Spitfire on landing on the 9th; this time the culprit was Lt Van Schalkywyk. One again the pilot was unhurt.

On the 12th ground targets were the priority, and nine Spitfires attacked and strafed German radar stations in southern France, wreaking considerable damage. A second, equally successful, sortie, again hitting radar stations, was flown on the 13th. Dickie Bird flew a dawn patrol in MJ901:RN-B, chasing an enemy aircraft:

Dawn patrol. Chased a Ju 88 or 410 from Corsica into S. France – could not get nearer that 10 miles – landed base 8 galls.

A second Spitfire Mk VIII had been received by the squadron. However, a decision had been made that 43 Sqn would fly all of the Mk VIIIs allocated to the wing, and it was transferred to that squadron on the 14th.

On the 15th the squadron took off before dawn to cover the landings on the invasion beaches. They were the first Spitfires to operate in the area. Sorties continued throughout the day of the landings, but the *Luftwaffe* failed to make an appearance. The following day the *Luftwaffe* eventually turned up in the form of three Fw 190s sighted five miles from St Raphael. After a long chase WO Wood (MK134) caught up with one of them and damaged it. Throughout the 18th the squadron was over the beaches constantly, putting up seven sorties of four aircraft each; however, the Germans declined to come up and fight.

On the 20th a rather unusual flight was carried out by Flt Lt Prince Emanuel Galitzine. Instead of his usual Spitfire he was airborne on the Group Captain's personal captured Saiman 200 biplane. The aircraft had been given a very swift daily inspection, during which the tyres were

'Pop' Wood in Italy, 1944. (72 Sqn)

inflated in the fervent hope they would stay that way on landing. Galitzine climbed in with his passenger, the squadron intelligence officer, Flt Lt Brill, clutching a Russian guitar, and took off. Both were grateful for the escort of a 284 Sqn Walrus amphibian, which flew with them on the journey from Corsica to France, where they were relieved to make a safe landing at Ramatuelle.

Fourteen of the squadron's Spitfires operated from Ramatuelle on the 25th, but two days later aircraft and ground crew were reunited at Sisteron. Operations from Sisteron commenced on the 28th, and on the second sortie of the day Flt Lt J.A. Ormerod burst a tyre on take-off and crash-landed, luckily without injury. The final sortie of the day was a strafing mission by four Spitfires led by Sqn Ldr Arthur south of Valence, and six vehicles were damaged. The last sortie on the 29th was almost a carbon copy, with six more vehicles damaged in the same area. The penultimate day of the month was taken up with more strafing missions. On the first, Gp Capt Duncan Smith led the squadron, which bagged ten trucks destroyed, sixteen damaged, one tank damaged and ten cycling troops scattered! The second sweep tallied three trucks destroyed, two damaged, two cars and a large coach damaged, as well as strafing the German troops scattering from the disabled vehicles. The final sortie was a recce led by Flt Lt Galitzine, during which two staff cars were destroyed for flak damage to one Spitfire in return.

Armed sweeps over France continued into September, and on the 2nd four pilots flew an armed recce of the Rhône valley. One pilot, Lt Grieve SAAF, encountered problems with his fuel supply and the Spitfire's engine cut out. Grieve baled out, landing to the west of Grenoble, where he was picked up by American troops and royally entertained by them. The following day it was all hands to the shovels once more, as torrential rain caused flooding in the campsite and drainage ditches had to be dug to divert the floodwater away.

Three four-aircraft strafing sorties were flown on the 4th in the Rhône valley, where six trucks and four horse-drawn vehicles were destroyed, and a further four vehicles damaged. The squadron did not have it all its own way, however, and on the first sortie Flt Lt Galitzine's Spitfire was damaged by flak, while on the last sortie Sgt R.H. Fenton had his Spitfire hit by flak also. Fenton was forced to bale out north-east of Grenoble, where he was picked up by American troops.

Like a band of Gypsies, the squadron began packing again on the 4th, having received orders to move to Bron airfield on the outskirts of Lyon. The 'A' party left on the 5th for the new base, stopping for the night in Valence, where its members were enthusiastically greeted and entertained as the first British troops to pass that way. Arriving at Bron the following day they set up the new campsite in record time: hardly surprising, given the practice they had had in the preceding months! Once established, they were treated to a plentiful supply of watery beer by the locals. The Spitfires flew in on the 7th and a curfew was imposed on Lyon at 2100 hrs, though this did not stop the local population wandering onto the airfield, examining the aircraft and generally causing a nuisance to the busy ground crew. The 'B' party left Sisteron on the 8th, arriving at Bron the following day, many of the men the worse for wear due to the hospitality of the towns they stopped in on the way! Jack Lancaster remembers the reception they received when arriving at Bron:

Once the local population heard that the RAF was going to Bron airfield they came out in droves, and they were asking people to go and have dinner with them or have a meal with them, a drink or whatever. Dickie Bird and I were invited by an American lady and her sister and the American lady's husband, who was a Frenchman, to their house for dinner. When we got there I'd never seen such a spread in all my life. They obviously weren't short of any food whatsoever. As I spoke a bit of French I was sort of pushed off to talk to the Frenchman while Dickie Bird and the other chaps were talking to the young ladies who had been invited. Just my luck.

Over the next few days the squadron flew numerous ground-attack sorties, but the tasking was having trouble keeping up with the Allied advance, and often Allied troops and vehicles were sighted well ahead of the bomb line. On one sortie the pilots returned just in time to pass valuable intelligence about twenty to twenty-five trains that had been spotted to an American P-47 Group which was about to take off. The P-47s had a field day train busting as a consequence.

It seemed that the squadron was destined to chase the enemy all the way to Berlin when it was ordered to move to Besançon on the 13th. The by now routine moves of ground parties commenced, and the aircraft flew in on the 16th. The squadron was not completely happy however, as it had been informed that it would soon be returning to Italy. This was not to its liking, as it had hoped for a different outcome. The weather then took a hand, postponing the move to Besançon, though the 'A' party had arrived there. Both Bron and Besançon were unfit for flying several times over the next few days, and after a week at Besançon the ground crew returned to Bron. Jack Lancaster, once again, drove up to the new base:

While we were going through Bonne on the road up from Lyon we experienced the sight of some French girls having their hair shorn off by some local people due to the fact that they had been cavorting or consorting with the German troops. We got to Besançon and it was pouring down. It rained the whole time we were there, so the aircraft never came. We spent one or two nights in the local hostelries, where we had a lot of fun, and then we were told to report to La Jasse down near Marseille. We were to go back to Italy, which was very disappointing because we thought we were on the way home.

They were not to stay long. By the 25th the 'A' party was on the move to La Jasse near Salon in preparation for the move to Italy. By the 27th the aircraft had joined them with the 'B' party. Throughout September the squadron began turning in its increasingly war-weary Spitfire LF Mk IXs for standard Mk IXs and replacement LF Mk IXs.

CHAPTER SIX

Italy Again

La Jasse was little more than a staging point for the squadron awaiting return to Italy, and no operational flying was carried out from this airfield. A small servicing party left for Florence by air on 2 October, followed by the Spitfires in the afternoon. The reminder of the squadron departed for the staging area in Marseille on the 3rd, and embarked on LSTs *32, 141* and *903* late on the 4th. By the 8th they were still at Marseille awaiting the sailing of the convoy, finally setting off with nine more LSTs on the 9th for Leghorn. After disembarking, the convoy headed for Florence, with the first party reaching the airfield at 0200 hrs on the 10th. The final groups did not arrive until the 13th. The move from La Jasse almost turned into a major catastrophe for the wing, as Dicky Bird relates:

72 Squadron, as part of the wing, took off from La Jasse and flew in mixed squadron flights of six aircraft in line astern, and comprised some fifty Spitfires. I was flying as No. 3 in the first flight of six aircraft, which was being led by Gp Capt Duncan Smith, Officer Commanding 324 Wing. We refuelled at Calvi, Corsica, and flew on to Florence. As we approached the coast of Italy, it appeared we were flying into a large thunderstorm. It did not take too long to realize that it was not a storm, but in fact night falling. The one-hour difference has not been allowed for.

The airfield at Florence has no ground-to-air control and no runway lighting. By the time we arrived it was getting very dark, and the runway, which was a black concrete dumbbell, was very hard to see. Being in the first six, it was more or less a straight-in approach and landing. The first two aircraft landed, followed by myself. It was now quite dark on the ground, and I was very conscious of all the aircraft behind. I made a fairly fast landing and turned off the runway onto the grass and taxied as far from the runway as I could, hoping there were no obstructions. I am not certain if anyone landed behind me, but by the time I had stopped and switched off someone had crashed at the end of the runway and was on fire. A few aircraft made an approach over the burning aircraft but were unable to land. It was now fully dark on the ground and visibility was only a few yards. It now looked a hopeless situation, and those of us on the ground decided to collect any vehicles we could find, even stopping vehicles on the road just outside the airfield and placing them with their headlights on by the side of the runway at about thirty degrees.

I am not sure if anyone managed to land at this time, as I was on the outside, stopping vehicles on the road, but I did hear a few aircraft make an approach but open-up at the last minute. Just as I returned with a jeep I had stopped on the road, someone made an approach and attempted to land, but smashed into one of the vehicles and burst into flames, killing the pilot and a number of people on the ground. At least one other aircraft made an attempt to land, but crashed into the wreckage. It was now impossible for anyone to land, and the only contact with those still in the air was via the R/T on one of the aircraft on the ground.

At this point the general consensus was that the only solution was for everyone to fly due west over the sea and bale out. Fortunately all the chatter on the R/T was picked up by the Americans stationed at Pisa airfield, and as they had installed runway lights, they opened up the airfield, and all forty-eight or so aircraft still in the air landed safely at Pisa, even one of 72 Squadron's aircraft flown by Dennis Degerlund, which ran out of fuel in the circuit and force-landed safely.

I am not sure how many died, but at least two pilots and a number of people on the ground. I saw and heard one pilot burn to death, and tripped over a mutilated body in the dark. It was a very upsetting experience, and once all the aircraft had left the circuit I was taken into Florence and installed somewhere, I can't remember where. I was three or four days in Florence before I returned to the airfield, by which time all the squadron's Spitfires had flown back from Pisa and the airfield had been cleared, and my aircraft had been parked with the rest of the squadron. On the night when I left my aircraft somewhere on the airfield I was unable to find it again. If Pisa had not opened with the runway lights, the whole of 324 Wing would have been lost, including 72 Squadron.

Wrecked Spitfires at Florence on 2 October 1944. (J. Lancaster)

While the squadron was returning from France to Italy, the battle for the Gothic Line was being fought, and on 1 October Monte Battaglia was captured by the US Fifth Army after a four-day battle. The Eighth Army was also heavily involved in the fighting, and had resumed its offensive against the Gothic Line on the 4th.

The first operations were flown on the 14th and met with immediate success. Six Spitfires flew a sweep of the Bergamo area and came across a solitary bomber. Six pilots shared in the kill: Sqn Ldr Arthur (PL319), Flt Lt J.N.M. McKinnon (MK171), Flt Lt D.C. Dunn (PT485), Flg Off W.E.C. Bunting (PL444), Flg Off D.G. Crawford (PL322) and Sgt Denis Degerlund (PT594). Three British, two Canadians and an Australian – a truly international effort. The victim was Ju188D-2 F6+AP of *6(F)/122. Oberleutnant* B. Friesenhausen, *Oberfeldwebel* J. Franken and *Obergefreiter* F. Regitz were all killed. One other crew member survived.

The squadron continued to settle in at Florence, taking over many buildings, including one complete with a dance hall and billiard tables, which was turned into the airmen's mess.There was no operational flying until the 19th, and then on the 21st the squadron increased its collective score again in a dogfight over the southern corner of Lake Garda. Eight Bf 109s were sighted and the fight commenced. New Zealander Flg Off R.B. Hendry (MJ631) shot down a Bf 109, Sgt A. Bell (MK553) probably destroyed another, and Flt Lt Galitzine (PL465) and Lt J.F. Jackson (PT594) damaged one each for no loss. There were no further

Spitfire undergoing maintenance on a PSP dispersal in Italy in 1944. (via L.J. Barton)

operations until the 31st, when an eight-aircraft sweep was flown over Lake Garda, but no opposition was found.

November 1944 opened to a ten-day period without operational flying, during which the squadron entertained itself with football, art lessons and two wild dances where large quantities of wine were consumed. The holiday could not last, though, there was still a war to fight, and operations recommenced on the 11th. The commanders must have believed 72 Sqn suitably refreshed during their sojourn at Florence, and they ordered yet another move, this time to Rimini. The 'A' party set off on the 12th, routeing through the mountains and halting at Fologna for the night. The journey was resumed the following day, with the party reaching Rimini at dusk. Jack Lancaster described life at Rimini as winter set in:

From Florence we set off for Rimini and stopped at Perugia. We camped there overnight and set off for Rimini the following day. We got to Rimini eventually, all in good shape, and found the war had started all over again. We bagged a bombed-out house, which was quite a nice house really, on the seashore, but unfortunately the bombing had deprived it of all its windows. So it had to be make-do-and-mend to try and get some sort of covering over the window holes, and this is where bits of tent and goodness knows what came in.

The boys were in a much better situation, because they were quartered in a hotel a bit further down the road from us, which looked quite a big, modern building, and nobody ever complained about their situation. It was very, very cold that winter in Rimini, and we managed to build a large oil drum into some sort of fire. We built chimneys for it and we got a drum of diesel oil or paraffin, and manufactured a heating arrangement that was very successful.

We started putting bombs on the aircraft, which was quite new to us, really, and there was a lot of quacking and gnashing of teeth about this. However, the people who were in authority decided that was what the fighters would do, they would carry bombs.

At Rimini another sad incident happened. I was down at the billets collecting some lads to go up to the aerodrome for relief duty, and someone said one of the airmen around the cookhouse had been shot by a bullet. They didn't know where it had come from, but thought it had come from the aerodrome. However, the aerodrome was at least a mile away. Then we noticed some smoke up on the aerodrome, and we hastened back and found that our intrepid Bence had been cleaning his engine with petrol sprayed from a stirrup-pump. The pump was put into a tin of petrol and sprayed through the nozzle. This had not dried at all properly, and he decided that he'd start up the engine before putting his cowlings back to make sure everything was all right, no oil leaks or anything like that. Of course, there must have been a spark somewhere because the petrol ignited and the plane set on fire. It burnt for quite a long time and the guns fired one round and the bullet found this chap down at the billets and killed him.

The Spitfires flew into Rimini on the 16th and flew twenty-two non-operational training sorties the next day. On the 18th Sqn Ldr Arthur was posted to HQ324 Wing and was replaced by Sqn Ldr P.L. 'Polly' Parrott DFC. The training sorties continued until the 21st, when 72 Sqn flew its first fighter-bomber sorties. The work to convert the Spitfires into fighter-bombers saw intensive labour by electricians and armourers fitting bomb-racks and wiring. Six Spitfires carrying bombs, and apprehensive pilots, bombed a cluster of houses, and though none of the houses were hit all of the bombs landed within the target area. The returning pilots reported it was 'good fun', and they were all for it. Not all came back immediately from the sortie. Plt Off L. True (PT411) was hit by light flak and baled out on 'no-man's

Jack Lancaster and Eric Boddice. (J. Lancaster)

72 Sqn ground crew at Rimini. (J. Lancaster)

Spitfire Mk IX RN-H at Rimini. (72 Sqn)

land'. With the help of an Italian, he was able to return safely to Allied lines. Several more fighter-bomber missions were flown during the rest of the month, and, perhaps an indication of how hard the enemy were being pushed back toward their homeland, German lessons commenced on the squadron.

By 5 December the Eighth Army had captured Ravenna and cut the rail link between there and Bologna. Sporadic fighter-bomber missions continued throughout December, but they were disrupted by periods of bad weather and high winds. On the 11th the squadron flew five missions, each of six aircraft, and on the fourth of these Sgt C.K. Griffin (PL465:RN-T) was hit by flak, crash-landing shaken and bruised just north-west of the runway at Forli. Clearly the flak at low level was going to be a much more dangerous proposition than fighters.

On the 14th four aircraft were quickly scrambled to assist the Army which was in trouble near the Bagnacavallu Canal. The aircraft were ordered to strafe observation positions in the town, such as church steeples and clock towers, to keep the Germans' heads down while the troops crossed the canal. The pilots had a grand time hitting anything that moved, and the Army later reported that a terrific job had been done, with a large number of enemy casualties from the Spitfires' strafing. Flt Sgt W.D. 'David' Park arrived on the squadron in December 1944 and flew his first operation on the 15th. He recalls the excitement, trepidation and confusion of this first sortie:

Of all the operational missions one flies the one that is most imprinted on one's mind is the first one. I arrived on the squadron for the first time at night, and was shown

72 Sqn Spitfire armed with a 500 lb bomb at Rimini. (72 Sqn)

to a camp bed in this room. The 'room' was in a bombed-out villa and we were in the basement. It was dark and the 40-Watt bulb did not give much light in the room. I decided to go to bed and get up early the next morning. I went for breakfast at about 8 a.m. Three or four pilots were also having breakfast; not a word was said, and it was obvious that everyone was waiting for the 'panic' phone to ring. Suddenly it rang! One of the chaps dived to the phone and took the message. The others forgot heir breakfasts in anticipation of what was coming. The chap on the phone called out four names and 'Ninety-gallon tanks'. This meant that the four named were to go to the airstrip to be briefed on an operation requiring aircraft to carry long-range tanks which could be jettisoned as soon as they were empty, or sooner if they met enemy fighters.

The mess was now empty apart from myself. I rapidly finished breakfast, got my flying-gear together and made my way to dispersal to await developments. The person I saw first was a squadron leader whom I took to be the CO, and I made myself known to him. I asked him when I would be able to 'crack off', meaning take part in operations. Before he could utter a word there was a squeal of brakes and a voice shouts, 'Park. Briefing.' I looked over to the jeep from which the shout had come and saw an Australian warrant officer of indeterminate age at the wheel. As I got into the jeep he says to me, 'We're throwing you in today, Park!' The briefing was a blur. The job, as far as I can remember, was to have a look at an airfield, which the enemy was suspected of reinforcing overnight with a large number of fighters. The laconic Aussie, by name 'Old Jake', turns to me and says, 'Park, you stick to me like shite to a blanket, whatever happens.' We take off and Jake tells us on the R/T to go over to Channel C for Charlie. This is the operational channel, and everything seems to be happening on it! Our callsign was Malvol Red. The thing that I remember was one of the boys calling, 'Malvol Red, 'Bogeys' at 3 o'clock high.' Old Jake, 'Roger, watch 'em, 109s. Here they come, break starboard, Malvol Red!' Like a flash Jake's aircraft vanished! Panic stations on my part. I slam my aircraft into what I consider a tight turn. Straining from the effects of 'G' and fright, I can hear nothing on the R/T. After what seemed like an eternity I decided to straighten up and try to see what was happening. Just as I accomplished this a 109 flashed across my front at about thirty yards' range! Very obviously he hadn't seen me. Several thoughts crossed my mind at that moment. There was the Hun at very close range and he looked exactly the same as the outlines we were shown in aircraft recognition. FIRE, you fool! But suddenly the Hun pilot looked over his shoulder and saw the business end of a Spitfire at very close range, stuck his nose down and was gone into the next country. We were flying Spit Vs at this time, and they did not have direct-injection carburettors, which meant that I had to roll on my back to follow him, and he was out of sight before I completed the manoeuvre. It took me some time to catch up with the section, and when we landed Old Jake says to me, 'I see you don't want to live too long, Park.' So ended my first 'show'.

By the 17th the Christmas rations had arrived at Rimini, and everyone on the squadron was taking a keen interest in the quantity and variety of the fare, particularly the officers, who had a great interest in the liquid ration as their mess had been dry for eleven days and nights! The Christmas festivities started early, with the officers inviting those of 324 Wing HQ to a 'bash' in the mess, where, in the words of the operations record book, 'Everybody got tight, but nobody got bent!' The war did not stop for Christmas Day, and the squadron flew a first-light weather recce, followed by four ASR missions searching for a pilot reported to be in a dinghy off Fano. Unfortunately the pilot was not found. Operations ended in time for everyone to take part in the Christmas Dinner held in the airmen's dining-hall. This was followed by a concert attended by those still able to stand or sit!

Hangovers notwithstanding, operations were on again on Boxing Day with a long-range sweep north of Lake Garda and a bomber escort to Comegliano. Fighter-bomber missions followed over the next few days, and following the precedent set by the squadron at Christmas, the New Year celebrations started on the 30th with a party in the officers' mess.

The squadron rounded off 1944 with a fighter-bomber mission, destroying heavy artillery pieces, and an escort to twenty-four Marauders bombing the marshalling yards at Castel Franco. The operations record for 1944 ended with the comment, 'New Year's Eve – Well, shall we say it was just like most other places.'

Spitfire Mk IX being refuelled. (via L.J. Barton)

Citation for Bar to DFC

LONDON GAZETTE, 29TH DECEMBER 1944

Arthur, S/L Charles Ian Rose

Squadron Leader Arthur has continued to lead his squadron with skill and determination. Since the award of the Distinguished Flying Cross he has completed many sorties and has destroyed at least one enemy aircraft. During the invasion of the South of France he has led his squadron in many sorties, which resulted in the destruction of 37 mechanical transport and other vehicles, and damaged many others. His coolness, determination and outstanding leadership have largely contributed to the successes achieved by the squadron.

Allied advance to the Gothic Line between 5 June and 25 August 1944, and gains between 29 August and 31 December 1944.

Sqn Ldr Parrott noted in the diary the following comments on the change to the fighter-bomber role:

Undoubtedly the pilots prefer the close-support missions to longer-range jobs such as armed recces. The latter definitely have a tiring effect on the pilots, whereas the close-support work tends to brace them up and increase their morale. 88 mm flak frightens them a good deal more than light 20 and 40 mm, of which nobody takes very much notice, except for deciding whether to strafe or not. Light flak has no effect on the bombing, 88 mm can have a bad effect.

Poor weather halted operations for the first few days of 1945, but on the 3rd the squadron again began hitting gun positions, enemy headquarters and strong points. By the 4th the Spitfires were using the 'cab rank' technique of operation whereby aircraft waited above until called in onto suitable targets by a ground controller (normally an RAF officer) in his own radio-equipped vehicle or armoured car, working with the forward troops, codenamed 'Rover David'. On the first mission of this type Flt Lt Jimmy Gray (PT475) was hit by flak and failed to return to base. A further loss was suffered on the 10th when Flg Off A. Crawford (MJ203), known to his friends as 'Al-Er-Bam', was hit by flak as his section of four Spitfires attacked a train near Canaro, and was posted missing. Des Gorham (EN253:RN-L) came back early minus part of his propeller.

By the 27th Rimini was suffering heavy falls of snow, and the following day the squadron personnel were kept busy clearing snow from the runway. Operations recommenced on the 30th, and on the last day of the month two armed recces were flown. On the first of these Plt Off Connon (PV123) was hit by flak and the tail of his Spitfire was blown off. The Spitfire crashed out of control in the River Adige. Ground attack may have been to the pilots' liking, but they were beginning to learn a healthy respect for flak, and Sqn Ldr Parrott wrote in the Squadron diary:

Unfortunately the squadron activities were again hampered by Old Man Weather, but what operations were called out proved that the pilots were on form. Flak during the month reached a high peak and certainly proved to be accurate, as can be seen by the loss of three excellent pilots. Flak maps are increasingly important items, and are proving their value.

February saw very few missions due to the weather, so the squadron took the opportunity to play sport, attend lectures and organize liberty runs to San Marino. On the 15th Sqn Ldr P.L. Parrott DFC was posted to Advanced HQ, Desert Air Force, and promoted wing commander. His replacement was Sqn Ldr K.N.R. Sissons from 43 Sqn. Flt Lt D.M. Leitch also arrived at this time to take over from Flt Lt D.C. Dunn as 'A' Flight commander, and the squadron began yet another move of base, with the 'A' party setting off for Ravenna airfield. On arrival the men were billeted in a large hospital near the strip with the airmen of three other squadrons, while the officers and SNCOs and HQ staff were in houses a mile or two to the north of the airfield. Operations continued at Rimini until the 17th, when the Spitfires flew into the new base. By the 18th the rear party had also reached Ravenna, and operations recommenced. The airfield was quite close to the front lines, and Jack Lancaster recalled the proximity of the enemy:

From Rimini we moved to Ravenna. When we stood on the balcony of the house at night you could hear the German guns going, and then reprise from our side, and the difference in sound was quite considerable. There was only a large marsh in between the Germans and us, there were no British troops in front of us until one morning we were wakened with a great banging which seemed to shake the whole place, and woke up to find that a battery of 4.5 in. guns had come in overnight and set their guns in our compound, and were battling away with the Germans.

The SNCOs went up to Forli to visit the sergeants' mess of the 7th Armoured Brigade, and we had quite an interesting day with them. One of our pilots, a flight sergeant, asked for a ride in a Sherman, and they said, 'Yes, sure you can.' He mistook an order while he was driving this tank and careered right through an old building. Unfortunately, the gun was facing forwards when it should have been facing rearwards to do something like that, and so it caused a bit of a ruction. When the 7th Armoured Brigade lads visited us on our airfield, the one thing they loved

Des Gorham on the wing of Spitfire Mk IX PV123:RN-K. (D. Gorham)

most was to be able to sit in a Spitfire, and if they could sit in it while the engine was running then they were over the moon.

Dickie Bird flew a dive-bombing sortie on the 21st, recording, 'Good target six barges unloading into MT. D/H [direct hit] on barges.' The following day he flew another dive-bombing sortie, noting, 'Found 12 MT dropped bob just in front – wizard strafe 3 destroyed rest damaged.' After four days of heavy fighting the US Fifth Army controlled the Upper Reno Valley between Bologna and Florence, and the Germans were being pushed into a reducing area of Italian soil. Flak took its toll again on the 23rd during a

Ground crew convoy on the road. Jack Lancaster on right. (J. Lancaster)

twelve-aircraft sortie to attack barges in the River Po. Flt Sgt T.N. 'Tommy' Ninan (JK659) was the victim, crash-landing in enemy territory and being posted missing. Sqn Ldr Sissons commented on the lack of air activity, and the large amount of work carried out to make the new base fit to live in, in the squadron diary:

Very little flying was done during the first half of the month, mainly due to bad weather in the form of ground mist. But, for the later part of the month we were kept busy both in the air and on the ground – this latter occupation being centred on our squadron billets, which are now quite reflective of the labour expended. The squadron figured prominently during the week 19th to 26th and was well reported in the Wing Gen Sheet.

The first sorties of March were on the 2nd, and were dive-bombing attacks, followed by another attack using a new method, bombing by radar. In this fashion the bombs were dropped through the cloud cover on command from a radar controller directing the Spitfires to overhead the target. On the 3rd, four Spitfires set out to bomb railway cuttings, and Plt Off Denis Degerlund (PT485), leading the sortie, had the misfortune to hit overhead power lines while strafing, and crashed his Spitfire behind enemy lines.

The losses in ground-attack sorties continued to mount, and were often caused by targets exploding rather than flak or fighters. On the 6th, four Spitfires led by Flt Lt D.M. Leitch (PL128) were bombing and strafing a road target. Leitch cut the road with his bomb and then commenced strafing an object he had sighted in a nearby field. The other pilots could only watch in horror as Leitch flew through the blast of the exploding object, crash-landing at high speed in the next field, followed by a large cloud of black smoke appearing above the wrecked aircraft. Flt Lt Leitch was posted missing, believed killed. David Park was lucky not to be shot down on the same sortie:

When I was climbing away I was hit by a burst of '88 which carried away the oil tank on the Merlin. Being a Rolls-Royce engine, it kept going until I made base.

As secret negotiations were taking place in Bern, Switzerland, between representatives of the American OSS and the German High Command in Italy for an early surrender of German forces in Italy, a sugar factory at Migliarino was the target for four Spitfires led by Sqn Ldr Sissons on the 8th. The bombing was successful, and the Army later reported that the ruined factory had burned until late the following day. The factory had been producing alcohol fuel for hard-pressed enemy transport. On the 9th Dickie Bird hit a truck with his wingtip while coming in to land, but escaped with only light damage to his Spitfire.

An early afternoon sortie on the 10th found six Spitfires attacking a small arms ammunition dump. Suddenly the Spitfire flown by Canadian Flt Sgt P.S. 'Bert' Jennings (RK916:RN-H) burst into flames in mid-air and spiralled in a sheet of flame to the ground. No parachute was seen, and Jennings was believed killed. David Park flew the same sortie:

Pat Jennings was killed on 10 March when we were attacking an ammo dump. I suddenly saw what looked like 'telegraph poles' fleeing past my aircraft, and hearing a chap by the name of Griffin coming on the R/T and saying, 'The bastards have got Pat!' When I was getting out of my aircraft on returning, Jock Mann came up to me and asked where the Canuck was? When I told him, I have never seen a man so badly affected! Pat was a great favourite on the squadron.

As for the other pilot in that section, the Aussie, he had a remarkable experience. We were both pulling up after a strafing run when he was hit at about 600 ft, and, I thought, went straight in! In actual fact he managed to bale out and landed safely. He buried his watch and escape kit before he was taken prisoner by German parachute troops, who took him in before their colonel. The colonel asked Phil his name, and when Phil told him it was Schneider the colonel nearly fell off his seat. Only two days before, another Aussie had been brought before him and his name was Redenbach! 'It's all Germans who are fighting us!' he said, but Phil assured him he was a 'fair dinkum' Australian! After quite a number of adventures, including contact with a clandestine outfit, he walked into the mess seventeen days later. He then went back to Australia.

The squadron extracted some measure of revenge for Jennings later in the day when four Spitfires attacked an enemy headquarters and wiped it out. Dickie Bird recorded the loss:

L to R: Dickie Bird, Jock Park, Dennis Degerlund, unknown ground crew. (72 Sqn)

Paddy missing (bod). Bert shot up, made our lines – crash-landed and killed himself landing.

On the 13th he noted:

Schneider [Australian WO P.F. Schneider] baled out three miles the other side.

And the following day he noted the wounding of another pilot:

Levvik wounded with 20 exp in cockpit. Port aileron shot – brought a/c back belly flopped on 'drome – good show.

That day the squadron was informed of immediate awards of the DFC to Capt K.F. D'Arcy SAAF and Plt Off Dickie Bird. The latter had joined the squadron several months before as a sergeant pilot. On the 15th another old hand turned up. Flg Off Laurie Frampton had already flown one tour with 72 Sqn, and was back for a second. On arrival he was given some advice on dive-bombing in the Spitfire:

The Luftwaffe had concentrated all aircraft in the Fatherland for home defence and so the Spitfire squadrons were carrying 500 lb bombs to discomfort German ground forces. Having had a basic grounding in the art of dive-bombing, I was advised in conversation in the mess that some bombs might have over-sensitive fuses and had been known to explode on release. It was wise, therefore, to watch your speed in the dive.

Escorts to B-26 Marauders were the favourite sorties tasked by headquarters in the days that followed, and the squadron escorted them to bomb such targets as Gorizio, Carlino and Spilinmergo. On the 20th six Spitfires attacked a concrete railway bridge near Vicenza, followed by five more Spitfires. In the second group Plt Off Dickie Bird scored a direct hit, leaving a large crater on the bridge and blowing away a large part of the side structure. He noted in his log:

Rail bridge. One hit – I claimed near-miss – PRU photo shows it as a D/H.

A second 72 Sqn old-stager arrived on the 20th when Flt Lt J.F. King also returned to the squadron for a second tour of operations. Australian Flt Lt Dudley Dunn was also awarded the DFC on this date.

The 21st was a busy day, with sorties to targets at Vicenza, Cittadella, Treviso and Castel Franco among others. Six aircraft attacked targets between Treviso and Castel Franco. The recently returned Laurie Frampton's Spitfire (MA583:RN-B) was last seen in a steep dive at 3,000 ft over the target. The Spitfire had been at 7,000 ft when a large black puff of smoke was seen near it as it entered a bombing dive. No one saw Frampton bale out, but he did survive the loss of his Spitfire:

Capt K.F. D'Arcy SAAF at Rimini in February 1945. (72 Sqn)

Our target was a rail cut between Treviso and Castiglione, and on sighting the target area several wagons were seen on the track. Dickie and his No. 2 dived on the wagons and seemed to have hit them as a great cloud of black smoke billowed up. I aimed for the centre of the smoke, released my bomb, pulled out of the dive and opened the throttle – a slight pause, then a very loud bang. I came round in the said cloud of smoke, and as I entered clear air the ground was approaching quite rapidly. Chop the throttle, heave back on the stick, she slowly came out of the dive but continued turning to port while still losing height. Using full right rudder and aileron and with the stick hard back, I just managed to keep straight and level while clipping the tops of some trees. The left side of the cockpit was getting warm so I assumed we were on fire. I tried to jettison the hood, but it stuck a few inches open; I dare not release the control column to bash it with my elbows in the approved manner. There was a farmhouse to the left of my line of flight, and doing my best to avoid it is the last thing I remember. Presumably I made some sort of crash-landing. I woke up sitting on the brick floor of a farmhouse, propped up against a heap of hay, with the family standing round wondering what to do with me. Since there were no enemy aircraft and no flak, the bomb must have exploded just after I released it. Thus was my second tour with 72 brought to a rapid end.

After being patched-up by the local medic I was temporarily housed in the guardroom of Treviso airfield. While still under German control, the guards were Italian Air Force and quite pleasant. Instead of keeping me locked in a cell all day, I was allowed out onto the balcony in the front. Some two or three days after my arrival a local cart came through the gate. On it was a Merlin engine, two Spitfire wingtips about 6 ft long and a tail unit, badly charred, which I believe was all that remained of my aircraft.

Laurie Frampton was in the bag.

More DFC awards arrived for 72 Sqn on the 21st, with a Bar to Sqn Ldr Polly Parrot's DFC and new DFCs for Flt Lt D.C. Dunn and Australian Plt Off Alf Taylor, who had both recently left the squadron, tour expired. Bomber escorts continued alongside fighter-bomber missions until the 26th, when heavy rain made the airfield unserviceable and halted operations. Dickie Bird recorded the results of one fighter bomber mission on the 25th: 'Strong point – strafed hell out of it.' The weather improved by the 28th, when a paddle-boat on the River Po was attacked. This was followed up by attacks on rail targets on the 29th. The last sortie of March was flown on the 31st: a fighter escort to B-26s bombing Manzano and Comegliano.

Winter still held a grip on the Italian mainland, and it managed to disrupt operations throughout the month, but when flying was possible the squadron had many successes, though countered by losses, as noted in the squadron diary by Sqn Ldr E. Cassidy (who would become CO in May 1945):

In spite of bad weather during the last week, the squadron carried out more than the missions of the previous month, which fact pleased everybody. We were given a very satisfactory proportion of Army targets, and these proved far more popular than the rail cuts. Four pilots were shot down – three of them are MBK [missing believed killed] and the fourth safe in hospital. A good month and all pilots are in fine fettle for the final offensive when it comes.

April 1945 saw bomber escorts and fighter-bomber missions continue, with the first day of the month bringing two escort missions to Marauders and two fighter-bomber missions, including an attack on a bridge at Adria. The net was closing in on the Germans from all sides, and the end of the war seemed close.

Recce photo showing Dickie Bird's direct hit on the Vicenza Bridge on 20 March 1945. (J. Bird)

However, the German troops fighting a desperate battle in Italy showed no sign of giving up. The *Luftwaffe*, starved of fuel and with few aircraft left in the theatre, may not have shown much of a presence over the battlefield, but the flak still came up thick and fast in almost every attack made by the Spitfires. On the 3rd, Sqn Ldr Sissons was replaced by Maj H.E. Wells SAAF posted in from No. 43 Sqn, and operations continued apace.

By the 9th the Allies were determined to finish off the Germans in Italy, and in preparation for the final assaults over 800 heavy and medium bombers attacked enemy positions on the River Senio. The 9th saw the Eighth Army launch its final offensive in Italy on German positions east of Bologna, aided by 1,800 aircraft and a 1,500-gun bombardment. The US Fifth Army also thrust toward Bologna and the River Po valley. 72 Sqn flew three missions in support of these attacks, striking at gun positions on the river banks with napalm bombs, which were used very successfully for the first time by the squadron. The squadron operations record noted that this attack in support of Polish troops crossing the river resulted in 'one colossal bloody blaze along target'.

The squadron diary also noted:

Everybody was excited to know that this was really it. We were finally going to drive the Germans out of Italy.

Des Gorham noted in his logbook, 'Bombing attack. Direct hit. The Great Attack. House exploded beautifully.' Some were destined never to see the Germans driven out. On the 10th four Spitfires were bombing targets north of Portomaggiore when WO Williams's Spitfire (MJ632:RN-A) caught fire during a bombing dive and crashed into the ground. No parachute was seen. Later in the day Flt Lt King

---

Bar to DFC Citation

LONDON GAZETTE, 20TH MARCH 1945

Parrott, Peter Lawrence, Acting Squadron Leader DFC

Squadron leader Parrott is now engaged on his second operational tour in the Mediterranean area. He has also completed a previous tour from England. Since the award of the Distinguished Flying Cross he has completed numerous sorties and has destroyed at least one enemy aircraft. He has led his squadron with skill and determination. During the landing at Anzio, his formation engaged and drove off a large number of enemy fighter-bomber attacks, contributing materially to the success achieved by his squadron. In all, Squadron Leader Parrott has destroyed at least six enemy aircraft.

Telephone No. : GERRARD 9234
Trunk Calls and
Telegraphic Address :} "AIR MINISTRY," LONDON

P. 430852/P.4.A.2.

AIR MINISTRY,
(Casualty Branch),
73-77 OXFORD STREET,
LONDON, W.I.
3 / March, 1945.

Sir,

    I am commanded by the Air Council to confirm the telegram in which you were notified that your son, Flying Officer Laurence Alfred Frampton, Royal Air Force, is missing as the result of air operations/on 21st March, 1945.

    The telegraphic report from Air Force Headquarters, Algiers, states that your son set out in a Spitfire aircraft to attack rail communications between Tevislo and Castel Franco, Northern Italy, and that the aircraft was last seen in a steep dive attacking railway trucks near Castel Franco. Your son was not seen to bale out.

    This does not necessarily mean that he is killed or wounded, and if he is a prisoner of war he should be able to communicate with you in due course. Meanwhile enquiries are being made through the International Red Cross Committee, and as soon as any definite news is received you will be at once informed.

/If

G.H. Frampton, Esq.,
  66, Meadway,
    Freeze Water,
      Enfield, Middlesex.

    If any information regarding your son is received by you from any source you are requested to be kind enough to communicate it immediately to the Air Ministry.

    The Air Council desire me to express their sympathy with you in your present anxiety.

    I am, Sir,

      Your obedient Servant,

The Air Ministry letter sent to Laurie Frampton's father after he was shot down. (L. Frampton)

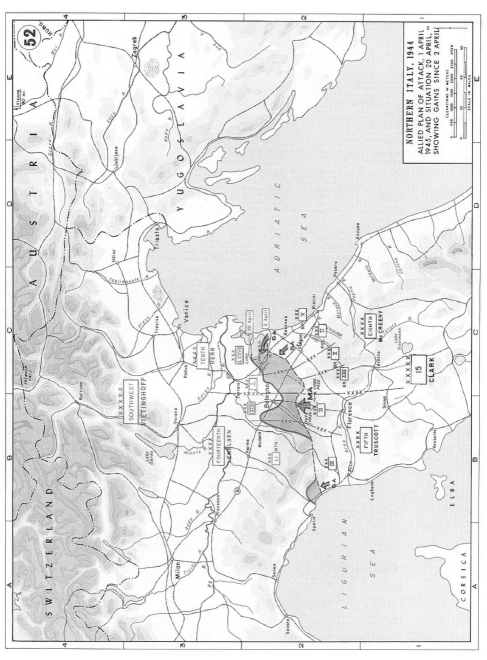

Allied plan of attack 1 April 1945

DFC Citation

LONDON GAZETTE, 13TH APRIL 1945

Pilot Officer Jeffrey Bird

This officer has completed a large number of sorties during which he has attacked a variety of enemy targets with much skill and determination. On a recent occasion, Pilot Officer Bird took part in a sortie during which six barges and a number of mechanical vehicles were most effectively attacked. This officer has invariably displayed a high degree of courage in his attacks on the enemy and among his successes is the destruction of 3 enemy aircraft.

---

brought his damaged Spitfire (RR259) back to Ravenna from a sortie attacking targets south-west of Fusignana. King made a wheels-up landing on the strip, but his aircraft veered and crashed into a tree, and the pilot was killed.

Napalm was being used fairly regularly now and was an extremely effective method of eliminating enemy strongpoints, and on the 12th Gp Capt Beresford DSO DFC led twelve Spitfires loaded with napalm to attack positions on the west bank of the River Santerno. Des Gorham noted, 'Bombing attack. Used blaze bombs on Santerno banks. Frizzled Fritz.' The following day saw a large number of sorties, and on one of these Australian WO P.F. Schneider was hit by flak. His Spitfire (MK687) crashed and was burnt out; however, Schneider was seen to take to his parachute, landing behind enemy lines, where he was last seen taking his parachute off. The squadron was hopeful he would evade capture, and he was posted 'Not Yet Returned'.

DFC Citation

LONDON GAZETTE, 13TH APRIL 1945

Captain Kenneth Frederick D'Arcy SAAF

In February, 1945, this officer piloted an aircraft in an attack against the railway sidings at Vicenza. The area was heavily defended. Nevertheless, Captain D'Arcy executed a perfect bombing run and obtained 3 hits on the target. Later in the day he took part in an attack on a number of barges, one of which he destroyed. This officer has taken part in a large number of varied sorties and has set a fine example of skill, courage and resolution.

The Eighth Army captured the Bastia Bridge intact on the 14th as Hitler rejected requests from his generals to withdraw north to the River Po. Operations continued apace as the Army demanded more and more air support to neutralize enemy positions. The 17th was the heaviest day yet in the offensive, with the squadron flying nine missions, eight of them in close support to the Army. The last attack of the day was on a pontoon bridge over the River Po.

Heartening news of Flt Sgt T.M. Ninan was received on the 17th. He had been posted missing on 23 February, and had been captured by the Germans. Released by the Americans, he had returned to England.

By now the strain on the pilots was beginning to show, particularly the flight and section leaders, and the Group Captain asked for details of the efforts made by each pilot. On discovering that Capt Colehan and Flg Off Craig had each led three missions that day, he ordered that in future no pilot would be allowed to fly more than twice a day. The hopes that WO Schneider, shot down on the 13th, would return were dashed when it was reported that he was a POW. The information came from one of Schneider's captors subsequently taken prisoner himself.

On the 20th the US Fifth Army reached the Po river plain as the Germans began to retreat, and 20 April found the squadron in need of a new commanding officer when Maj H.E. Wells (ML146) crash-landed south of Argenta on an armed recce sortie. Wells was badly hurt, and moved through several hospitals before reaching No. 66 General Hospital at Riccione at midnight that night. He was visited by Gp Capt Beresford and the medical and intelligence officers, who found him on a stretcher waiting to go into the operating-room. He was in a very dazed state and had suffered severe hand and shoulder injuries. With the CO in hospital, Capt W.E. Colehan SAAF assumed command of the squadron on the 21st. The 2nd Polish Corps and the US 34th Division of the Eighth and Fifth Armies respectively combined operations to capture Bologna on the 21st, and had reached the Po north of Bologna two days later.

On the 24th the Eighth Army captured Ferrara, thirty miles north-east of Bologna, and crossed the Po after fierce engagements with the enemy. The US Fifth Army captured Spezia on the Gulf of Genoa. The next day Mantua, sixty miles north-west of Bologna, was captured by the Fifth Army, which continued its advance up the coast. The Eighth Army crossed the Po and captured Parma. Genoa was captured by Italian partisans, and the people of Milan staged a revolt on the 26th, while the Fifth Army captured Verona and entered Genoa on the 27th. On the 28th word of another downed squadron pilot was received. Flt Lt J.A. Gray was now a POW, and on this day was awarded the DFC. The last operations of the month were offensive patrols carrying ninety-gallon overload tanks, and the five missions brought a good bag of destroyed and damaged enemy transport. Sqn Ldr Cassidy wrote of the month's operations in the squadron diary:

The Grand Finale was quite as hectic as we had anticipated, and once more the previous weight of bombs dropped was doubled. There were enough close-support targets to satisfy the most ferocious Hun Hater, and everybody went all out, having what we all knew was to be our last crack at the enemy in Europe.

Bombing accuracy was very satisfactory. The squadron dropped blaze bombs [napalm] for the first time, and very popular they proved. Pilots got a great kick out of seeing the sheets of flame cover the flood banks, which were infested with Huns. Casualties during the month were fairly heavy but not as bad as might have been expected considering the effort put up.

The Americans, meanwhile, had captured Brescia on the 28th, and the Eighth Army reached Venice. Mussolini and his mistress, Clara Petacci, and twelve Fascist cabinet ministers were captured trying to escape in a German convoy, and all were shot. The bodies of Mussolini and his mistress were brought to Milan the following day and hung upside-down from lampposts, where the bodies were shot at and spat upon. The German armies in Italy surrendered on the 29th, and the Eighth Army secured Venice before advancing on Trieste. The Fifth Army entered Milan and linked up with the Eighth Army at Padua. On the 30th, the Fifth Army in north-west Italy also linked up with French troops advancing eastwards at the French–Italian border.

May 1945 saw a gradual wind-down in offensive operations for the squadron, with only one uneventful armed recce north of Udine by four Spitfires on the 1st, while Sqn Ldr E. Cassidy DFC arrived from No. 92 Sqn to take command of the squadron. The squadron's final operational sortie of the Second World War was flown on 2 May when Flt Lt R. Rayner (MJ668) and another pilot, whose name is not recorded in the operations record book, but was flying Spitfire MJ571, took off at 1405 hrs for an offensive patrol, landing back at 1520 hrs and closing the book on 72 Squadron's war.

Fighting on the Italian Front ceased at 1200 hrs, and though the thoughts of many on the squadron probably turned to the possibility of being posted home, this was not to be. Almost as soon as the fighting finished the squadron was ordered to move again.

On the 3rd the 'A' party set off, led by the intelligence officer, Flt Lt Brill, for the Udine area. It halted for the night outside Padua. The following day it set off for, and arrived at, the new airfield at Rivolto. The squadron's sixteen Spitfires flew in later in the day. The 'B' party also set off, under the command of Flt Lt True, and stopped at Ferrara for the night. On the 5th it continued its journey, which was delayed by road blocks and traffic jams and did not reach Padua till late that night. Setting off early the next morning, the party joined the rest of the squadron at Rivolto.

News reached the squadron on the 7th that Plt Off Denis Degerlund was safe and had been taken POW. He had only had to endure a few weeks in captivity, as the war in Europe ended the next day, 8 May 1945, with Germany's surrender.

Ground crew weighting the tail of Spitfire MK IX MJ629:RN-F as it is run up. (via L.J. Barton)

Des Gorham with his Spitfire, Italy 1945. (D. Gorham)

With the war over, the squadron was quickly moved into Austria as part of the occupation forces, but the journey was far from a safe one, as Jack Lancaster recalls:

We left Ravenna and crossed the Po on a huge pontoon bridge which the Army had built, and that was quite an experience. We arrived at a little place called Udine about twenty miles north of Trieste on 7 May 1945. We didn't know what was happening at the time or where the enemy was, but we settled in there for the night, and next morning we heard that the end of the war had come and that we were to go immediately up into Austria, to Klagenfurt.

During our stay in France the squadron had managed to purloin a Studebaker truck which had belonged to the Germans, and I believe had previously belonged to the French. We found that this would make a very nice flight office, and so we took it with us back to Italy. I was detailed to drive this, along with Flt Sgt Mann, to go up into Austria.

We found that the main road up to Villach was closed due to the fact that the Germans had blown a bridge, and we had to make a detour through the north-west corner of Yugoslavia to get up into Austria. While going up this very narrow road we were suddenly met by a bunch of partisans, Yugoslav partisans, who jumped

Des Gorham with a Spitfire Mk IX at Ravenna. (D. Gorham)

Des Gorham in Spitfire RN-E with ground crew on wing. (D. Gorham)

Des Gorham at the tail of his Spitfire, with Mk IX RN-P behind. (D. Gorham)

A closer view of Des Gorham at the tail of his Spitfire shows that it was named 'Betty'. (D. Gorham)

Sgt Chas Cousins inspecting *Luftwaffe* wrecks at Udine. (via L.J. Barton)

out into the road and pointed rifles at us, so we came to an abrupt halt. We were told to get out of the vehicle, and we were pushed against the side of the vehicle with our hands above our heads and wondered what on earth was going on. We'd been separated from the squadron because we had set off a bit early, and we had no back-up at all. I don't think the Yugoslavs knew what or who we were. All we had on the vehicle was 72 Sqn written on the door and a very small roundel on the front bumper. However, they didn't seem to bother, they wanted the vehicle and its contents, and that was all they cared about. Just about that time, down the road came a convoy of German soldiers in half-track vehicles, and sitting in the front of one of these was a German officer, who stopped the vehicle and got out to ask what was going on. He asked me who I was and what we were doing, and I informed him that we were RAF and we were going up into Austria. He said that he was not going to surrender to these partisans, and said, 'If you can tell me where the nearest British officer is I'll surrender to him according to the armistice which has been signed.' I gave him instructions as to where to find the British military post, and he said, 'Well, good luck to you.' Just before he left I said to him, 'You speak very good English.' And he said, 'Well, I should, shouldn't I, I was educated at Oxford.' I reckon my guardian angel was right on the ball that day.

We arrived at Klagenfurt later that day, and it was reassuring to see hangars and good sound buildings of the **Luftwaffe**, *so we were not going to be living in tents. We settled in there pretty well. The partisans, Yugoslavs, were raiding the Austrian border, taking whatever they could while they had the opportunity, and I think our pilots were observing what was going on rather than having to defend anything.*

CHAPTER SEVEN

Austria

The RAF in Italy was not slow to revert to peacetime routine, and Wednesday afternoon sports were reintroduced, as were half-day off on Saturdays and all day off on Sundays. Rivolto turned out to be only a staging-point, and on the 10th the squadron was on the road again, heading for Klagenfurt in Austria. The 'B' party followed on the next day, and the Spitfires flew up, along with a Junkers Ju F.13 found at Udine. Once again the squadron had not been slow to collect a few war prizes.

The European war may have been over, but the squadron began flying sorties again from Klagenfurt. On the 12th, two 'Tac R' missions and a search for a

Junkers F.13 being inspected at Klagenfurt by Flg Off Newman and Sgt Lancaster. (J. Lancaster)

72 Sqn sergeants' mess members at Klagenfurt in September 1945. (72 Sqn)

missing Anson were flown. The 'Tac R' missions continued to be flown in the days that followed, and word arrived of the award of the DFC to Maj H.E. Wells SAAF on the 13th.

There was still some concern in mid-May that some German forces might try to hold out and disregard the surrender order. Consequently, the squadron flew ten Spitfires alongside one of 43 Sqn, led by the wing leader, Gp Capt Beresford, in a demonstration of force in the Bleiberg area. As they flew over the town, red stars and banners were seen festooned everywhere. The Russians held the town.

In a continuation of the return to peacetime normality, the khaki battledress worn by the squadron since North Africa was exchanged for RAF Blue Service Dress, and daily bathing runs began to the Werther See on the 16th. A rest camp was established there, and the squadron was soon taking advantage of it. On the 21st Capt W.E. Colehan was awarded the DFC, and a few days later news reached Klagenfurt that Flt Lt W.J. Cameron, posted missing on 26 July 1943, was safe in England after liberation from a POW camp.

On the 28th thirteen of the squadron's Spitfires flew down to Campoformido airfield to take part in the Desert Air Force flypast celebrating the end of hostilities. The Australian and Canadian personnel, who had served the squadron so well, began leaving for repatriation on the 30th, and at the end of the month Sqn Ldr Cassidy recorded in the diary:

Menu from the WO and sergeants' mess
at Udine. (A.E. Allen)

The inside of the Udine menu, showing the reason for the dinner – a gunnery course in
October 1945. The signatures of those attending are on the left. (A.E. Allen)

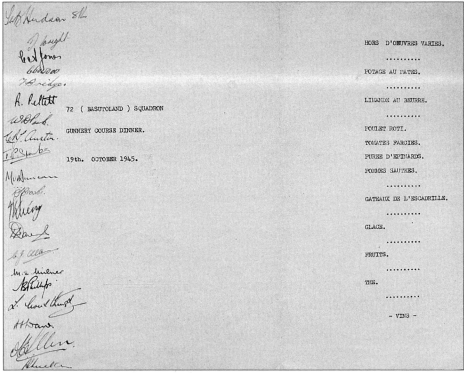

With the cessation of hostilities on the Italian Front on 2 May, the squadron's operations for the month were virtually non-existent. On 10 May, the squadron moved into Austria to play its appointed role in the occupation, and flew a number of Tac/R patrols to cover movement of Yugoslav partisan troops and POW columns. From 18 May, the squadron's flying activities were limited to training. Great efforts were made within the squadron to further sports, entertainments and general welfare.

June opened with a four-aircraft search for a missing Baltimore, but with no luck. More news of missing airmen began to filter in during the month, with reports that WO G.H. Turgeon and Flg Off Laurie were safe and well. By the 8th the return of airmen completing their period of overseas duty was in full swing, and thirteen airmen with low

A.E. 'Wink' Allen. (E. Boddice)

release-group numbers were posted to other units in Italy pending repatriation. To prepare others for the return home a lecture on 'Release and Rehabilitation' was held on the 9th and was well attended. By the 10th the South Africans were also on their way home. On the 18th, two members of the ground crew, Sgt G.H. Gilbert and Sgt I.A. 'Rio' Wright, were Mentioned in Dispatches, and the following day several airmen who saw a career in the services had applied for transfer to the Fleet Air Arm and underwent medical examinations.

On 4 July the airmen of the squadron took part in voting in the first British elections for ten years, some 120 casting votes. On 14 July Sqn Ldr Cassidy was promoted to Wing Commander Flying for 324 Wing, but remained temporarily with the squadron. On the 15th the 'non-fraternization' rule was lifted, and in the words of the squadron diary, 'Morale rose.' On the 27th Sqn Ldr D.J. Johnson arrived to take command of the squadron.

72 Sqn flight line at Klagenfurt. (J. Lancaster)

DFC Citation

LONDON GAZETTE, 13TH JULY 1945

Captain William Edward Colehan SAAF

This officer is an exceptionally able pilot and a fearless fighter. He has completed very many sorties during which he has successfully attacked a wide range of enemy targets. In April, 1945, Captain Colehan led a small section of aircraft in an attack against an enemy strongpoint consisting of one large and three smaller heavily defended houses. The attack was pressed home with great skill and vigour. The objective was completely destroyed. As a result our ground forces were able to advance for some distance. Some days later, Captain Colehan led a section in an attack against another heavily defended strongpoint. In spite of considerable enemy fire the attack was pressed home with great success. The determination shown by this officer was in keeping with that which he has shown throughout his tour of duty.

By August the squadron had settled into Klagenfurt as part of the forces of occupation, and into a routine of flying training, leave, rest and recreation, courses and lectures. VJ Day was announced on the 15th, and the squadron was stood down to celebrate the end of the Second World War. On the 28th the CO, adjutant and engineering officer travelled up to Zeltweg to inspect the squadron's next base of operations. They found sufficient hangars and accommodation for the squadron, including administration offices and permanent barrack blocks for the airmen. The SNCOs were to live in a combined wing mess, while the officers would move into a *Schloss* (castle) four miles from the airfield. Jack Lancaster recalls the change of pace during this period and the opportunities available for rest and relaxation:

We settled in for a week or two and then someone decided that we ought to have a spot of holiday, and quite a few of us were sent down to Venice for a week, which was very good for us after all the problems we had previously. When I came back from the holiday I was called in to the CO, and he said, 'I understand you speak German, so I'd like you to go out and find some liquid refreshment for the mess.' Which I did. I was given the authority to do a bit of bartering with sugar, etc., and I came back with a Bedford 15 cwt loaded with schnapps and soda water.

By 6 September the squadron was packing its equipment again in preparation for the move to Zeltweg, with the Spitfires arriving at the new base on the 8th. By the 10th all had arrived and the routine of settling in began. By mid-

Jack White on wing, with 'Wink' Allen in cockpit, of Spitfire Mk IX RN-Q at Klagenfurt.
(J. Lancaster)

September many members of the squadron, who had been with the unit since
North Africa, were on their way home, replaced by airmen from other units.
The poor weather during the month had severely curtailed flying, and home
leave and releases left the squadron under strength.

On 1 October the pilots began packing bags in preparation for a detachment
to Campoformido and an armament practice camp. The aircraft took off at 1100
hrs the following day, and flew over the Alps at 17,000 ft an hour later in a
rainstorm. Air-to-ground firing and bombing commenced on the 3rd, and the
following day air-to-air firing started, but the effort was severely reduced when
the second detail shot away the towed drogue being used. This left only one
towing Harvard available due to lack of spare drogues for the second towing
aircraft.

Sqn Ldr T.W.B. Hudson took over command of the squadron on 14 October,
and by the 18th the squadron had steadily improved its bombing and air firing,
but had gone through all the available drogues, and as it was impossible to get
more, it began packing for home, and all were back at Zeltweg by the 22nd.

By October 1945 old alliances between the Western Allies and the Soviet-
dominated Eastern Bloc were becoming strained, and the first signs that all
might not be well in the future were beginning to show. Lack of spares, personnel

---

DFC Citation

LONDON GAZETTE, 21ST AUGUST 1945

Rayner, Ronald, Flight Lieutenant

This officer has completed numerous operational sorties. On one occasion he was detailed to lead six aircraft in an attack on an enemy occupied house near Argenta. Despite heavy anti-aircraft fire the house was completely destroyed, and a second house destroyed 15 yards away. Flight Lieutenant Rayner is an outstanding leader.

---

and equipment, coupled with poor weather, severely limited the squadron's operations, and Sqn Ldr Johnson made his views felt in the squadron diary at the end of the month:

The major part of the month has been spent at the practice camp at Campoformido, where we had very good weather. This enabled us to complete bombing and air-to-ground on schedule. The air-to-air was abruptly curtailed because using gyro sights we blew away several drogues. This had a misleading effect on the scoring, because we were only able to assess on the drogues which came back.

Jack Lancaster, 2nd left, and other servicemen on R&R in Austria. (J. Lancaster)

Zeltweg, summer 1946. L to R: Flg Off Wink Allen, Flg Off Levick Coulthurst, Flg Off Jock Park. (A.E. Allen)

On returning to base we continued the routine Yugoslavian border patrols and occasional 'Rover Paddy' work. The weather at base is deteriorating steadily and we shall soon have snow. When not flying, pilots are constructing their own information room. Towards the end of the month lack of personnel forced us to become part of a composite squadron under the command of Wing Commander Flying, and we are still on that basis.

November 1945 found the squadron still at Zeltweg, something of a luxury following their travels through Italy, Corsica and France. They were still flying patrols along the Yugoslavian border; however, these were severely curtailed by bad weather in the first fortnight of the month. Flying recommenced on the 19th, but was still limited in scope due to the poor weather. Taking advantage of this, preparations for the squadron's first peacetime Christmas celebrations were in full swing, and it planned to have a memorable one.

The weather in December was little better for flying; however, it was very good for skiing, and the squadron began sending groups for two-week courses on the 7th. On 19 December the squadron had its first peacetime flying accident. Flt Lt Wood, commanding 'B' Flight, was going round again after a failed landing

Spitfire Mk IX RN-S coming in to land. (72 Sqn)

attempt when he had an engine failure. He immediately made a wheels-up forced landing, stepping out of the damaged Spitfire (PT552) unhurt.

Christmas celebration began on the 22nd with a draw in the sergeants' mess, and continued till Boxing Day. There was a short break before they recommenced on the 30th in the work-up to the New Year and, for some, an all-night party in the pre-war style.

Having rounded out the year in some style, the squadron was able to look back on it and reflect on its achievements and what the future held. The sudden end of fighting in Italy left many wondering what to do to keep occupied, but the squadron soon found them plenty of activity, as the CO noted in the diary:

And so an eventful year concluded. A year which saw first victory in Italy – the theatre immediately concerning the squadron – followed quickly by the collapse of resistance in Germany and finally cessation of hostilities with Japan.

It has been a difficult year. The first few months saw the endeavours of all the squadron personnel strained to the utmost as the tempo of warfare increased towards the final result which was to so successfully [... indecipherable ...] with the route of the German forces behind the Po. The anticlimax of the collapse in our theatre found many bewildered and at a loss as to what to do with themselves, once the war was

324 Wg Inspection by ACM Barrett at Zeltweg in 1946. L to R: Gp Capt B. Kingcome DSO DFC; ACM Barrett; Wg Cdr E.J. Cassidy (Wg Cdr Flying); Sqn Ldr Bert Ambrose (OC 43 Sqn); Sqn Ldr J.R. Cock (OC 72 Sqn); Flt Lt F. Cox (Intelligence); Sqn Ldr Dennis (OC 111 Sqn); Sqn Ldr 'Skip' Evans (Maintenance); Sqn Ldr M. Rees (Sqn Ldr Operations); WO Sharp (Discip). (via Erik Mannings)

over they could relax. Luckily, however, the move up to Klagenfurt and the lakes of Corinthia in time to catch the latter position of South Austrian summer solved some of these problems, since everyone was able to enjoy the sunshine and warmth of lakeside rest camps. Outdoor activities – swimming, boating, riding, fishing – in this beautiful country provided a near-perfect stopgap for the confusion felt by most individuals between the rapid severance from operational existence and necessity for settling down to comparative peacetime standards as RAF Occupation Austria.

Early September saw the wing, minus our old friends 93 Squadron, who were disbanded at Zeltweg, on the main route from Klagenfurt to Vienna. A well-established Luftwaffe station this, about which the only unfortunate part was its locality – there being none of the attractions of the more populated areas available. Despite the shortage of personnel that occurred as more and more of our old-timers left us, time expired, the squadron settled into its winter quarters quite quickly, and

No. 324 Wing officers' mess at Zeltweg, Austria, July 1946. 72 Sqn pilots in the photo are: Rear row, L to R: 2nd Mike Duncan, 4th Levick Coulthurst DFC, 10th Johnnie Woodside, 11th Charlie Cowood, 12th Bob Austin. Middle row, L to R: 6th 'Mo' Milner, 7th Jones, 13th Aubrey Allen, 14th Johnny Spiers. Front row, L to R: 5th Sqn Ldr Dennis (OC 111 Sqn), 6th Wg Cdr Cassidy DC (Wg Cdr Flying and ex-OC 72 Sqn,) 7th Gp Capt Brian Kingcome DSO DFC, 9th Sqn Ldr Johnnie Cock DFC (OC 72 Sqn), 10th Sqn Ldr Bert Ambrose (OC 43 Sqn). The dogs are named Vodka, Vilma, Mellie and Fritz. (A.E. Allen)

internal squadron activities, clubs of all descriptions and social activities, even if on a modified scale, were re-established.

The Austrian winter has unfortunately played us false this year, and snow is conspicuous with its absence. This has seriously interfered with an ambitious Winter Sports programme which had been arranged in the late autumn; and naturally this has proved a great disappointment to the skiing enthusiasts to a great extent, and has cut down what was to have been our major sporting activity to a very minor proportion.

The main difficulty that the squadron has overcome during the occupation has been the lack of personnel. Leave to England, but principally release, has literally reduced us to a mere skeleton formation, and at some critical period to just a handful of men with few, if any, SNCOs. Nevertheless, by ingenuity and resource they have found ways of keeping the squadron going as a reduced operational formation.

Spitfires RN-M, P and V in the squadron hangar at Zeltweg in 1945.

The year has been in no way an easy one. The sudden cessation of hostilities, the transition from war to peace and the inevitable sense of frustration brought by the task of winning the war suddenly coming to an end with nothing tangible to take its place have been problems of some account. I have no hesitation, however, in saying that throughout this period in facing these many problems and changes the squadron has, to a man, risen splendidly to the task.

Flying recommenced in the New Year. However, it was still hampered by poor weather and a lack of pilots to fly the aircraft as more and more were demobbed. A further lack of ground crew to service and maintain the aircraft almost brought the squadron's flying to a standstill by the end of January.

On 8 February Sqn Ldr J.R. Cock DFC arrived to take command and replace Sqn Ldr Hudson, and officially took over on the 11th. By the 16th, Spitfire serviceability had dropped so low that only four aircraft could be found for flying. By the 19th the squadron was using those aircraft which were flyable to practise supply dropping, using canisters.

The weather in early March seriously affected flying, but there was some good news as replacement ground crew began to arrive in the middle of the month; in fact, by the 13th the squadron had more fitters on strength than it could use! The weather also cleared, and flying recommenced, with a large number of dive-bombing practice sorties being flown.

By mid-April the old wartime 72 Sqn was almost all gone, with seventeen airmen leaving on the 14th, tour expired. On the 15th two pilots had a lucky escape during a wing formation practice. Flt Sgt Brooks (MH884:RN-E) and Flt Lt Lynn (NH453:JU-V) of 111 Sqn collided. Both pilots baled out and were unharmed. The incident happened in full view of the AOC; his comments were not recorded.

As April progressed the wing continued to practise formations for the Desert Air Force air display to be held later in the month. A fly-off was held between Flg Off Cowood of 72 Sqn and Flt Lt Skinner of 43 Sqn for the solo aerobatic display, and Charlie Cowood won, albeit scaring everyone in the process with his display. The twelve Spitfires of 72 and 43 Squadrons took off for Campoformido on the 26th, and took part in the flypast, which went off without a hitch, despite previous worries that it might not. In addition to the hectic flying practice sorties, the squadron continued to fly Yugoslav border patrols.

With the improvement in the weather, May saw an increase in flying, including a flypast over Graz by the wing as part of the VE Day Anniversary celebrations. On 30 May the Inspector-General of the RAF, Air Marshal Sir Arthur Barrett KCB MC, arrived to inspect 324 Wing, and as he left after a very detailed inspection of the squadron his only comment to the CO was:

I have no criticisms to make other than your chief cook needs a hair cut!

June 1946 saw a major improvement in the weather, and much flying was done. One highlight of the month was the arrival of Flt Lt Fifell of the Central Fighter Establishment at West Raynham, who flew in with a de Havilland Hornet. He put on an excellent demonstration of the twin-engined fighter's abilities, including a flypast with both propellers feathered.

June also found dark political clouds looming on the horizon in a precursor to the soon-to-arrive 'Cold War'. Italy and Communist Yugoslavia had been arguing politically over the ownership of Trieste, and things threatened to become heated. With this in mind the squadron stepped up its battle formation practice sorties. By the 7th, Desert Air Force HQ was requesting maximum serviceability from the squadrons, and flying ceased in order to allow the ground crew to get all of the Spitfires ready. On 13 June some of the hard work to get all of the aircraft serviceable was undone when Sgt Cowell taxied into the tail of WO Pettitt's Spitfire. As the Sabres continued to rattle over Trieste, the pilots helped out by belting-up 20 mm and 0.5 in. ammunition, 'just in case'.

By the 20th the squadron had been bought up to three hours' operational notice, and the pilots continued to belt-up ammunition, becoming thoroughly bored in the process. In order to bring the Desert Air Force wings up to operational standard, a simulated attack on the St Stino bridge over the Piavi river in northern Italy was laid on under the codename Operation Bedlam for the 25th. No. 324 Wing was to provide top cover to 244 Wing, while 239 Wing would play the part of the defending force. OC 72 Sqn noted the day's operation in the squadron diary:

The weather didn't look too good at briefing time with 7/10th–9/10th cloud at 6,000 ft, but nevertheless, eighteen aircraft (six each from 43, 72, 111) took off at 0930. The clouds proved to be about 1,000 ft above the Alps, so we were able to get through OK. En route to the rendezvous at Castel Franco, we were intercepted by four 'defenders', but as this was 'before game was due to commence', we ignored them. Rendezvous was made thirty seconds ahead of time, and 244 was one minute late. However, we joined up OK and proceeded to the target area. Ten miles west of the target, the attacks by the defenders commenced in earnest. The attacks by the Mustangs were hardly what one would term 'good tactics', as they were doing vertical dives through 'gaggles' and single head-on attacks on fighter formations – I consider they would all have been 'chopped' quite quickly, with little loss to ourselves. A first-class mêlée ensued for nearly fifteen minutes, very reminiscent of a 'dawn patrol' show, and one had views of aircraft from every conceivable angle – some unpleasantly close. After fifteen minutes the wing leader 'called us off', and quite the most impressive part of the show was that, despite the constant breaks and turn-abouts, the wing was still in one piece and had re-formed and set course in under two minutes. We landed at Treviso, refuelled and returned to base, having done three hours' flying for each aircraft. Altogether an informative and pleasant operation.

The CO also commented on the heightening of tension in the region with the dispute over Trieste in his end-of-month diary summary:

The next point of interest has been the reversion to the 'good old days' of a tentative readiness and a general air of flap. Movements have been confined, in general, to a ten-mile radius of camp, although Velden and Venice leave continued, but active pilots on tour-ex or release have been held up, pending an easing of tension.

The pilots have been active belting-up and generally servicing ops equipment – good practice for them, as in many cases it is new to them. The wing has been on its 'mobile toes', ready for the practice Operation Shambles – when one squadron at a time will move on a war basis to the far side of the 'drome and live under canvas. One can't help but feel, in view of the fact that we have become infinitely more static than mobile, that the operation was aptly named.

As July opened, the dispute over Trieste continued, and the squadron was ordered to prepare a forward operating base at Lavoriana in Italy. Believing itself safe from being called to take part in Operation Shambles for at least another week, the squadron was somewhat shocked when it was ordered to up sticks and join 111 Sqn in the field on the 5th. It was fortunate that, though showing signs of wear, its tentage was in a much better condition than 111's. Nevertheless, after three days of heavy downpours, the squadron was ordered back to the other side of the airfield, much to the relief of those involved. The two objects of the move into the field had been achieved by ironing out the snags thrown up by being static for so long and acclimatizing the new personnel to rapid moves and living in the field, even if most of those involved left for home on release about a week later.

August opened with the wing taking part in the DAF Arms Test on the 2nd, followed the next day by the event of the year, the Wing Officers' Dance. This in turn led to a stand-down the next day. By the 7th the squadron could only muster one Spitfire per day for flying, due to a tyre shortage. By the 12th there were still no tyres available, and the pilots were reduced to cleaning and polishing Perspex canopies and testing the jettisoning of the aforementioned items.

Squadron pilots living under canvas in Austria in 1945. (via L.J. Barton)

72 Sqn was not the only unit affected, and the lack of spares for the wings in the region was becoming critical, grounding most Spitfires except for essential flying. By the 15th the situation had improved very slightly, and the squadrons were allowed two aircraft per day for flying. The pilots now turned their hands to respraying the Spitfires, which had not been repainted for years, during this period of enforced idleness.

At long last some tyres arrived for the wing on the 29th, and limited flying recommenced. All was not well, however, as not long after the tyres were fitted Flt Sgt Cowell came back from an aerobatics sortie to make a dead-stick landing, out of fuel. He had been flying Spitfire RN-A fitted with a Merlin 70 engine, and had been using high revs and boost; it was a lucky escape.

By September the weather was beginning to affect flying again, and the tyre shortage once more reared its head, reducing the squadron's effort to have four aircraft flying per day. Throughout this period the squadron was plagued with persistent rumours of a move of base, and consequently the flying effort was cut to two per day just in case.

On the 12th, Flt Sgt Roberts, a pilot on loan to the squadron for training, was on his second solo in a Spitfire when he burst a tyre on landing. He was able to keep the Spitfire straight and undamaged, and his creditable performance was noted. Unfortunately Flt Sgt Boddice did not do quite so well that day. Flying as Red 2, his engine cut out over Knittelfeld at 5,000 ft, and he attempted a glide-landing. Unfortunately his speed dropped off and the Spitfire (ML194) spun in from 50 ft on the edge of the airfield. The Spitfire was a complete write-off, with the port wing and engine ripped off. Boddice escaped with minor bruises.

On the 13th the persistent rumours came true, and the squadron was informed that 244 Wing would move in from Treviso, while 239 Wing would move from Tissano to Treviso and 324 Wing would move to Tissano. The squadron was very disappointed to be leaving Zeltweg.

In scenes reminiscent of the advance up the length of Italy, the squadron's 'A' party began loading vehicles for the move on the 16th, and left early on the 17th for Tissano, arriving later in the day. On the 23rd the Spitfires flew in to the new base, taking an hour to fly over. The squadron took over the 93 Sqn dispersal, and found it to be 'a pretty disgusting mess'. The hard standing for the Spitfires was a section of runway which was in bad repair and covered in loose stones. The runway in use was little better, and one of 43 Squadron's pilots ran off it on landing, turning his Spitfire over. The pilot was unhurt. The squadron immediately began to settle in and sort out the mess left by 93 Sqn. The rear party arrived on the 24th.

By the 28th the squadron was making good progress in settling in to its new quarters but two problems were limiting flying. The first was the lack of tyres once more, and the second the need to restrict flying to mornings only, to allow repairs to be carried out to the runway in the afternoon. The squadron's wing partner, 43 Sqn, was still having little luck with the poor state of the runway, and another Spitfire ran off the runway on the 30th, collapsing its undercarriage.

Spitfire Mk IX ML194:RN-C crashed by Eric Boddice at Zeltweg. (E. Boddice)

The whole wing was kept busy as October opened with bombing practice on the Tagliamento range; however, the run of bad luck for 43 Sqn continued, with the loss of a pilot and Spitfire on the 9th, when the pilot failed to recover from a bombing dive. The following day 72 Sqn was lucky not to have lost a pilot. During an interception exercise, following which 72 claimed to have shot down the whole of 111 Sqn, Flt Lt Garnham dislocated his left shoulder while closing the canopy after take-off. He made an excellent job of landing the aircraft, despite the pain and discomfort he was suffering.

Eric Boddice aged 17. (E. Boddice)

On the 16th the squadron took part in a twenty-seven-aircraft flypast in honour of General Eisenhower, who was inspecting a guard of honour at Campoformido. The General sent his congratulations to the wing following the flypast. The remainder of the month was taken up with bombing and strafing practice on the nearby ranges.

November brought a worsening in the political situation over Trieste, and on the 5th there was a bit of a flap when the squadron was ordered to bring twelve aircraft to armed readiness at 0310 hrs. The panic subsided at 1000 hrs, but the squadron remained at fifteen minutes' readiness until 1730 hrs. The next day it was a repeat performance, with 43 Sqn holding readiness this time. On the 8th the readiness reverted to 72 Sqn, and this situation continued until the 14th, when the readiness state was reduced to thirty mins, alternating between the squadrons of the wing. By the end of the month the readiness flap was over, and in any case the weather as December opened was so poor that flying ceased for long periods. The weather had not improved by Christmas Eve, but this did not stop the wing from pulling all the stops out to celebrate. The festivities continued through Christmas Day and Boxing Day, and flying resumed on the 27th. As the squadron celebrated, though, rumours of impending disbandment had been heard, and the CO closed the squadron diary for the year with the following comment:

If the rumour is correct, 72 will cease to be early in the New Year, at the end of a highly creditable and eventful life in peace and war – a name and number which will live for always in the memories of those who served in it, and a just place for it will be found in the illustrious annals of the Royal Air Force.

The rumours were true, and the squadron did disband in January 1947 – but not for long.

Squadron Commanders, 1942–47

22 Aug 1942 to 23 Apr 1943	Sqn Ldr R.W. Oxspring DFC
24 Apr 1943 to 19 Dec 1943	Sqn Ldr S.W. Daniel DFC
19 Dec 1943 to 3 Jan 1944	Maj A.C. Bosman DFC SAAF
3 Jan 1944 to 12 Apr 1944	Sqn Ldr J.M.V. Carpenter DFC
12 Apr 1944 to 18 Nov 1944	Sqn Ldr C.I.R. Arthur DFC
18 Nov 1944 to 15 Feb 1945	Sqn Ldr P.L. Parrott DFC
15 Feb 1945 to 3 Apr 1945	Sqn Ldr K.N.R. Sissons
3 Apr 1945 to 21 Apr 1945	Maj H.E. Wells SAAF
21 Apr 1945 to 1 May 1945	Capt W.E. Colehan SAAF
1 May 1945 to 27 Jul 1945	Sqn Ldr E. Cassidy DFC
27 Jul 1945 to 14 Oct 1945	Sqn Ldr D.J. Johnson
14 Oct 1945 to 11 Feb. 1946	Sqn Ldr T.W.B. Hudson
11 Feb 1946 to Jan 1947	Sqn Ldr J.R. Cock DFC

Squadron Bases, 1942–47

NORTH AFRICA

Gibraltar	Nov 1942 to 16 Nov 1942
Maison Blanche	16 Nov 1942 to 18 Nov 1942
Bone	18 Nov 1942 to 20 Nov 1942
Souk el Arba	20 Nov 1942 to 15 Jan 1943
Souk el Khemis	15 Jan 1943 to 12 May 1943
La Sebala	13 May 1943 to 23 May 1943
Utique	23 May 1943 to 26 May 1943
Mateur	26 May 1943 to 10 Jun 1943

MALTA

Hal Far	10 Jun 1943 to 16 Jul 1943

SICILY

Comiso	16 Jul 1943 to 30 Jul 1943
Pachino	30 Jul 1943 to 29 Aug 1943
Panebianco	29 Aug 1943 to 2 Sep 1943
Cassala	2 Sep 1943 to 13 Sep 1943

ITALY

Tusciano	13 Sep 1943 to 11 Oct 1943
Naples	11 Oct 1943 to 16 Jan 1944
Lago	16 Jan 1944 to 5 Jun 1944
Tre-Cancelli	5 Jun 1944 to 13 Jun 1944
Tarquinia	13 Jun 1944 to 25 Jun 1944
Grosetto	25 Jun 1944 to 5 Jul 1944
Piombino	5 Jul 1944 to 20 Jul 1944

CORSICA

Calvi	20 Jul 1944 to 25 Aug 1944

SOUTHERN FRANCE

Ramatuelle	25 Aug 1944 to 27 Aug 1944
Sisteron	27 Aug 1944 to 7 Sep 1944
Bron	7 Sep 1944 to 27 Sep 1944
La Jasse	27 Sep 1944 to 2 Oct 1944.

ITALY

Florence	2 Oct 1944 to 16 Nov 1944
Rimini	16 Nov 1944 to 17 Feb 1945
Ravenna	17 Feb 1945 to 4 May 1945
Rivolto	4 May 1945 to 11 May 1945

AUSTRIA

Klagenfurt	11 May 1945 to 8 Sep 1945
Zeltweg	8 Sep 1945 to 2 Oct 1945
Campoformido (detachment)	2 Oct 1945 to 22 Oct 1945
Zeltweg	22 Oct 1945 to 23 Sep 1946

ITALY

Tissano	23 Sep 1946 to Jan 1947

Aircraft Operated by No. 72 Squadron, 1942–47

SUPERMARINE SPITFIRE Mk Vb

P8541	To 64 Sqn
P8545	To 72 Sqn 30 Apr 1942. To 350 Sqn 20 May 1942.
P8560	From 74 Sqn 19 Jun 1941. To ASTH 14 Aug 1941.
P8600:RN-L *Lady Linlithgow*	Missing 10 Jul 1941.
P8604	Missing 10 Jul 1941.
P8609 *Heart of England II*	To 72 Sqn 27 Jul 1941. Ran out of fuel on return from sweep and abandoned 3 miles off Ramsgate, 27 Aug 1941.
P8700	To 72 Sqn 7 Dec 1941. To 154 Sqn 16 Mar 1942.
P8713	To 72 Sqn 27 Jul 1941. Missing escorting Blenheims to Hazebrouck 29 Aug 1941.
P8741	
P8744 *Wonkers*	To 72 Sqn 21 Nov 1941. To Westlands 11 Jan 1942.
P8749	To 72 Sqn 9 Jul 1941. To 610 Sqn 11 Jul 1941.
P8750	To 72 Sqn 9 Jul 1941. To Scottish Aviation 1 Aug 1941.
P8751	To 72 Sqn 10 Jul 1941. To Scottish Aviation 29 Jul 1941.
P8757:RN-Q *Quthung*	To 72 Sqn 14 Jul 1941. To 154 Sqn 13 Jun 1942.
P8783	To 72 Sqn 12 Jul 1941. To 401 Sqn 31 Dec 1941.
R7219 *Absque Labore Nihil*	From 74 Sqn. Shot down by fighters escorting Blenheims to Hazebrouck l4 Jul 1941.
R7228	From 74 Sqn 29 Jul 1941. Wheels prematurely raised on take-off; hit ground and crash-landed 1½ m SW of Valley, 26 Aug 1941.
R7265 *Grimsby I*	To 72 Sqn 30 Sep 1941. Engine failed on take-off at Gravesend 5 Dec 1941. To Westland.
R7298	To 72 Sqn 28 Oct 1941. To ASTE 5 Dec 1941.
W3168	From 92 Sqn 24 Oct 1941. To 133 Sqn 15 Jun 1942.
W3170:RN-H *Henley on Thames*	From 74 Sqn 27 Jul 1941. Overturned on downwind landing at Martlesham Heath 5 Apr 1942.

W3178 *Thebe*	To 72 Sqn. To 401 Sqn 27 Sep 1941.
W3181 *City of Leeds I*	From 92 Sqn 9 Jul 1941. Ditched in English Channel while escorting Stirlings to Lille 19 Jul 1941. Sgt R.F. Lewis killed.
W3229	To 72 Sqn 8 Jul 1941. To 306 Sqn 3 Sep 1941.
W3256	To 72 Sqn 8 Jul 1941. Missing escorting Blenheims to Mazingarbe 23 Jul 1941.
W3259	From 74 Sqn. To 74 Sqn.
W3316:RN-M *City of Salford*	To 72 Sqn 29 Jun 1941. Missing escorting Blenheims to Hazebrouck 24 Jul 1941.
W3321 *Elcardo The Thistle*	From 74 Sqn 19 Aug 1941. To 124 Sqn 29 Jun 1942.
W3367 *Lerumo*	From 74 Sqn 29 Jul 1941. Shot down by fighters on sweep to St Omer 7 Nov 1941. Plt Off H. Birkland (RCAF) POW.
W3380 *Basuto*	From 74 Sqn 27 Jul 1941. To ASTH 29 Aug 1941.
W3406:RN-I *Auckland II Mission Bay*	From 452 Sqn 13 Feb 1942. Shot down by Bf 109 escorting 6 Bostons to Abbeville marshalling yards 25 Apr 1942.
W3408 *Mr and Mrs Albert Ehrman*	To 72 Sqn 8 Jul 1941. Missing escorting Blenheims to Rotterdam 28 Aug 1941.
W3411	From 74 Sqn. Missing (Fruges) 10 Jul 1941.
W3429 *Mohale's Hoek/ Berea*	To 72 Sqn 20 Jul 1941. To 222 Sqn 15 Feb 1942.
W3430	*President Roosevelt I* To 72 Sqn 20 Jul 1941. To 222 Sqn 14 May 1942.
W3431:RN-K *Kaapstad III*	To 72 Sqn 24 Jul 1941. To 403 Sqn 31 Dec 1941.
W3437:RN-L	
W3440 *Trengganu*	To 72 Sqn 10 Jul 1941. To 401 Sqn 8 Dec 1941.
W3441 *Alloway*	To 72 Sqn 10 Jul 1941. To 417 Sqn 24 Apr 1942.
W3446:RN-J *Jennifer/ Richards Basuto*	To 72 Sqn 1 May 1942. To 350 Sqn 20 May 1942.
W3511	To 72 Sqn 27 Jul 1941. Missing escorting Hurricanes to St Pol 8 Nov 1941. Plt Off N.E. Bishop killed.
W3513	To 72 Sqn 31 Jul 1941. To 54 Sqn 10 Oct 1941.
W3516	To 72 Sqn 27 Jul 1941. Missing on ground attack mission to Calais area 19 Sep 1941.
W3618	To 72 Sqn 30 Aug 1941. To 315 Sqn 1 Sep 1941.
W3624	To 72 Sqn 2 Jan 1942. To 504 Sqn 8 Jul 1942.
W3630 *Kuwait*	From 403 Sqn 20 Oct 1941. To 124 Sqn 17 Nov 1941.
W3648 *Wisbech*	From 609 Sqn 20 Aug 1941. To AST.
W3704 *Quacha's Nek*	To 72 Sqn 19 Sep 1941. Missing presumed shot down by Bf 109 near Dunkerque during sweep 25 Oct 1941. Plt Off Falkiner missing.

W3771	To 72 Sqn 30 Aug 1941. To ASTH 9 Sep 1941.
W3841	To 72 Sqn 14 Apr 1942. To 121 Sqn 29 May 1942.
AA749 *Moshesh*	To 72 Sqn 3 Oct 1941. Missing from a ground-attack mission 8 Dec 1941.
AA841	From 412 Sqn 14 Apr 1942. To 121 Sqn 24 May 1942.
AA854	
AA864	To 72 Sqn 19 Oct 1941. Missing from sweep near Hesdin 8 Dec 1941.
AA867	To 72 Sqn 22 Oct 1941. To 222 Sqn 14 Mar 1942.
AA913	To 72 Sqn 12 Nov 1941. To 303 Sqn 8 Apr 1942.
AA914	To 72 Sqn 12 Nov 1941. Swung while taxiing in crosswind into an excavation at Biggin Hill 15 Apr 1942.
AA915	To 72 Sqn 12 Nov 1941. To 145 Sqn 15 Nov 1941.
AA920	To 72 Sqn 30 Nov 1941. To 124 Sqn 26 Mar 1942.
AA924	From 501 Sqn 26 Apr 1942. To 306 Sqn 18 May 1942.
AA945:RN-C	To 72 Sqn 11 Dec 1941. To 306 Sqn 22 Aug 1942.
AB150	To 72 Sqn 16 Dec 1941. Abandoned after engine cut 15 miles off Dunkerque 29 May 1942. Flg Off B.O. Parker (RCAF) killed.
AB152	From 124 Sqn. Spun into ground near Biggin Hill on 28 May 1942.
AB194	To 72 Sqn 16 Dec 1941. To 111 Sqn 28 Feb 1942.
AB258	To 72 Sqn 28 Dec 1941. Missing presumed shot down near St Omer 4 Apr 1942.
AB260	From 611 Sqn 4 Aug 1942. To 504 Sqn 21 Jun 1943.
AB283:RN-F, RN-E	To 72 Sqn 2 Jan 1942. To ASTH.
AB324 *Mafeteng*	To 72 Sqn. To Middle East 3 May 1942.
AB375	From 124 Sqn. Shot down by Bf 109s near Calais on 24 Apr 1942.
AB806	To 72 Sqn 22 Aug 1941. To 401 Sqn 21 Oct 1941. To 72 Sqn 23 Mar 1942. Shot down by Spitfire off Beachy Head 1 Jul 1942. Gp Capt P.R. Barwell DFC killed.
AB817 *Leribe*	To 72 Sqn 29 Aug 1941. To 452 Sqn 5 Mar 1942.
AB818 *Maseru*	To 72 Sqn 30 Aug 1941. To AST 7 Dec 1941.
AB822 *Harding*	To 72 Sqn 30 Aug 1941. Shot down by Bf 109 10 miles off Dover, 26 Oct 1941, Sgt L. Stock killed.
AB843	To 72 Sqn 28 Jul 1941. Missing from sweep to Mazingarbe, presumed shot down by Bf 109s near Mardyck 27 Sep 1941. Sgt A.F. Binns killed.
AB848	To 72 Sqn 28 Dec 1941. To 332 Sqn 20 Aug 1942.
AB854	To 72 Sqn 27 Jul 1941. To AST 23 Aug 1941.

AB855	From 611 Sqn 24 Oct 1941. Missing near St Pol 8 Nov 1941, Sgt D.R. White killed.
AB864 *Makesi*	To 72 Sqn 30 Sep 1941. To AST 23 Dec 1941.
AB870	To 72 Sqn 18 Nov 1941. To 308 Sqn 24 Aug 1942.
AB879 *Hawkes Bay I Dannaevirke*	To 72 Sqn.
AB893 *Lilepe*	To 72 Sqn 20 Aug 1941. Abandoned after engine problems on return from sweep 19 miles E of Dungeness, 8 Nov 1941.
AB922 *Liphamola*	To 72 Sqn 29 Aug 1941. To 401 Sqn 26 Oct 1941.
AB979	To 72 Sqn 4 Apr 1942. Collided with AB150 while taxiing at Biggin Hill 13 Apr 1942. To Westland.
AD134	To 72 Sqn 30 Aug 1941. To 401 Sqn 17 Mar 1942.
AD183:RN-H	To 72 Sqn 30 Sep 1941. On return from Boston escort the pilot baled out over Brighton. Crashed near Ditchling, Sussex, 15 Mar 1942.
AD274 *Mokhotlong*	To 72 Sqn 11 Oct 1941. To ASTH.
AD324	To 72 Sqn 24 Oct 1941. To GAL.
AD347:RN-C	To 72 Sqn 2 May 1942. Damaged Cat B on ops 8 Jun 1942. To Westland.
AD375	To 72 Sqn 23 Mar 1942. Missing presumed shot down by Fw 190s SE of Calais, 12 Apr 1942.
AD386	To 72 Sqn 5 Apr 1942. To 133 Sqn 15 Jun 1942.
AD467	To 72 Sqn 28 Oct 1941. To ASTH 28 Nov 1941.
AD513	From 121 Sqn. To 340 Sqn.
AR347	To 167 Sqn
BL267	From 610 Sqn 29 Jul 1942. To 222 Sqn 15 Aug 1942.
BL318	To 72 Sqn 15 Dec 1941.
BL331	To 72 Sqn 8 Jan 1942. To 616 Sqn 8 Jan 1942.
BL334:RN-I	From 222 Sqn 26 Apr 1942. To 411 Sqn 18 May 1942.
BL338	To 72 Sqn 21 Nov 1941. To ASTH.
BL345	To 72 Sqn 8 Jan 1942. To 616 Sqn 8 Jan 1942.
BL418	From 611 Sqn 4 Aug 1942. To 71 Sqn 12 Aug 1942.
BL496	To 72 Sqn 26 Jan 1942. To 65 Sqn 26 Jan 1942.
BL516	To 72 Sqn 13 May 1942. To USAAF 6 Sep 1942.
BL636	From 611 Sqn 4 Aug 1942. To 71 Sqn 13 Aug 1942.
BL638 *Borough of Acton*	To 72 Sqn. To VASM 10 Oct 1942.
BL721 *Garut*	To 72 Sqn 22 Feb 1942. Escort Bostons to St Omer, hit by flak and shot down 4 Apr 1942.
BL728	To 72 Sqn 15 Mar 1942. To 111S 16 May 1942.
BL733	To 72 Sqn 4 Apr 1942. To ASTH.
BL763	To 72 Sqn 26 Apr 1942. To 340 Sqn 18 May 1942.
BL773	To 72 Sqn 22 Feb 1942. To GAL 15 Mar 1942.

BL810	From 611 Sqn 4 Aug 1942. To 303 Sqn 1 Jun 1943.
BL857	To 72 Sqn 15 Feb 1942. Engine cut, force-landed 2 miles N of Eastchurch 12 Apr 1942.
BL864	To 72 Sqn 17 Mar 1942. SOC 13 Apr 1942.
BL935	To 72 Sqn 3 Mar 1942. Missing presumed shot down by fighters near St Omer, Flt Sgt T. Watson killed.
BL941	To 72 Sqn 13 Apr 1942. To 411 Sqn 18 May 1942.
BL979	From 401 Sqn 4 Apr 1942. To AST.
BM117	From 611 Sqn 4 Aug 1942. To AST 29 Oct 1942.
BM122	From 611 Sqn 4 Aug 1942. To Scottish Aviation.
BM125	To 72 Sqn 4 Apr 1942. Missing presumed shot down by Fw 190s SE of Calais 24 Apr 1942. Sgt R.P.G. Reilly killed.
BM143	From 611 Sqn 4 Aug 1942. To HAL 3 Nov 1942.
BM189	From 611 Sqn 4 Aug 1942. Hit h/t cables in mock attack and made a wheels-up landing at Dalmellington, Ayr, 6 Aug 1942. To Scottish Aviation.
BM192	From 611 Sqn 4 Aug 1942. To HAL 9 Nov 1942.
BM193	From 71 Sqn.
BM195	From 611 Sqn 29 Jul 1942. To 610 Sqn 27 Dec 1942.
BM210:RN-Z	
BM211	From 611 Sqn 4 Aug 1942. To 416 Sqn 29 Mar 1943.
BM253	From 501 Sqn 16 May 1942. To 65 Sqn 4 Aug 1942.
BM256:RN-F *Dorothy Mary*	From 501 Sqn 16 May 1942. To 65 Sqn 4 Aug 1942.
BM265:RN-T *The Pride of Newport*	From 331 Sqn 12 May 1942. To 243 Sqn 30 Aug 1942.
BM271 (LF Mk Vb) *Kenya Daisy*	From 133 Sqn 15 Jun 1942. To 65 Sqn 29 Mar 1943.
BM290	To 72 Sqn Summer 1942.
BM291	To 72 Sqn.
BM300:RN-E	From 133 Sqn 15 Jun 1942. To 65 Sqn 4 Aug 1942.
BM313:RN-H *Connie*	From 331 Sqn 12 May 1942. To 234 Sqn 4 Jun 1942.
BM326	From 501 Sqn 14 May 1942. To 65 Sqn 4 Aug 1942.
BM327	To 72 Sqn 10 May 1942. To AST 16 Jul 1942.
BM345	From 331 Sqn 12 May 1942. To AST 16 May 1942.
BM361	From 41 Sqn 28 Jul 1942. To 71 Sqn 2 Aug 1942.
BM366	To 72 Sqn 29 Jul 1942. To 41 Sqn 2 Aug 1942.
BM384	To 72 Sqn 17 Apr 1942. Crashed into the sea while checking a raft off Dungeness 9 May 1942. Plt Off D.O. Waters RNZAF killed.
BM402	To 72 Sqn 15 May 1942. To RAE Jun 1942.

BM413	From 611 Sqn 4 Aug 1942. To 232 Sqn 23 Sep 1942.
BM418	From 133 Sqn 15 Jun 1942. To 65 Sqn 4 Aug 1942.
BM450	To 72 Sqn. Force landed at Biggin Hill 5 June 1942. To 65 Sqn.
BM470	From 133 Sqn 15 Jun 1942. To 52 OTU 5 Feb 1943.
BM484	To 72 Sqn 16 May 1942. Shot down by Fw 190s near Calais 26 Jul 1942. Sqn Ldr H.R. Tidd killed.
BM485	To 72 Sqn 16 May 1942. To 65 Sqn 14 Aug 1942.
BM490	From 132 Sqn 15 Jun 1942. To 322 Sqn 3 Aug 1942.
BM492	From 132 Sqn 15 Jun 1942. To VASM 18 Aug 1943.
BM495	To 72 Sqn.
BM515	From 133 Sqn 15 Jun 1942. To 65 Sqn 4 Aug 1942.
BM516	To 72 Sqn 10 May 1942. To 65 Sqn 14 Aug 1942.
BM518	From 133 Sqn 15 Jun 1942. To 65 Sqn 4 Aug 1942.
BM529	From 133 Sqn 14 Jun 1942. To 65 Sqn 4 Aug 1942.
BM591	To 72 Sqn 7 Jun 1942. To 133 Sqn 15 Jun 1942.
BM636	From 71 Sqn.
BM653	To 72 Sqn 12 Jul 1942. To 315 Sqn 4 Sep 1942.
EN793	From 121 Sqn 28 Jul 1942. To 306 Sqn 20 Aug 1942.
EP181	To 72 Sqn 10 Sep 1942. To 602 Sqn 18 Dec 1942.
EP183	From 302 Sqn 10 Sep 1942. To 610 Sqn 25 Mar 1943.
EP285	To 72 Sqn 28 Jul 1942. To 52 OTU 27 Jan 1943.
EP597	To 72 Sqn 30 Aug 1942. To VASM 21 Jun 1943.
EP904	To Gibraltar 14 Sep 1942. To 72 Sqn. Damaged Cat 2 5 Jan 1943.
EP911	To Gibraltar 1 Nov 1942. To 72 Sqn. SOC 31 Dec 1942.
EP914	To Gibraltar 1 Nov 1942. To 72 Sqn. To NW Africa 28 Feb 1943.
EP962	To Gibraltar 6 Nov 1942. To 72 Sqn. To NW Africa 28 Feb 1943.
EP981	To 72 Sqn 1 Nov 1942. To NW Africa 28 Feb 1943.
ER142	To Gibraltar 1 Nov 1942. To 72 Sqn. To Malta 1 Jul 1943.
ER257	To Gibraltar 1 Nov 1942. To 72 Sqn. SOC 31 Jan 1943.
ER307	To Gibraltar 9 Nov 1942. To 72 Sqn. To NW Africa.
ER490	To Gibraltar 6 Nov 1942. To 72 Sqn. To NW Africa 28 Feb 1943.
ER555	To Gibraltar 6 Nov 1942. To 72 Sqn. SOC 31 Jan 1943.
ER564	To Gibraltar 6 Nov 1942. To 72 Sqn. To NW Africa 28 Feb 1943.
ER586	To 72 Sqn. Belly-landed near Mateur 21 Dec 1942.
ER589	To 72 Sqn.

ER590	To Takoradi 27 Dec 1942. To 72 Sqn. To Middle East 18 Jan 1943.
ER598	To Gibraltar 6 Nov 1942. To 72 Sqn. To Middle East 23 Dec 1942.
ER603	To Gibraltar 6 Nov 1942. To 72 Sqn. SOC 31 Dec 1942.
ER615	To Gibraltar 6 Nov 1942. To 72 Sqn. To 111 Sqn.
ER620:RN-Z	To Gibraltar 6 Nov 1942. To 72 Sqn. Nosed over on landing Souk el Khemis, damaged Cat 2 17 Dec 1942.
ER635:RN-M	To Malta 1 Jul 1943. To 72 Sqn. SOC 26 Apr 1945.
ER656	To Gibraltar 6 Nov 1942. Crashed in forced landing 15 miles S of Souk el Khemis 8 Feb 1943.
ER660	To Gibraltar 9 Nov 1942. To 72 Sqn. To NW Africa 28 Feb 1943.
ER678	To 72 Sqn. Collided with ER589 and crashed W of Jefra 26 Jan 1943.
ER726	To 72 Sqn. FTR ops 2 Jan 1943.
ER732	To 72 Sqn. Damaged in air raid at Souk el Arba 31 Dec 1942.
ER808	To 72 Sqn. To Middle East 19 Jan 1943.
ER812	To 72 Sqn. Damaged Cat 3 on ops 17 Jan 1943.
ER878	To 72 Sqn. Hit by ER598 after landing at Souk el Khemis, 23 Jan 1943.
ER962	To 72 Sqn. Missing from ground-attack mission 5 Jan 1943.
ER964	To 72 Sqn.

SUPERMARINE SPITFIRE Mk Vc

EE799:RN-K	Probable serial error, as this aircraft crashed in UK.
EE811	To 72 Sqn Nov 1943. To NW African AF 11 Jan 1944.
EF599:RN-F	To Malta 1 Aug 1943. To 72 Sqn. To NW African AF 1 Nov 1943.
EF640:RN-V	To 72 Sqn 30 Nov 1943. SOC 26 Apr 1945.
EF648:RN-M	Missing from ground-attack mission near Rome 2 Dec 1943.
EF656	To 72 Sqn Oct 1943. To NW African AF 30 Nov 1943.
ER635:RN-M	To 72 Sqn Oct 1943. SOC 26 Apr 1945.
ES107:RN-C	To 72 Sqn Jul 1943. To N Africa 30 Nov 1943
ES281	To 72 Sqn. To Sicily 1 Aug 1943.
JG746:RN-B, RN-E	To 72 Sqn. To Malta 1 Jul 1943.
JG771:RN-K	To 72 Sqn. To Malta 1 Jul 1943.
JG793:RN-E	To 72 Sqn. To Malta 1 Jul 1943.
JG806:RN-E *Port of Sudan Kassala*	To 72 Sqn. To Malta 1 Jul 1943.

JK132:RN-B *El Fasher Darfur Province*	From 154 Sqn. To 3 Sqn SAAF.
JK173	To 72 Sqn 1 Jul 1943.
JK180	To 72 Sqn Aug 1943. To NW African AF 1 Nov 1943.
JK271	To 72 Sqn Dec 1943. SOC 26 Apr 1945.
JK275:RN-F	To 72 Sqn. To Malta 1 Jul 1943.
JK322	To Gibraltar 24 Mar 1943. To 72 Sqn. To Malta 1 Jul 1943.
JK364:RN-H	To 72 Sqn Oct 1943. To NW African AF 1 Nov 1943.
JK368:RN-J	To 72 Sqn. To N Africa 1 Jan 1944.
JK372	To 72 Sqn Jul 1943.
JK429:RN-N	To Malta 1 Jul 1943. To 72 Sqn. Missing from sweep over Sicily 12 Jul 1943.
JK450:RN-X	To 72 Sqn. To Malta 1 Jul 1943.
JK456	To 72 Sqn Oct 1943. To NW African AF 1 Nov 1943.
JK460	To 72 Sqn Aug 1943. To NW African AF 30 Sep 1943.
JK466	To 72 Sqn Jul 1943.
JK468:RN-H	To 72 Sqn 1 Jul 1943. To Middle East 30 Sep 1943.
JK549	To 72 Sqn Aug 1943. To Italy 1 Nov 1943.
JK599	To 72 Sqn.
JK637	To 72 Sqn. To Malta 1 Jul 1943.
JK659:RN-D	To 72 Sqn Feb 1945. FTR ops 23 Feb 1945.
JK786	To 72 Sqn Jul 1943.
JK806	To 72 Sqn Jul 1943. To Armée de l'Air GC2/7 31 Aug 1943.
JK826	To 72 Sqn. Hit a soft patch and overturned on take-off at Falcone 10 Sep 1943.
JK878	To 72 Sqn Dec 1943. SOC 31 May 1945.
JK930:RN-G, RN-K	To 72 Sqn Jul 1943.
JK944	To 72 Sqn Oct 1943. SOC 29 Aug 1946.
JK990:RN-M	To 72 Sqn Jul 1943. To Sicily 1 Aug 1943.
JL127	To 72 Sqn Dec 1943. Engine cut, ditched off Corinth 15 Oct 1944.
JL176	To 72 Sqn Dec 1943. To Middle East 30 Nov 1945.
JK180:RN-S	To 72 Sqn. To NW African AF 1 Nov 1943.
JL365	To 72 Sqn Dec 1943.
JL368	To 72 Sqn Oct 1943. To SS703 1 Jun 1944.

SUPERMARINE SPITFIRE Mk VIII

Possibly MK118	To 72 Sqn 6 Aug 1944. Crashed on landing at Calvi 8 Aug 1944.
**760	To 72 Sqn Aug 1944
MT786	To 72 Sqn Aug 1944. To 43 Sqn Aug 1944.

SUPERMARINE SPITFIRE Mk IX

BR623	From 611 Sqn 24 Jul 1942. To 401 Sqn 27 Jul 1942.
BR626	To 72 Sqn 24 Jul 1942. To 401 Sqn 27 Jul 1942.
BR628	To 72 Sqn 24 Jul 1942. To 401 Sqn 27 Jul 1942.
BR630	To 72 Sqn 24 Jul 1942. To 401 Sqn 27 Jul 1942.
BR981	To 72 Sqn 24 Jul 1942. To 401 Sqn 27 Jul 1942.
BR982	To 72 Sqn 24 Jul 1942. To 401 Sqn 27 Jul 1942.
BR985	To 72 Sqn 24 Jul 1942. To 401 Sqn 27 Jul 1942.
BR986	To 72 Sqn 24 Jul 1942. To 401 Sqn 27 Jul 1942.
BS104	To 72 Sq. 25 Jul 1942. To 401 Sqn 27 Jul 1942.
BS119	To 72 Sqn 24 Jul 1942. To 401 Sqn 27 Jul 1942.
BS120	To 72 Sqn 24 Jul 1942. To 401 Sqn 27 Jul 1942.
BS157	To 72 Sqn 24 Jul 1942. To 401 Sqn 27 Jul 1942.
BS159	To 72 Sqn 24 Jul 1942. To 401 Sqn 27 Jul 1942.
BS172	To 72 Sqn 24 Jul 1942. To 401 Sqn 27 Jul 1942.
BS176	To 72 Sqn 24 Jul 1942. To 401 Sqn 27 Jul 1942.
BS177	To 72 Sqn 24 Jul 1942. To 401 Sqn 27 Jul 1942.
BS180	To 72 Sqn 24 Jul 1942. To 401 Sqn 27 Jul 1942.
BS337	To Gibraltar 6 Feb 1943. To 72 Sqn. To NW Africa 31 Mar 1943.
BS358	To 72 Sqn 12 Feb 1943.
BS500:RN-V	
BS550	To Gibraltar 6 Feb 1943. To 72 Sqn. To NW Africa 28 Feb 1943.
BS553	To 72 Sqn 12 Feb 1943.
BS558	
EN107	To 72 Sqn Jul 1943.
EN116:RN-A	To 72 Sqn 12 Feb 1943. Collided with Bf 109 and crash-landed at Oued Zarga 19 Apr 1943.
EN135:RN-E	To 72 Sqn 12 Feb 1943.
EN136	Abandoned near Medjez el Bab 25 Mar 1943.
EN144:RN-D	To 72 Sqn 1 Jul 1943. To Middle East 30 Oct 1943.
EN147	To 72 Sqn Jul 1943. To NW African AF 1943.
EN148:GK-G	To 72 Sqn. Wg Cdr Gilroy, 324 Wg leader's aircraft. To Malta 1 Jul 1943.
EN152	To 72 Sqn Feb 1945. SOC 14 Mar 1946.
EN191	From 1435 Sqn. To 72 Sqn. Tyre burst on take-off and swung off runway at Ravenna 4 Mar 1945.
EN195:RN-H	
EN200	
EN201	
EN242:RN-D	To 72 Sqn 12 Feb 1943.
EN244	From 81 Sqn 26 Apr 1943. To Middle East 21 Feb 1945.

EN245	To 72 Sqn 12 Feb 1943.
EN246	Stalled on approach at Souk el Khemis, 25 Feb 1943.
EN250:RN-J	To 72 Sqn 12 Feb 1943. Damaged by Bf 109s and crash-landed near Medjez el Bab, 3 Apr 1943.
EN251	
EN252	To 72 Sqn. To Malta 1 Jul 1943.
EN258:RN-Y	To 72 Sqn 1 Jul 1943. To N African ASC 31 Oct 1943.
EN259:RN-K	To 72 Sqn Jul 1943. To 111 Sqn.
EN278	
EN289	
EN291:RN-S	To 111 Sqn.
EN292	To 72 Sqn 12 Feb 1943. Shot down by Bf 109s near Medjez el Bab 11 Apr 1943.
EN294	
EN298:RN-J, RN-B	To 72 Sqn 12 Feb 1943. Shot down by fighters near Biscari 20 Jun 1943.
EN299:RN-H	To 72 Sqn 12 Feb 1943.
EN301:RN-Z	
EN303:RN-G, RN-F	
EN309:RN-Q, RN-N	To 72 Sqn 12 Feb 1943. Hit by debris from Bf 109 and crashed near Augusta 16 Jul 1943.
EN311:RN-G	To 72 Sqn 12 Feb 1943.
EN312	To Gibraltar 6 Feb 1943. To 72 Sqn.
EN351	To 72 Sqn 12 Feb 1943.
EN356	
EN357	
EN358:RN-J	To 72 Sqn 1 Jul 1943. Missing presumed shot down S of Messina 26 Jul 1943.
EN359	
EN368:RN-H	
EN391	
EN394	Swung on landing and tipped up at Hal Far 15 Jun 1943.
EN398	To 72 Sqn
EN416	
EN461:RN-A	To 72 Sqn May 1943. To N Africa 30 Nov 1943.
EN491:RN-C	From 81 Sqn. To 93 Sqn.
EN517	To Gibraltar 24 Mar 1943. To 72 Sqn. To NW Africa 30 Apr 1943.
EN518:RN-G	
EN521	To 72 Sqn. To 1435 Sqn.
EN534:RN-D	From 232 Sqn.
EN553:RN-Y	To 72 Sqn Jul 1943. To Middle East 1 Aug 1943.

EN556:RN-D	To 72 Sqn Feb 1945.
EN640	To 72 Sqn Jan 1944.
JG722:RN-D	To 72 Sqn. Hit by flak and abandoned 25 Dec 1943.
JK429	To 72 Sqn 1 Jul 1943. Missing from sweep over Sicily 12 Jul 1943.
JL384:RN-A	From 53 OTU. To 72 Sqn. To 29 MU 5 Aug 1945.
LZ861	To 72 Sqn Dec 1943.
LZ915	From 111 Sqn. To 253 Sqn.
LZ949	To 72 Sqn Aug 1943. To NW African AF 1 Nov 1943.
MA245	To 72 Sqn Jul 1943. To Middle East 1 Aug 1943.
MA413	To 72 Sqn Jan 1944. SOC 29 Feb 1944.
MA425	To 72 Sqn Apr 1944. To 241 Sqn.
MA443:RN-T	To 72 Sqn Nov 1943. Engine cut, abandoned on convoy patrol off Anzio 21 Jan 1944.
MA444:RN-B	To 72 Sqn. Hit by flak and abandoned 3 miles SW of Ceprano 16 Mar 1944.
MA449	To 72 Sqn Mar 1944. SOC 14 Mar 1946.
MA458	To 72 Sqn Mar 1944. Crashed 6 Apr 1946.
MA462	To 72 Sqn Oct 1943. To NW African AF 1 Nov 1943.
MA511 *Uruguay XI*	To 72 Sqn Nov 1943. Shot down by flak while chasing Bf 109 4 miles south of Ceccaro 19 Dec 1943
MA520:RN-B, RN-S	To 72 Sqn. Undershot landing, hit tree and u/c collapsed
Sunshine	Falcone 6 Sep 1943
MA521:RN-S	To 72 Sqn Dec 1943. Missing presumed shot down by fighters over Anzio 17 Mar 1944.
MA530	To 72 Sqn Mar 1944. To Med AAF SOC 31 Oct 1946.
MA538	To 72 Sqn Feb 1944. Engine cut and abandoned near Lake Comacchio 25 Apr 1945.
MA546	To 72 Sqn Mar 1944. To Middle East 5 Jul 1945.
MA560	To 72 Sqn. Dived into the sea off Nettuno 27 Mar 1944?
MA561	To 72 Sqn Mar 1944. Shot down by flak 15 miles NW of Anzio 26 Mar 1944.
MA583:RN-B, RN-S	To 72 Sqn Feb 1945. Dived into ground near Castelfranco 21 Mar 1945.
MA637:RN-Y	To 72 Sqn Oct 1943. Crash-landed near Nettuno 19 Feb 1944.
MA884	To 72 Sqn Aug 1944. SOC 30 Aug 1945.
MB807:RN-Q	To 72 Sqn Mar 1944. SOC 31 Mar 1944.
MH329	To 72 Sqn Apr 1944. Lost power on take-off, crash-landed and overturned at Lago 4 Apr 1944.
MH336	To 72 Sqn Jan 1944.

MH560	To 72 Sqn. Dived into the sea off Nettuno 27 Mar 1944.
MH562:RN-V	From USAAF. To 72 Sqn. To 93 Sqn.
MH604	To 72 Sqn Jan 1944. To USAAF 31 Jan 1944.
MH607	To 72 Sqn Mar 1944. To Middle East 28 Dec 1944.
MH611:RN-M	To 72 Sqn Jan 1944.
MH623	To 72 Sqn. To 93 Sqn.
MH635	To 72 Sqn Mar 1944. To Med AAF 21 Jun 1945.
MH655	To 72 Sqn Jan 1944. To USAAF 31 Jan 1944.
MH658:RN-F	
MH669:RN-N	From 232 Sqn Jan 1944.
MH673	To 72 Sqn. To 243 Sqn.
MH699:RN-E, RN-N	To 72 Sqn Jan 1944. SOC 31 Mar 1944.
MH710	To 72 Sqn Feb 1945.
MH893	From 43 Sqn. To 225 Sqn.

SUPERMARINE SPITFIRE LF.Mk IX

EN253:RN-L	To 72 Sqn Feb 1945. To Middle East 5 Jul 1945.
EN583	To 72 Sqn Apr 1944. To Italian AF 30 May 1946 as MM4038.
JL354	To 72 Sqn May 1944. SOC 26 Sep 1946.
JL362	To 72 Sqn Jun 1944. To Turkey 30 Nov 1944.
JL364	To 72 Sqn May 1944. SOC 22 Nov 1945.
MA537:RN-C	To 72 Sqn Aug 1944. SOC 20 Sep 1945.
MH426	To 72 Sqn May 1944. Engine cut and abandoned near Pistoia 8 Mar 1945.
MH690:RN-E	To 72 Sqn Feb 1945.
MH699	To 72 Sqn Feb 1945. SOC 20 Sep 1945.
MH763	To 72 Sqn Jul 1944. To Med AAF 21 Jun 1945.
MH766	To 72 Sqn Aug 1944. To Med AAF 21 Jun 1945.
MH784:RN-E	From 208 Sqn May 1944. To 3 Sqn SAAF.
MH884:RN-E	To 72 Sqn. In collision with NH453, crashed and abandoned at Rutterfeld, Austria, 15 Apr 1946.
MJ128:RN-F	To 72 Sqn Apr 1944. SOC 15 Mar 1945.
MJ134	From 43 Sqn. To 87 Sqn.
MJ190:RN-D	To 72 Sqn May 1944. Hit by flak and crash-landed near Ravenna 18 Apr 1945.
MJ200:RN-D	To 72 Sqn. Stalled on landing and u/c collapsed at Rimini 11 Jan 1945.
MJ203	From 451 Sqn Dec 1944. To 72 Sqn. Hit by flak near Canaro and abandoned 10 Jan 1945.
MJ248	To 72 Sqn Apr 1944. To 253 Sqn.
MJ256	To 72 Sqn May 1944. To Middle East 9 Aug 1945.
MJ407	To 72 Sqn Apr 1944. SOC 18 Aug 1944.

MJ420	To 72 Sqn Mar 1945. SOC 13 Dec 1945.
MJ552:RN-F	To 72 Sqn Jun 1944. Crashed on take-off at Grossetto 3 Jul 1944.
MJ561	To 72 Sqn Apr 1945. To Italian AF 26 Jun 1947 as MM4131.
MJ571	To 72 Sqn Apr 1945. To Italian AF 26 Jun 1947 as MM4102.
MJ620	To 72 Sqn Jun 1944. To 2 Sqn SAAF.
MJ625	To 72 Sqn Apr 1944. To Middle East 31 May 1945.
MJ626:RN-D	To 72 Sqn Apr 1944. SOC 18 Aug 1944.
MJ629:RN-F	From Middle East 1944.
MJ631	From 232 Sqn Dec 1944. To 72 Sqn. SOC 14 Mar 1946.
MJ632:RN-A, RN-E	To 72 Sqn Aug 1944. Caught fire in bombing dive and crashed 5 miles N of Porto Maggiore 10 Apr 1945.
MJ653	To 72 Sqn Mar 1945.
MJ668	To 72 Sqn Apr 1945. To Italian AF 26 Jun 1947 as MM4058.
MJ673	To 72 Sqn Apr 1944. To Italian AF 30 May 1946 as MM4059.
MJ681	To 72 Sqn Apr 1944. SOC 15 Mar 1945.
MJ718:RN-H	To 72 Sqn Apr 1944. To Middle East 31 May 1945.
MJ739	To 72 Sqn Apr 1944. To 4 Sqn SAAF.
MJ778:RN-J	To 72 Sqn May 1944. To Italian AF 26 Jun 1947 as MM4137
MJ784	To 72 Sqn Jul 1944.
MJ786	To 72 Sqn Aug 1944.
MJ829:RN-E	To 72 Sqn May 1945. To Italian AF 26 Jun 1947 as MM4108.
MJ885	To 72 Sqn. To 4 Sqn SAAF.
MJ901:R-:B	To 72 Sqn Apr 1944. To 7 Sqn SAAF.
MJ992:RN-M	To 72 Sqn Apr 1944. To 73 Sqn.
MK111	
MK134:RN-T	To 72 Sqn Apr 1944. SOC 23 Dec 1944.
MK171:RN-O	To 72 Sqn Apr 1944. Swung on landing and hit ambulance at Rimini 31 Jan 1945.
MK353:RN-Z	To 72 Sqn. Hit by flak over Bologna and abandoned near Firenzuola 26 Jun 1944.
MK375	To 72 Sqn Feb 1945. To Italian AF 27 Jun 1946 as MM4077.
MK422	To 72 Sqn. Damaged by flak and abandoned 12 miles NE of Grenoble 23 Oct 1944.
MK553:RN-B	From 43 Sqn. To 72 Sqn. SOC 18 Oct 1945.
MK664	From 43 Sqn. To 72 Sqn. Engine cut and abandoned W of Grenoble 2 Sep 1944.

MK687	To 72 Sqn Mar 1945. Combat with Fw 190s and Bf 109s, hit by flak and abandoned 13 Apr 1945.
MK679	To 72 Sqn May 1945. To Italian AF 26 Jun 1947 as MM4135.
MK736	To 72 Sqn Mar 1945. SOC 30 Apr 1947.
MK845	To 72 Sqn Apr 1945. SOC 14 Jun 1945.
ML142:RN-B	To 72 Sqn Apr 1945. SOC 18 Oct 1945.
ML146	To 72 Sqn Apr 1945. Hit by flak and crash-landed 3 miles S of Argenton 20 Apr 1945.
ML194	To 72 Sqn. Spun in on powerless approach at Zeltweg, Austria, 12 Sep 1946.
ML416	To 72 Sqn May 1945. To Italian AF 26 Jun 1947 as MM4125.
NH19407	To 72 Sqn Mar 1945. SOC 30 Aug 1945.
NH431	To 72 Sqn 21 Sep 1944. To AST.
NH603	To 72 Sqn Apr 1945. SOC 18 Oct 1945.
PL127	To 72 Sqn Sep 1944. To Italian AF 26 Jun 1947 as MM4099.
PL128	From 225 Sqn. To 72 Sqn. Damaged by explosion of target and crashed 6 Mar 1945.
PL319:RN-P	To 72 Sqn Sep 1944. To 43 Sqn.
PL321	To 72 Sqn Sep 1944. SOC 30 Apr 1947.
PL322	To 72 Sqn Nov 1944. Hit by flak and abandoned on ground-support mission 4 Dec 1944.
PL444:RN-X, RN-V	To 72 Sqn Nov 1944. SOC 11 Apr 1946.
PL453:RN-X	To 72 Sqn Mar 1945. Wings wrinkled in bombing dive 2 Apr 1945.
PL465:RN-T	To 72 Sqn Sep 1944. Hit by flak and crash-landed NW of Forli 11 Dec 1944.
PL498	To 72 Sqn Apr 1945. 30 Apr 1947.
PL594:RN-F	
PT364:RN-O	To 72 Sqn Sep 1944. To 601 Sqn.
PT396	To 72 Sqn Apr 1945. To Italian AF 26 Jun 1947 as MM4025.
PT411	To 72 Sqn Sep 1944. Hit by flak and abandoned SE of Faenza 21 Nov 1944.
PT475:RN-N	To 72 Sqn Nov 1944. Hit by flak on ground attack mission near Argenta 4 Jan 1945.
PT485:RN-H	To 72 Sqn Oct 1944. Hit cable while attacking transport and crash-landed near Legnano 3 Mar 1945.
PT552	To 72 Sqn. Engine cut on overshoot, belly-landed at Zeltweg 19 Dec 1945.
PT594	To 72 Sqn Oct 1944. To Middle East 9 Aug 1945.

PT774	To 72 Sqn Dec 1944. To 9 Ferry Unit.
PT849:RN-U	To 72 Sqn May 1945. SOC 10 Jun 1948.
PV121	To 72 Sqn Apr 1945. SOC 14 Mar 1946.
PV123:RN-K	To 72 Sqn Dec 1944. Shot down by flak near River Adige 31 Jan 1945.
PV152	To 72 Sqn Dec 1944. SOC 13 Sep 1945.
PV308	To 72 Sqn Mar 1945. To 43 Sqn.
RR259:RN-K	To 72 Sqn Mar 1945. Hit tree and belly-landed 2 miles SW of Fusignana 10 Apr 1945.
SM176:RN-R	To 72 Sqn Mar 1945. To 43 Sqn.
TA863	To 72 Sqn Feb 1945.

SUPERMARINE SPITFIRE HF Mk IX

PV321	To 72 Sqn. To 601 Sqn.
RK916:RN-H	To 72 Sqn. Caught fire and spun into ground 10 Mar 1945.
RR246:RN-M	To 72 Sqn Mar 1945. To 43 Sqn.
TA772	To 72 Sqn Mar 1945. To Middle East.

CAPRONI SAIMAN 200

***** RN:I	Captured at Comiso Jul 1943.

MESSERSCHMITT Bf 109G-4

1150	Captured at Pachino Aug 1943.

MESSERSCHMITT Bf 109G-6

12.30.1160	Captured at Comiso Jul 1943.

Appendix Four

Operational Statistics, November 1944 to May 1945

FIGHTER-BOMBER SORTIES

	Nov 44	Dec 44	Jan 45	Feb 45	Mar 45	Apr 45	May 45
Operational Flying Hours	56.00	233.00	230.05	244.10	497.50	774.00	98.00
Non-Operational Flying Hours	109.00	11.00	27.40	22.15	35.05	27.00	178.00
Operational Sorties	48	225	205	197	418		
Weight of Bombs Dropped (lb)	14,550	94,300	87,000	62,500	140,000	277,000 and 24 napalm bombs	
DIRECT HITS:							
Enemy-Occupied Houses and Strongpoints		28	16	11	53	126	
Roads		9	4	4	5		
Guns			1				
Causeway			1				
Rail Cuts		1	2	7	19		
Enemy HQ			4				
Trucks (3-ton)			1	7	1	35	
Trucks (Rail)			3	2	6	8	
Bullock Carts			2				
Barges				8		3	
Bridges				2			
Ammunition Dumps				3			
Factories		2					
TOTAL		40	34	44	84	172	

	Nov 44	Dec 44	Jan 45	Feb 45	Mar 45	Apr 45	May 45
DAMAGED:							
Trucks (Rail)					16	15	
Staff Cars			2				
Barges			2	12	2	10	
Bridges					1		
Motor Transport				45	4	54	
TOTAL			4	57	23	79	

'Pilot's Notes' for Messerschmitt Bf 109G

While in Sicily, the squadron found several abandoned Axis aircraft on Comiso airfield. With a little work, a Messerschmitt Bf 109G was made serviceable, and Tom Hughes was the 'lucky' pilot to fly it. Tom wrote his own set of 'Pilot's Notes' for the aircraft and used them while test-flying it. They are reproduced here:

NOTES ON MESSERSCHMITT 109G

Before starting:

1. Petrol on (P1&2).
2. Main electric switch on (Trigger on st'bd side forward).
3. Main airscrew control press-button on (A14).
4. Airscrew pitch selector switch to 'Hand' (E26).
5. Radiator open – control to 'AUF'.
6. Check green U/C lights.

Starting:

1. Switches on (M1&2).
2. Inertia flywheel turned by hand.
3. Petrol pump press-button on (A21).
4. Throttle open a quarter-inch.
5. Five or six strokes with priming-pump.
6. Pull starter engaging gear handle.

Taxiing:

Sand-filter closed (N.B. Powerful toe-operated brakes).

Take-off:

1. Trim – elevator indicator to zero.
2. Pitch – indicator to twelve o'clock (Control on throttle).
3. Open throttle gently.
4. U/C up – squeeze spring safety-catch and push red knob in. Check red lights and visual cable indicators.
5. Throttle back and reduce pitch setting (Then E26 to 'AUTO').
6. Radiator to 'AUTO'.
7. Open sand-filter.

Landing:

1. Radiator open ('AUF'). Sand-filter closed.
2. Reduce speed (300 KPH?). U/C down. Check green lights. (Note: nose drops considerably.)
3. Pitch-setting to twelve o'clock (E26 to 'HAND' first).
4. Reduce speed (200 KPH) and wind down flaps.
5. Approach at 160 KPH or less with slots open.

Switching off:

1. Allow engine to idle.
2. Pull yellow lever below throttle-quadrant back and down.
3. Switches off. Petrol off.
4. MAIN ELECTRIC SWITCH OFF. PRESS RED BUTTON ON LEFT OF INSTRUMENT PANEL (B5).

Engine data:

Take off: 2600 RPM at 1.4 ata at 12 o'clock pitch setting.
Cruise: 2300 RPM at 0.9 ata at 10 o'clock pitch setting.

Instruments:

All instruments are electrically operated.
Artificial Horizon can be caged by rotating the face from 'LOS' to 'FEST'. It is switched on by press-button (A12).
Compass is switched on with main electric switch. The course desired is set by rotating face until course is at the top.
The miniature aircraft indicates actual aircraft heading.
Temperature Gauge gives coolant temperature unless switch (M19) is held up. It then shows oil temperature.

Electric Press-buttons:

A8 – Generator	A12 – Artificial horizon
A9 – Pressure-head heater	A14 – Main airscrew control
A10 – Cockpit lights	A21 – Fuel-pump
A11 – Navigation lights	B5 – MAIN ELECTRIC CUTOUT.

Emergency U/C Selector (*NOTZUG FUR FAHRWERK*) releases U/C from locked-up position.

This aeroplane is very light on the ailerons but exceptionally heavy on the elevators, making constant use of the elevator-trim necessary. There is no rudder-trim and it is never required.

T.B. Hughes
HUGHES' SCHOOL OF AERONAUTICS
2nd AUGUST 1943

Appendix Six

Squadron Song, 1943

(Sung to the tune Jerusalem)

Who as a Squadron came
Out overseas to fame
Flying to dusk from early sunrise
Chasing the Hun from Africa's skies
Who feared throughout the land
Who were that gallant band
Known as Basutoland
Who – Why – Seventy Two.
Who, with their hopes of home
Moved on a Malta 'drome
Keeping their kills away up ahead
Chasing the Luftwaffe out of the Med
Who on a record day
Got the old Hun to play
Put fourteen of them away
Who – Why – Seventy-Two.
Who as Who, on their new campaign
Are sweeping the skies again
Out every day defending the ports
Or up at the front as bomber escorts
Who'll make old Goering pack
Who, when thoughts going back
Can say – well we've done our whack
Who – Why – Seventy-Two.

Appendix Seven

Luftflotte 2 Order of Battle
Operation Husky, 10 July 1943

Throughout the campaigns in Tunisia, Sicily and Italy the main opponents of the squadron were *Luftflotte* 2 fighting alongside Italian Air Force units. The order of battle for *Luftflotte* 2 during Operation Husky is tabled below:

LUFTFLOTTE 2

III/TG1		Junkers Ju52
III/TG2		Junkers Ju52
IV/TG3		Junkers Ju52
I/TG5		

FLIEGERKORPS II

ITALY

II/JG27		Messerschmitt Bf 109
I/JG53		Messerschmitt Bf 109
II/ZG1		Messerschmitt Bf 110
ZG26	*Stab, III, 10*	Messerschmitt Bf 110
II/SKG10		Focke-Wulf Fw 190
III/SKG10		Focke-Wulf Fw 190
KG1	*Stab, I, II*	Junkers Ju 88
KG6	*Stab I, III*	Junkers Ju 88
KG26	*Stab, I, III*	Heinkel He 111
KG76	*Stab, I, II*	Junkers Ju 88
III/KG30		Junkers Ju 88
II/KG54		Junkers Ju 88
II/KG77		Junkers Ju 88
I/LG1		Junkers Ju 88
1(F)/123		Junkers Ju 88
Feldluftgau XXVIII		
3 Flakbrigade		

SICILY

JG53	*Stab, II, III*	Messerschmitt Bf 109
JG77	*Stab, I, II*	Messerschmitt Bf 109
IV/JG3		Messerschmitt Bf 109
II/NJG2		Junkers Ju 88
SKG10	*Stab, II*	Focke-Wulf Fw 190
2(F)/122		Junkers Ju 88
		Messerschmitt Me 210
		Messerschmitt Me 410

Feldluftgau Sizilien
22 Flakbrigade

Fliegerfuhrer Sardinien

II/JG51		Messerschmitt Bf 109
III/JG77		Messerschmitt Bf 109
SchG 2	*Stab, I, II*	Focke-Wulf Fw 190
		Henschel Hs 129
3(F)/33		Junkers Ju 88
4(H)/12		Focke-Wulf Fw 189

Fliegerdivision 2

KG100	*Stab, II, III*	Dornier Do 217

No. 72 Squadron Pilots, 1943–44

RANK	NAME	POST
Sqn Ldr	Robert 'Bobby/Oxo' OXSPRING	Commanding Officer
Flt Lt	'Tiny' LE PETIT	Adjutant
Flt Lt	Derek 'Fordy' FORD	Flight Commander
Wg Cdr	'Sheep' GILROY	
Wg Cdr	Piet HUGO	
Flt Lt	David 'Chumley' COX	
Flt Lt	HAGGER	
Flt Lt	Ian KROHN	
Flg Off	Owen HARDY	
Flg Off	Peter 'Juppy' JUPP	
Flg Off	Dalton 'Pryth' PRYTHERCH	
Flg Off	WALKER	
Flg Off	WATSON	
Plt Off	George KEITH	
Plt Off	Jerrold 'Chem' LE CHEMINANT	
Plt Off	'Johnny' LOWE	
Plt Off	George MALAN	
Plt Off	Ken SMITH	
Plt Off	'Lew' STONE	
WO	Charles 'Chas' CHARNOCK	
WO	Sexton 'Sex' GEAR	
WO	'Red' HUNTER	
Flt Sgt	Eric SHAW	
Sgt	BROWN	
Sgt	K.E. CLARKSON	
Sgt	DEWAR	
Sgt	Laurie 'Fram' FRAMPTON	
Sgt	GRIFFITHS	
Sgt	Roy 'Huss' HUSSEY	
Sgt	MOORE	
Sgt	MOTTRAM	
Sgt	George PASSMORE	
Sgt	PEARSON	
Sgt	M. 'Po' POCOCK	
Sgt	'Robbie' ROBERTSON	
Sgt	H.B. SMITH	
Sgt	SMITH	
Sgt	SOLLITT	

Bibliography and References

——, *The War Years 1939–1945, Eyewitness Accounts*, Marshall Cavendish Books, 1994

Bowyer, Chaz, *History of the RAF*, Bison Books Ltd, 1977

Bradford Telegraph & Argus articles – 22 March and 17 Nov 1943

Corbin, William James, and Mannings, Erik, Monograph: 'Memories of 72 Squadron', privately published, August 2006

Elliot, Gp Capt R. Deacon, OBE DFC RAF, 'World War II December 1939 to December 1940', RAF Museum Ref. X002-5542

Frampton, Laurie, and Mannings, Erik, Monograph: 'Into The Blue – With Seventy-Two', privately published, 2007

Hooton, E.R., *Eagle in Flames, The Fall of the Luftwaffe*, Brockhampton Press, 1999

Lake, Alan, *Flying Units of the RAF*, Airlife Publishing Ltd, 1999

Lancaster, Jack, with Mannings, Erik, Monograph: 'All The Way With 72 Squadron', privately published, 2007

London Gazette

No. 72 Sqn Form 540 Operations Record Book, 1939–1947

Rawlings, John, *Fighter Squadrons of the RAF and their Aircraft*, Crecy Books Ltd, 1993

Richards, Denis, and Saunders, Hilary St G., *Royal Air Force 1939–45, II, The Fight Avails*, HMSO, 1954

Scrase, Rodney, and Mannings, Erik, Monograph: 'Spitfire Saga', privately published

Shaw, Michael, *No. 1 Squadron*, Ian Allan Ltd, 1986

Shores, Christopher, and Williams, Clive, *Aces High*, Grub Street, 1994

Useful website:

RAF History: www.rafweb.org

Index

166 Sqn 53
225 Sqn 67
232 Sqn 71, 75
241 Sqn 66
243 Sqn 68, 95, 129
284 Sqn 166
309 Sqn 62
417 Sqn 141
616 Sqn 53
1435 Sqn 97

RAF Units
239 Wing 208, 211
242 Group 9, 38, 67, 81, 86
244 Wing 208, 211

322 Wing 9, 69, 94, 129
324 Wing 9–10, 20, 51, 58–9, 69, 75,
  90, 94–5, 101–2, 117, 125, 128–9, 133,
  145, 159, 161, 168–9, 172, 175, 199,
  208, 211
325 Wing 9
4350 AA Flt, RAF Regt. 45
Central Fighter Establishment 208

SAAF Units
7 SAAF Wing 133

USAAF Units
6th FW 146
31st FG 62